Kirtley Library
Columbia College
8th and Rogers
Columbia, MO. 65201

WITHDRAWN

The Process of Group Communication

The Process of Group Communication

Ronald L. Applbaum

California State University, Long Beach

Edward M. Bodaken

University of Southern California

Kenneth K. Sereno

University of Southern California

Karl W. E. Anatol

California State University, Long Beach

SCIENCE RESEARCH ASSOCIATES, INC.
Chicago, Palo Alto, Toronto, Henley-on-Thames, Sydney, Paris
A Subsidiary of IBM

©1974, Science Research Associates, Inc.
All rights reserved.
Printed in the United States of America.
Library of Congress Catalog Card Number 73–91961

ISBN: 0–574–19000–7

Contents

PREFACE

AN ORIENTATION

    1. An introduction   5

THE GROUP-COMMUNICATION PROCESS

    2. The communicator   29

    3. Verbal messages in small-group communication   49

    4. Nonverbal messages in small-group communication   73

    5. Problem solving   93

    6. Norms and roles   133

    7. Cohesiveness   159

    8. Conflict   183

    9. Leadership in small groups   215

CONTROLLING THE GROUP-COMMUNICATION PROCESS

    10. Methods of discussion   249

    11. Small-group techniques   275

REFERENCES   295

INDEX   307

Preface

It would certainly seem unnecessary to document man's involvement with group behavior. We are all familiar with the pervasive influence of group experiences in our own lives. Whether such experiences involve social groups or work groups, the bulk of our energy is expended in interaction with others.

And just as our personal involvement in groups has grown, so too has the academic study of group behavior. The burgeoning number of college and university courses dealing with group activity run the gamut from the family to the impact of large social-movement groups. But perhaps the most common focus of study for group-related behavior has been the group-communication processes. Sociology classes spend a great deal of time looking at the basic interactive nature of people in group settings. Social psychology courses are devoted to personality differences of individuals who participate in group activities. Students in business administration classes study the effects of organizational changes on work groups. And speech communication classes in group discussion examine the many formats and types of problems that small groups of people come together to solve.

In addition to the fact that the viewpoints on group behavior are as diverse as the fields looking at group behavior, the factors or variables of interest have grown. Thus, such traditional concepts as leadership, norms, and roles, while occupying a fair share of the attention, have been joined by variables of more recent interest. The latter include consideration of decision-making theories, conflict resolution, nonverbal dimensions of group behavior, language variables in group settings, and power functions of group members. While it is certainly true that knowledge of all these variables—and many more—is useful to the student of group behavior, it has often been the case that such information has been "dumped" upon the student in one of several ways.

For the most part, textbooks in group communication have tended to take either a theoretical or a practical bias in the presentation of material. In the former, students are introduced to a number of theoretical concepts and the research literature that describes those concepts. Books that operate from a practical bias are generally written for group-discussion courses—"how to" books. Such books are largely performance-oriented and deal with the types of groups and the kinds of communicative behavior that are appropriate to each.

It is of course unnecessary that one *or* the other approach be taken. Our general purpose in writing this book was to address ourselves to both perspectives. We attempted to integrate theoretical-conceptual positions in the area of group communication, with application of that information to practical problems and situations. But the task of integrating theory and application is not easy. So we looked to the various ways that we approached the group-communication process; we examined the crucial factors that we thought to be operating in group settings. This consideration led us to the development of the Group Process Model, upon which we based the book and around which we organized each part and chapter.

In approaching the book in this way we hoped to satisfy teachers and students who we felt wanted *both* theory and application. The application of general systems principles allowed us to provide a workable framework from which to operate. In taking this systems approach we were able to dispose of timeworn notions that many of our students found unpalatable. Such notions, for example, that there were "causes" of group phenomena and then there were "effects" in group experiences. As you will see, we take a pretty hard line, advocating the principle that any factor can be both cause and effect.

Thus we hoped through the development of the Group Process Model and the systems orientation to translate the findings of empirical research in small-group processes into workable ideas for the teacher and the student. To do this we found it necessary to write casually at times, more technically at others. From time to time we interrupted our writing to present an exercise that we thought would be helpful to the student in understanding the concepts or research that we had been discussing. And at the end of each chapter we provided annotations of readings that we thought would be helpful for the student or teacher who wished to go into more detail with the material.

In addition to these features, some unique and others timetested, we dealt with materials that stand out in small-group texts.

For example, the treatment of language variables is often left to more advanced communication texts. We think this is a curious practice and spent considerable time detailing the importance of language variables in group deliberations. Such factors as nonverbal communication—so important in group settings—and cohesiveness have been given exhaustive treatment with both textual and exercise materials.

Recent developments in group processes suggest that the role of conflict occupies an increasing importance in the way that groups proceed. In our discussion of conflict we considered the various implications of conflict in small groups and the methods of resolving particular types.

Finally, we presented a type of classification system for group format and kind. Discussion of T-groups and sensitivity groups is offered for the reader who may find them of interest.

In a sense, this book represents a significant accomplishment for a small group. At times the authors were in agreement, at others in conflict. We hope you will find the concepts discussed useful in your group experiences.

An Orientation

1. An introduction

PREVIEW

What are the functions of groups?
   They influence beliefs, values, feelings, and patterns of behavior.
   They fulfill many basic needs.
   They may have an impact beyond their immediate membership.
   They affect the strength of our democratic society.

What is a group?
   A group consists of two or more persons interacting with one another in such a way that each person is influenced by each other person.

What is communication?
   Communication is a process in which a message acts as a linkage between people.

What are the components of the group-communication process?
   Communicators
   Messages
   Interaction
   Situational context

What are the characteristics of the group-communication process?
   Communication occurs in a system.
   Communication is dynamic.
   Communication is complex.
   Communication dimensions are both causes and effects.

What are means of controlling the group-communication process?
   Methods of discussion.
   Techniques of discussion.
   Techniques for individual development.

We all live in a world that is oriented toward group activity. It has been estimated that most people belong to an average of five or six groups at any given time. With how many groups are you associated? How many academic, religious, athletic, social, economic, or political groups or organizations form a part of your life?

Man is a changing organism and the nature of his group associations necessarily changes. Most of us are born into a family group that plays a dominant role in our formative years. Then we go to preschool, kindergarten, and elementary school. We may join the Boy Scouts or Girl Scouts, a Pop Warner athletic league, the YWCA or YMCA. In high school we belong to the band, the science club, tennis team, or pep club. In college we may join a sorority or fraternity, the Newman Club, the Psychology Club, or the debate team. We may be nominated to Phi Beta Kappa. If we can afford it, we may live in a singles-only luxury apartment. After college, we may join economic organizations such as the Chamber of Commerce, and professional groups such as the American Bar Association and the International Communication Association. All the while, we might spend many hours working with the PTA and various religious, political, civic, and youth organizations, and belong to discussion clubs and automobile clubs. To relax we might have cocktails and dinner at our country club, and then pay for the bounties of the good life at Weight Watchers. Our list could be extended very easily; the number of existing small groups has been estimated to be as high as four or five billion.

The functions of groups

Groups are a constant fact of life and have a strong bearing upon how our lives are shaped. Most of our beliefs, values, feelings, and habitual patterns of behavior stem from our experiences in various groups, beginning with the family. Think, for example, of your religious or political views. Were they influenced by your family group? What other attitudes, values, or actions have been influenced by groups to which you have belonged? Clinical psychologists find a close relation between group membership and either pathological or healthy personalities.

Besides exerting influence, groups have the potential of satisfying many, if not most, of our basic needs or motives (Maslow, 1954). Except for *physiological* needs like food and rest, most of our needs may be gratified by membership in a group. We may satisfy *security* needs, such as the need for physical well-being and the need for a future free from danger, by joining various health and retirement groups. Also, groups typically have established ways of operating that create an atmosphere of stability and confidence. Our *social* needs, those yearnings to gather with people and to give and receive affection, obviously can be fulfilled only by group membership. *Prestige* needs—the coveting of a prominent position with corresponding high status—can be satisfied in groups. Group membership, finally, may gratify the need for *self-actualization*. This drive to fulfill one's highest potential, to find a more significant meaning in life is, for example, what possibly leads men and women to seek our highest political offices, or to work for the Indian, Chicano, black, and similar movements.

Groups may have an influence beyond their immediate membership. Government agencies, for example, as well as numerous groups in education, industry, and the military, have a significant impact upon the lives of millions of people. Recently the United States and the Soviet Union signed a nuclear arms limitation pact, one of the most significant political actions since Hiroshima and Nagasaki. This agreement could not have been reached without thousands of hours of negotiation by numerous American and Soviet groups.

On another plane, the strength of our democratic society depends on the efficient operation of the multitude of groups comprising it. Today, more than at any other time in our history, our schools and churches, our businesses and unions, together with government bodies and various citizen groups must function well if the larger system is to work successfully. Yet our society is so closely interrelated that no group can act independently, doing its own thing. Our democracy requires a coordinated interplay of its innumerable groups.

communication diary

1. *Which of your beliefs, values, and patterns of behavior have been influenced by groups?*

2. *What basic needs have you fulfilled through group membership?*

3. *What groups to which you belong or have belonged have had an impact beyond the membership of the group?*

The nature of groups

So far we have not answered the question you may have been asking: What is a *group?* There are numerous legitimate ways of defining a group; indeed, no single definition has proved satisfactory to all scholars in the area of group processes. Groups have been variously defined in terms of perceptions, motivations, goals, organization, interdependency, and interaction of the group members. For our purposes we may define a group as *two or more persons who are interacting with one another in such a manner that each person influences and is influenced by each other person* (Shaw, 1971). Some examples by Shaw may serve to clarify the definition. We may note the differences between collections of individuals that are not groups (we call these *aggregates*) and collections that are. "If one person, A, sees another person, B, with whom he wishes to speak and so approaches him, A is influenced by B but not vice versa; hence *interaction* does not occur, and A and B do not constitute a group. However, if B notices that A is attempting to get his attention, B may be influenced to also approach A. In this case, A and B are interacting and so compose a group. Or consider the case of a person, A, who is looking up at the sky and is approached, independently, by two other persons, B and C, who also begin looking in the same direction. Again, no group exists, despite the fact that B and C have been influenced by A, because A has not been influenced by B or C. These three persons become a group if they enter into a discussion (interaction) concerning the object of their attention. It should be clear that interaction requires *mutual* influence, and an aggregate of individuals is a group only if interaction occurs." (Shaw, 1971, p. 10)

Although interaction has been stressed as the distinguishing feature of a group, other characteristics are also very important. For the most part we will be interested in groups that (1) are relatively permanent, (2) have a common purpose, and (3) have an identifiable group structure.

Since we will be dealing primarily with communication processes in *small* groups, we should now answer the question What is a small group? Really, there is no clear line of demarcation between small groups and large groups. A group containing fewer than ten members will generally be considered a small group, and one containing a hundred members is certainly a large group, but a group containing between ten and thirty members is hard to classify. While we are indirectly interested in the dynamics of communication in large groups, the bulk of the literature on group behavior in communication and social psychology is based on research studies using five or fewer members. Fortunately, most groups in everyday affairs fall within the limits we have described for the small group.

A model of communication

So far we have avoided a discussion of the nature of communication. What is communication? The answer may appear at first to be fairly simple. Most of us have an intuitive notion of the concept. What we want to do in the remainder of this chapter is to increase our natural understanding of what communication is, and perhaps correct any existing misconceptions. Our aim is to understand what is essential to communicative behavior. In any act of communication, especially communication in a group context, we want to be able to identify the basic components or variables operating at the time. Without such knowledge it would be impossible to determine why communication was effective or ineffective, or to do anything about a problem or a communication breakdown that may have occurred. So now let us turn our attention to the analysis of elements and forces affecting the process and outcome of communicative behaviors—behaviors that are quite complex, as we shall see.

We might begin with a definition of communication. Most of us think of communication as the act of imparting, transmitting, or interchanging thoughts, opinions, or information by speech or writing. Let us modify this conception slightly. Let us think of communication as a *process in which a message acts as a linkage between people.* For the time being, the important thing about this definition is the role of the message as a means of connection between communicators. The role of the message as a linkage between people is the essence of the communication process. Communication is essentially the *relationship* set up by the sending and receiving of messages. This text stresses the critical function of communication in affecting social interaction in the group. No matter what the nature of the group may be, or what its purpose is, the tool it uses to establish social interaction to achieve its goals is communication. Communication is the glue that holds the group structure together; it is the enzyme that allows the group process to function. Without communication, groups could not exist; without communication, people could not interact.

How can we understand what is fundamental to the study of communication? We can build a model. We are all familiar with models. We have all seen miniature replicas of ships, cars, trains, planes, and rockets. A model is a way of representing an object, idea, or process. It allows us to clarify complexity by giving only the necessary details. It provides a frame of reference, a vantage point from which we can look at, examine, and describe complicated relationships.

Communication, however, is not something physical like a lunar rover. It is an activity, a process. We cannot use a replica to depict communication; we have to construct a different kind of model. Nevertheless, any model we construct should enable us to identify, describe, or categorize the relevant components of the process.

There exist numerous communication models. It is helpful to recognize that they are arbitrary creations of the people who developed them. If we remember this fact, we will avoid the fruitless search for the *correct* model of communication.

Bear in mind, also, that any model we build may have weaknesses. Perhaps the most serious is the possibility of oversimplifying and misrepresenting the process in order to make it more manageable or understandable. With this caution, let us start with a very simple model of communication.

The model has two basic components: people and messages. Although we can conceive of single individuals communicating with themselves about clouds, stop signs, and even rocks, we are only going to consider cases involving at least two people. A figure may help us here. Aside from the word *message*, the terms may be unfamiliar. The term *encoder* refers to the person creating the message. He takes the meanings he has in his head—his thoughts and ideas—and translates them into verbal, nonverbal, and vocal stimuli. He develops sounds, words, sentences, and paragraphs. He simultaneously sends out an array of nonverbal signals: the posture he assumes, his facial reactions, his gestures, and the intonation he gives to his words. The process is accomplished so effortlessly most of the time that we fail to realize how incredibly complex encoding really is. Speaking is probably the most complex activity man engages in. It requires thought combined with incredibly fine and coordinated activities of the diaphragm, lungs, larynx, tongue, pharynx, nasopharynx, teeth,

Figure 1. Model of communication

and lips. Under stress—for example when giving a speech to a strange audience—a person may not be able to speak well, and possibly not at all.

The expression *decoder* refers to the person receiving and translating the message. The message comes to him as verbal and nonverbal signals—more precisely as sound and light waves. In decoding, he translates these verbal and nonverbal stimuli into thoughts, ideas, and cognitions.

In attributing significance to a message, we should recognize that meaning is not something "out there." Meaning is something within us, something we create. "Meanings are in people" is a basic phrase in communication. (Berlo, 1960, p. 175) Meaning does not reside in the message. An identical message may produce distinctly different meanings in two listeners. For example, a coed representing the women's dorms on a university committee considering a twenty-four-hour visitation policy for coeds' rooms may perceive the pleas of a faculty member opposing such a policy to be grossly discriminating, male chauvanistic, and highly ineffective. Another coed, representing the university religious council, may perceive the request to be in the best interests of the women involved and very sensible. Obviously, the meaning is not *inherent* in the message.

Now that we have an understanding of the units of a model, let us examine how it functions. First, notice that there is a two-way exchange of messages. Communication is not a one-way street. Person A encodes a message and sends it to Person B. Person B, after decoding the message, encodes his own message and sends it back to A. This message is called *feedback*. The important thing to note about feedback is not that it is a second message following the first in a temporal sequence. What is important is that it serves the vital function of providing the sender of the initial message with information about the effects produced by his message. He thus can continue, backtrack, or do anything else he thinks appropriate. Without feedback he must operate in the dark and simply hope that he's getting through. Thus Person A's future messages are modified by the feedback sent to him by Person B. Likewise Person B's future messages are affected by the messages he has received from A. Persons A and B are said to be in a system. Second, we have discussed the processing of messages as occurring in sequence—that is, a person is alternately either a speaker or a listener. In actuality, decoding and encoding go on at the same time. Refer to the model again: within each person we have both processes going on at the same time. As Person A *sends* out a message he is *simultaneously receiving* the verbal and nonverbal messages of Person B. Finally, observe how messages serve as the linkage between the two parties.

Although we have introduced new terms—*encoding* and *decoding*—the model may appear pretty simple. One may be led to believe that the process of communication between two people, when we strip away the jargon, is not a very complex affair. Dispel that notion. Consider this situation: Person A is trying to communicate with Person B. Initially, A has the very difficult task of encoding or creating a message that will adequately express the meaning he wishes to convey. Creating words and sentences that express our precise meanings is very difficult, to which many of us will attest when we recall how difficult it is to handle an essay question on an examination. Try, for example, to define the word *time*. We all know what it means. But we have the devil's time trying to express its meaning precisely, especially without using the word *time* itself. This problem is even more apparent when the ideas to be expressed are involved and complex.

Add to this task the problem of creating a message with the other person in mind. Person A has to be thinking of Person B while creating his message. Person A has to have what is called a receiver orientation. He has to consider B's familiarity or lack of familiarity with the material, his interest, his age, and his level of education, perhaps his race and socioeconomic background, and so forth. A message that may be perfectly suitable for a college graduate may be completely misunderstood by someone with only an elementary school education. Assume now that Person A has created a message considering both of these factors—let us say a sentence. Person A at this point has to be very alert to the feedback that B provides him upon receiving the original message. B may indicate through words, facial expression, or both, that the sentence was not understood, or that it was understood but unappreciated or even rejected. In subsequent sentences A will also have to take account of this feedback.

Finally, added to this three-part process is the fact that Person A must also monitor himself. As he speaks he listens to his sentences. Should these fail to satisfy him, he has to make adjustments.

Communication and the group process

So far, we have been considering a simple model of communication, though we have discovered that the simple process of Mr. A talking to Mr. B is really not so simple after all. Let us now consider an expanded model of communication, one more appropriate to the group-communication process.

To begin with, let us note the components of our group model as illustrated in figure 2. There are four fundamental dimensions: the communicators, the message, interaction, and the situational context. First, a few words of caution. As in all models, these dimensions are arbitrary; they were created to help us more easily perceive the complex communication that occurs within groups. And though each dimension is identified as a separate entity, the distinction between dimensions is sometimes difficult to maintain, for they overlap. Nevertheless, we believe such analyti-

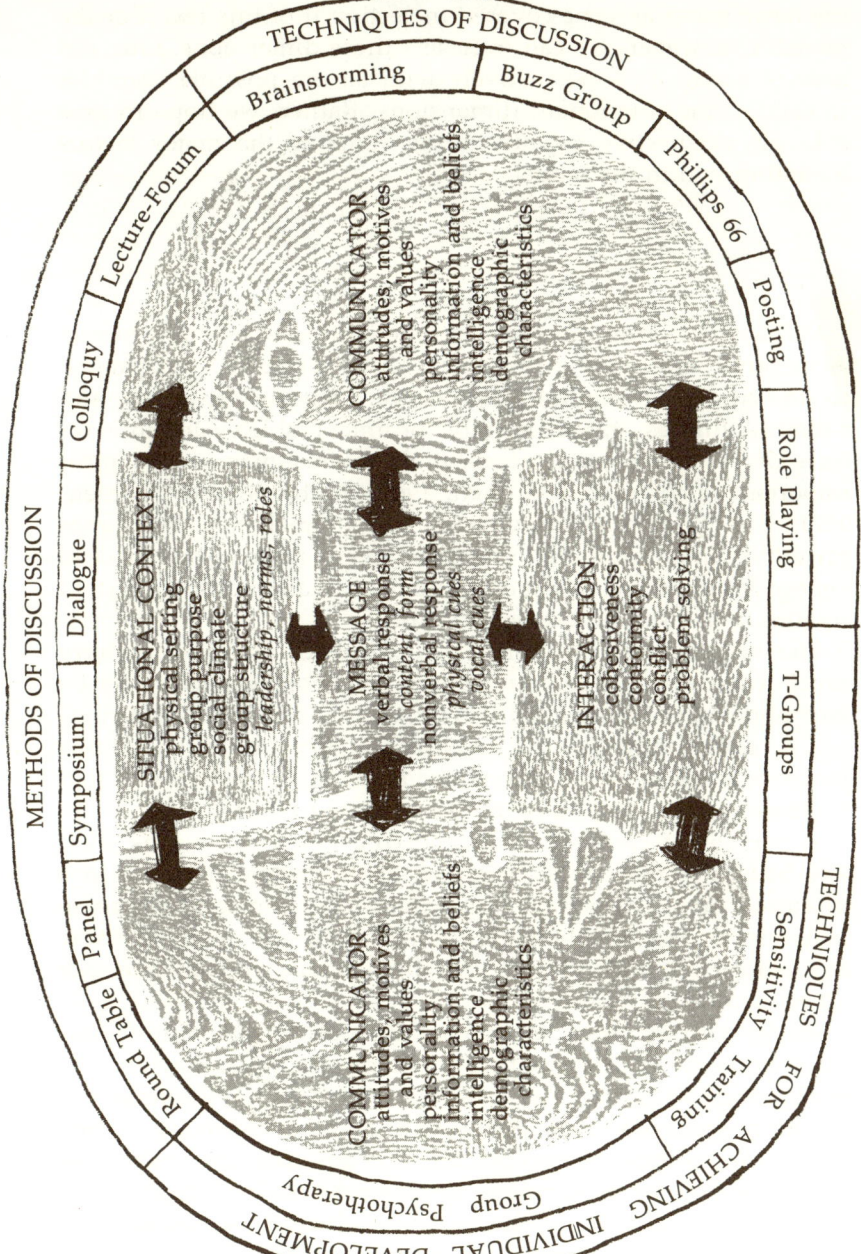

Figure 2. Group model

cal distinctions, though not quite justified in reality, have much to offer the student of the process. These four dimensions form the basic material to be covered in section II of this text. For the moment, however, we can overview these dimensions. Our aim here is not to deal exhaustively with all the possible variables in each of the component dimensions. Rather, we hope to give a broad perspective by illustrating some of the major factors operating within the model.

The communicators

Each communicator in a small group is affected by many factors as he sends and receives messages. Three variables having much to do with his communication are his attitudes, motives, and values. Attitudes—those favorable or unfavorable evaluations we have of people, objects, ideas, or behavior—may be the most important of the factors (Cohen, 1964; Zimbardo and Ebbesen, 1971). For example, a man who has an extremely negative stance toward Women's Liberation is not likely to be persuaded to change his mind on the issue. On a subject that is not so important to him, he is likely to be more flexible.

Likewise, a person's motives—his needs or drives—may have much to do with his communication behavior. Someone may be very obnoxious during a group deliberation, constantly interrupting or calling attention to himself. He may be driven to this behavior because he has strong needs for recognition, needs that he feels he may not be able to satisfy in any other way.

A person's values—his enduring conception of what is good and bad—also may be very important. A student involved in a discussion about the problem of uncontrolled population increase may respond very coldly to abortion as a solution, no matter how economical or practical. He may be Catholic and believe that aborting a fetus is murder.

Along with attitudes, motives, and values, personality factors often have much to do with our communicative behavior. The highly dogmatic group member (Rokeach, 1960), for example, has a strong dependency upon authority and has difficulty in distinguishing between what someone says and who he is, especially when the speaker is someone he perceives to have high status or prestige. Furthermore, he tends to adhere to a "party line" in his thinking. We generally describe such an individual as closed-minded.

The information and knowledge one possesses certainly have

a bearing on communicative behavior in a group. Someone with information that is necessary to the group may become a dominant influence, and an intelligent person may be a force to reckon with because of his capacity to evaluate critically the proposals of others.

Other characteristics of the communicator that may influence communicative behavior are demographic in nature. Clearly, race may have a major influence on communication. And all of us have attitudes about people of certain ages, sex, and looks. Depending on whether the attitude is favorable or unfavorable, communication may be easy or difficult.

communication diary 2

1. *What communicator characteristics of a helpful nature do you possess?*
2. *What communicator characteristics of a harmful nature do you possess?*

The message

The second major dimension of our group communication model is the *message*. Messages, as noted earlier, are the means by which people interact in groups. This linkage between individuals through messages is the heart of the process of communication. By message, we mean any communication factor that operates to link communicators. Messages include gestures, markings, commands, threatening nonverbal cues, or a tension release such as loud laughter.

Messages may be analyzed from two broad perspectives—their *verbal* and *nonverbal* features. The term *verbal* refers to the use of *words* to convey meaning. Words may be perceived through spoken or printed means. Right now you are reading words. Verbal messages may be divided into two subcategories: content and form.

Under content we include such factors as the purpose and topic of the message, the nature of assertions or arguments made, and the amount and type of evidence used to support a point. For example, the use of threatening messages is likely to influence one's attitude toward a group problem. Let's say we are asked to decide the final grades for each member of our class. One classmate intimates that if he gets anything less than a B, he'll break our necks. We are likely to avoid adopting a solution that would give the classmate less than a B.

Verbal messages can also be looked at in terms of their form. Here such factors as logic and message organization are considered. The reasonableness of any conclusion reached in a message depends on the logic used in reaching the conclusion. The understanding or acceptance of a message by the group may be influenced by its overall organizational pattern, the placement of arguments, and the presentation of all sides of an issue. In presenting a possible solution to a problem, a group member may present only the points in favor of his proposal. This procedure is particularly likely to backfire if the other members of the group are well educated; they are apt to be suspicious of and reject one-sided proposals.

A final aspect of form, embodying both organizational and stylistic characteristics, is the fleeting nature of messages in small groups. Unlike platform speeches, group members typically produce messages that are brief, fragmentary, and impromptu. There is a general give-and-take, with episodic building bit by bit upon preceding ideas and frequent digression and repetition.

The second major perspective from which we may analyze messages is in terms of their *nonverbal* features. For example, accompanying a person's words or verbal signals is a string of *physical* and *vocal* cues (Knapp, 1972). They are usually employed to reinforce or emphasize the verbal cues. It is when these nonverbal cues are in conflict with the words that possible problems in interpretation arise. One of the interesting aspects of communicative response is that when verbal and nonverbal cues are in conflict we often pay more attention to the nonverbal cues. We have all heard the committee chairman whose voice was shaky, whose face was immobile and perspiration-beaded, and whose body was rigid begin the meeting by saying how pleased he was to be there. We didn't believe him, did we?

Interaction

Interaction is the third major dimension of the model. Here we are talking about the dynamics of communication, the processes that result from the give-and-take between members of a group. Interaction involves analyzing sequences of behavioral exchanges that affect the behavioral and verbal responses of the other members of the group. One important aspect of interaction is *cohesiveness.* Cohesiveness refers to the feeling of "we-ness" or togetherness that members feel toward each other and the group as a whole. Cohesiveness is shown by a member's sense of identification with the group, his feelings of attraction for group membership or for other members of the group. Cohesiveness—generally regarded as a positive characteristic—has a definite bearing on receptivity to influence attempts within the group, on group productivity, and on individual member satisfaction (Shaw, 1971).

On the other hand, *conformity*, another product of interaction, is sometimes looked upon with distaste, although a certain amount of conformity is necessary. To many people *conformity* means that one sacrifices his feelings, opinions, and point of view to the group. Yet how could a group solve a problem if the members did not conform to certain standards of behavior? What if members decided not to follow any rules? The group would sooner or later disintegrate.

Another component of interaction is the process of *conflict*. Most of us give a negative connotation to the word. We think of conflict as something to be avoided. And indeed it should be avoided if it hinders the efforts of the group to reach an effective solution to a problem or if it leads to such social-emotional problems that prevent members from communicating. On the other hand, it can be said that the best solutions to difficult problems are often those that have been shaped in the forge of conflict.

A final factor of interaction to be considered is the vital function of *problem solving*. We come to grips with many problems facing us in our schools, churches, businesses, homes, and halls of government by means of conferences, committees, and small work groups. Successful handling of these tasks requires training in this vital aspect of group life. Cohesiveness, conformity, conflict, and problem solving are perhaps the most interesting aspects of communication within small groups.

Situational context

The final dimension of our group communication model is that of *situational context*. Communication is in no small measure influenced by the social context in which it occurs. Every situation forms a pattern, a context, that governs the ongoing flow and effectiveness of group communication.

Of initial interest in our consideration of situational context are characteristics of the physical setting. The objects surrounding us, the architecture, the esthetic factors of the situation, and possibly even the climate operate in subtle ways to influence our com-

Information sharing, self-maintenance, and problem solving

municative behavior (Knapp, 1972). The size of the room in which a group meets can have a bearing on the outcome. Consider having a discussion in one of these oversized broom closets called meeting rooms, or clustering five chairs together in the middle of the gym floor. Neither of these settings seems conducive to effective communication. Furniture arrangement can have an impact on communication. A simple way to decrease the communication between any two members of a group is to seat them side by side, for people tend to talk to those seated opposite themselves.

Though physical aspects are significant situational variables, group *purpose* or *task* is also a major influence. The circumstances that cause individuals to come together into groups are many and varied. Generally, however, they can be classified into three major categories: (1) information sharing, (2) self-maintenance, and (3) problem solving. We should note initially that these types of tasks are not mutually exclusive. In fact, elements of all three may be present in the same small group. Thus group task or purpose is primarily a matter of priority. In other words, a group may meet for information sharing only to find that it is necessary to engage in problem solving resulting from conflict of information.

A group whose task is primarily that of information sharing has as its primary purpose the communication of and interaction about new knowledge. Group members enter the situation with the purpose of imparting information and not necessarily of debating the views expressed in this information. Government leaders, businessmen, and students who meet to increase their knowledge and understanding of questions of interest to them are participating in an information-sharing discussion.

Groups concerned with self-maintenance focus their attention on their various members as individuals, or on the structure of the group itself. Members of such a group are engaged in communication that concerns member-to-member or member-to-group relationships. They seek to understand themselves and others better. Students discussing problems over coffee, or releasing their tensions and frustrations over beer after an examination are common examples. Sometimes the need for such a group takes a more formal approach and a permanent group is formed to provide the tension-releasing opportunity to communicate with others of similar interest. Alcoholics Anonymous, Weight Watchers, and Parents Without Partners are all examples of collections of individuals who have found that formal organization into groups provides needed support.

The third major task, problem solving, involves the intellectual chore of focusing on some difficulty and seeking to alleviate it. We have already stressed the importance of this group purpose. All three of these tasks or purposes may have a dominant influence upon the nature of the communication.

---

communication diary 3

1. What information-sharing group experiences have you had?
2. What self-maintenance group experiences have you had?
3. What problem-solving group experiences have you had?

The *social climate* of the group is yet another vital factor to be considered under situational context. The most extensively studied group climates are those dealing with cooperative and competitive orientations. In a cooperative climate group goals are similar, while in a competitive climate group members have different goals.

The last factor to be discussed under situational context is *group structure*. Structure includes group roles and norms. Most efficient small groups have a clearly defined group structure. One aspect of structure is the role of the *leader*. Effective leaders are characterized by task-related abilities, sociability, and motivation. Aside from the leader, other members of the group must fulfill their *roles* if the group is to fulfill its purpose or task. Roles may be defined as "the set of expectations which group members share concerning the behavior of a person who occupies a given position in the group." (Hare, 1962) In any group, we may play a number of roles or we may specialize in certain roles. For example, our role may be concerned with initiating group action or resolving group conflict. We may perform one role in one group and a totally different role in another group. The point to be stressed is that there are multiple roles to be performed in every group and many people play different roles in different groups.

Implied in a consideration of group roles is the topic of group norms. Norms are standards of behavior that are expected of group members. Regardless of the group to which one belongs, the ground rules, the expected patterns of behavior, are made quite clear. Departure from group norms may result in initial efforts to bring the deviate back to the fold. Continued deviation from the group's norms may result in the isolation, avoidance, or even expulsion of the offending member.

All aspects of structure influence the functioning of the group and affect the amount of satisfaction each member will experience in the group.

Before leaving our consideration of the fundamental dimensions of our model, we want to offer a few final observations. A clear understanding of the communication process in small groups cannot be obtained without taking cognizance of *all* the component dimensions. Do not assume, however, that each dimension is equally important in every occasion of group communication. While a single dimension may have a dominating effect upon group processes in one discussion, in another discussion this same dimension's impact may be relatively minor. The dynamic interplay of the four dimensions creates a fascinating, complex transaction. We hope to simplify the complexity to manageable proportions in succeeding chapters.

We have not quite completed the examination of our model of communication and group processes. Consider figure 2 again. The outer band enclosing the component dimensions illustrates a number of small group communication situations: methods of discussion, techniques of discussion, and techniques for individual development. These are the day-to-day circumstances in which our theoretical knowledge of group communication can be put into use. We assume that an understanding of the component dimensions will enhance participation in these various forms of small group communication. Productive, cooperative, and gratifying use of the communication process demands application of principles derived from theory, research, and past practice.

Characteristics of the group communication process

Now that we have taken a broad look at the components of our model, let us examine the characteristics of group communication depicted by the model.

Group communication occurs in a system. A system implies that there is a connection or interaction between all of the dimensions of the model. No dimension operates or exists as an isolated entity. A change in any dimension will tend to result in changes throughout the system. Likewise, a change in any one dimension is a result of multiple changes occurring throughout the system. Viewing group communication as a system suggests that no single dimension can be understood in isolation. And finally, an understanding of each dimension is necessary to understand the total system.

Group communication is dynamic. Communication is not an object or a thing. Rather it is a process, an activity occurring over time. As a process occurring in time, it is constantly changing, constantly in flux. These changes are continuous, irreversible, and unrepeatable. Once spoken, words can never be unspoken. And because of the systemic nature of the group communication process, each of these changes in the various dimensions produces a fluid, flexible, dynamic process.

Group communication is complex. There are two reasons why communication in a group is a complex affair. For one thing, all of the dimensions are operating (interacting) simultaneously. Secondly, characteristics under each of the basic dimensions are continuously changing while interacting. If you can conceive of this process with its interplay of multiple forces, all constantly changing while interacting, then you have a notion of the nature of complexity.

Group communication dimensions are simultaneously cause and effect. This idea has already been implied in the concept of communication as a system. For example, we may look at the message as a cause influencing the dimensions of communicator, interaction, and aspects of group context. From another perspective we can also observe how and why certain characteristics of communicators, interaction, or situational context affect the messages that are produced.

OVERVIEW

We will now survey the following ten chapters. As we focus on a dimension or one of its elements we will gain more detailed, concrete information. At the same time, we may lose our perspective of how each component relates to the larger system. It is important, then, not to lose sight of the postulate that *group communication occurs in a system*. We must remain conscious of this principle, which insists that no single aspect of group communication can be understood except as it relates to the whole.

Chapter 2. The communicator. This chapter examines how characteristics of group members affect communication in the group. Five factors are considered: (1) credibility, which refers to evaluative perceptions we have of other group members; (2) attitudes, which are tendencies we have to make favorable or unfavorable evaluations about ideas, things, and behavior; (3) the impact of sex roles; (4) personality, which may be thought of as tendencies to behave in consistent ways; and finally, (5) the influence of communicator intelligence upon group behavior.

Chapter 3. Verbal messages in the small group. In this chapter, we discuss the nature, form, and function of verbal messages in the small group. We consider how the message strategies of praise, criticism, censure, and giving instructions influence group members. We show how distortion, filtering, and overloading occur, and how acceptance of a message facilitates or hinders compliance. In terms of acceptance we discuss the way in which reality, ambiguity, credibility, and congruency influence the acceptance of messages. The chapter concludes with a description of how group members typically respond to verbal messages.

Chapter 4. Nonverbal messages in the small group. This chapter discusses nonverbal message cues in the small group. We consider nonverbal language as signals of emotions, control, and direction. We investigate nonverbal messages as signals of interpersonal orientation and as clarification of verbal messages. We also examine the effect of social distance and seating arrangement.

Chapter 5. Problem solving. We begin the chapter by offering our definition of problem-solving behavior—recognition and attempted alleviation of some relevant difficulty. We discuss three problem-solving patterns that focus on member interaction, thought processes, and group decision making: (1) Bales's Interaction Process Analysis, a method of analyzing interaction in group problem solving; (2) reflective thinking, a thought-process-oriented approach to problem solving; and (3) a model developed to identify phases in group decision making. We also present three formats for solving problems in group discussion. We conclude with a consideration of problem-solving behaviors as they relate to the Group Process Model.

Chapter 6. Norms and roles. This chapter examines the nature of norms and roles and their functions in small groups. Norms refer to group standards about acceptable and unacceptable behaviors within the group. Roles are the various positions a member occupies within a group and the behaviors required of each position. Both norms and roles develop to provide structure within a group. They are seen as necessary in accomplishing both group task and social-emotional goals. The manner in which norms and roles influence group members, the sending and receiving of messages within the group, and important aspects of group interaction are illustrated.

Chapter 7. Cohesiveness. We begin with a definition of cohesiveness, acknowledging the importance of attraction, motivation, and common goal as forces that keep members in groups. We examine member satisfaction and group productivity as factors relevant to group cohesiveness. We conclude our analysis with an examination of the communicator, message, and situational context as causes or effects of cohesiveness.

Chapter 8. Conflict. This chapter examines conflict behavior in the small group. We describe conflict on intrapersonal, interpersonal, and intragroup levels. Conflict is discussed as both productive and nonproductive in terms of group function and purpose. We examine conflict as it relates to the communicator, message, and situational context. We conclude the chapter by noting some communication principles pertinent to conflict behavior in the small group.

Chapter 9. Leadership. This chapter discusses leadership in terms of leader as communicator, the messages he sends, his interaction with group members, and the context in which he communicates. We suggest that leadership performance depends as much upon contexts or situations prevalent in or around the group, as it does upon the attributes communicated by the leader. The quality of interaction between a leader and group members is influenced by leadership style. Three styles of leadership —autocratic, democratic, and laissez-faire—are discussed.

Chapter 10. Methods of discussion. The chapter examines methods or procedures for presenting a group discussion. Group discussion is defined as the face-to-face interaction of two or more persons engaged in the task of information sharing, problem solving, and self-maintenance. Six methods of discussion are examined: (1) panel; (2) round table; (3) symposium-forum; (4) dialogue; (5) colloquy; and (6) lecture-forum.

Chapter 11. Small-group techniques. The chapter is concerned with an examination of five small-group techniques: (1) brainstorming, a technique for promoting free interchange of ideas among group members without fear of criticism or evaluation; (2) buzz groups and Phillips 66, techniques for providing more audience involvement in a formal group discussion; (3) posting, a discussion technique used for locating and clarifying group problems; (4) role playing, which is a dramatization of a problem or group situation to provide a group member with a clear understanding of his own role and the roles of the other group members; and (5) laboratory training, a tool for teaching group members proper behaviors in group task and social-emotional areas.

ADDITIONAL READINGS

Mortensen, C. David. *Communication: The Study of Human Interaction* (New York: McGraw-Hill, 1972). Chapter 1, "A Frame of Reference," presents a lucid discussion of the nature of communication. Chapter 2, "Communication Models," explains the nature, strengths, and weaknesses of models as a prelude to the review of major models of the communication process.

Shaw, Marvin E. *Group Dynamics: The Psychology of Small Group Behavior* (New York: McGraw-Hill, 1971). Chapter 1, "The Nature of Small Groups," presents a good overview of the various approaches that have been taken in defining the small group.

The Group-Communication Process

2. The communicator

PREVIEW

What five communicator characteristics have an impact on the group process?

Credibility
    Prior and ongoing determinants
    Dimensions
    Effects of credibility upon group processes

Attitude: tendencies to judge concepts, persons, objects, and behaviors in a favorable or unfavorable manner
    Measurement of attitudes
    Ego-involvement and effects upon group processes

Sex
    Sex roles and impact upon group processes

Personality: predispositions to behave in consistent ways
    Effects of six traits upon group processes
        Authoritarianism and dogmatism
        Social sensitivity
        Ascendant tendencies
        Self-reliance and dependability
        Unconventionality
        Emotional stability

Intelligence: ability to understand and solve problems
    Effects upon group processes

A case could be made for the claim that communicator characteristics are perhaps the most important of the various dimensions of group communication. For what a communicator intends to do or is inclined to do, and what he is able or capable of doing may have no small effect upon the successful operation of the group.

Qualities we bring to the group may affect our ability to lead, to accept influence uncritically, to enhance cohesiveness, to foster conflicts, to solve problems efficiently, and so on. Since all variables within the communication system affect one another, qualities of the communicator influence other dimensions. In turn, they are affected by other dimensions.

In this chapter we won't examine how every communicator variable influences every variable in all other dimensions. Nor will we enumerate effects of all other dimensions upon communicator characteristics. In the first place, we don't know how every communicator variable affects and in turn is affected by variables of other dimensions. We recognize in theory that they do affect one another. But quite frankly, we do not have research which, to date, has pieced together the puzzle of possible interrelationships among variables.

So we'll be selective. We're going to emphasize the factors that research has demonstrated to have some impact. And to be perfectly candid, we're going to look at variables reflecting our own biases. We hope, though, all of us will agree that characteristics emphasized will help in understanding better the role of communicator factors in affecting group processes.

We'll examine five major communicator characteristics: credibility, attitude, sex, personality, and intelligence. We'll examine each in turn and try to understand their nature and their influence upon group processes.

Credibility

Qualities we perceive in other members are among the most significant factors affecting behavior in small groups. We react quite differently to group members we judge to be competent, honest, and hard working as compared to those we believe are incompetent, care little about the group, and are goof-offs. Members perceived to have high credibility strongly influence crucial aspects of a group's life.

Credibility refers to evaluative perceptions we have of other group members. These can be looked upon as falling somewhere on a continuum ranging from high or positive to low or negative. Credibility is not a characteristic possessed by a communicator. It's the naive individual who believes that certain characteristics when possessed invariably lead to high or low credibility.

Depending upon other factors operating at the time, a group member's qualities may be viewed as being either an asset or a liability. Consider this cast of two characters. One has a bachelor's degree in applied physics from the California Institute of Technology. He comes from a family prominent in industry. He lives in a comfortable home in the wealthy suburb of San Marino. Let's add that he's intelligent, fluent, and personable. Let's really spice it up by saying he's a double for Robert Redford. Our second member of the cast lives in the Watts district of Los Angeles. She had to quit school after the ninth grade to help support her family. She's divorced, the sole support of four young children, and on welfare. And she's black. Remember our goal: to see whether possession of certain characteristics invariably leads to high or low credibility.

At first glance we might assume that our man from Cal Tech would have higher credibility than our welfare mother from Watts. But let's set up the group communication situation. Suppose our two individuals are members of a citizen committee appointed by the mayor investigating the effects of poverty upon quality of life of inner-city residents. Need we go on? Can we see why our fair-haired physicist would not be a particularly credible group member, while our high school dropout would? If we changed the group setting and task, we could easily reverse the credibility associated with our two communicators. Suppose our two individuals were members of a research team charged with developing new smog-control devices. Notice that both communicators remained constant, but they would be perceived to have opposite levels of credibility in these different situations.

Five communicator characteristics

Now that we have a general notion of how credibility is a result of source characteristics combined with other characteristics operating at the time, let's examine a little more systematically specific factors contributing to perceptions of credibility.

Determinants of credibility

A group member often brings with him certain characteristics already known to some or all of the group. Past experiences we may have had with him affect our responses to him within the group. In the absence of personal knowledge his reputation may influence us. In addition, a host of other factors enter in. His personal appearance, occupation, education, personal wealth, ethnic background, religion, marital status, number of arrests, and so forth may serve to modify our perception of his credibility.

What a communicator actually says and does in the group will interact with his prior characteristics to influence our perception of his credibility. Prime among these are the content expressed. We've all heard the cliché of the beautiful-but-dumb blonde. She perhaps has high credibility as a result of her appearance until she opens her mouth. Then it's all downhill as far as her credibility is concerned. Aside from content, other factors bearing upon perceptions of credibility are quality of reasoning, organization of ideas, delivery, and language. The list could easily be extended.

Dimensions of credibility

When we evaluate a group member as being high or low in credibility, we take into account all of his prior and ongoing characteristics. These multiple, interacting characteristics can be combined into a small number of basic or underlying factors or dimensions.

Two dominant factors have been consistently identified in research: *competence* or *authoritativeness*, and *trustworthiness* or *safety*. A member is said to have high competence if he is perceived to be knowledgeable about the discussion topic and demonstrates general ability. Trustworthiness, the second factor, is a result of perceptions of honesty, lack of ulterior motives, sense of fair play, concern for others, and the like.

No intent is implied that these are observations of truth. What we're talking about are *perceptions* of competence and trustworthiness. The successful con man becomes rich precisely because he is able to persuade his victims that he possesses both high competence and trustworthiness.

Effects of credibility

Prior experience or knowledge of a group member may establish a favorable or unfavorable predisposition on the part of other group members to him. It may be exhibited by a willingness or unwillingness to listen and quite possibly accept or reject his ideas, sometimes quite apart from the quality of what is said. The implications for leadership potential seem obvious. Certain people may never get the chance to advance to a position of leadership because their unsavory reputations precede them. These prior perceptions may lead other group members to "turn them off psychologically" before they ever get started. Conversely, a

Some determinants of credibility

person may have leadership thrust upon him because knowledge of his sterling qualities sets the stage for his entrance into the group.

Perhaps the most important consequence of perceived levels of credibility involves acceptance of ideas. Available evidence suggests that perceptions of competence and trustworthiness are very important in affecting acceptance of opinions (Cohen, 1964). Without being perceived as being highly credible, chances of having one's ideas accepted are slim, even if they have merit. Perceptions of low credibility seem to get in the way of our ability to objectively evaluate the intrinsic merits of content. Judy, a strong Women's Libber, may have difficulty in seeing any merit in anything someone may say whom she perceives to be a male chauvinist.

Let's probe the effects on perceptions of competence and trustworthiness upon group behavior. These two factors are not necessarily of equal importance. The nature of the discussion content and characteristics of the other group members will determine their relative importance.

If the discussion purpose requires special expertise, knowledge, and skill, then the factor of authoritativeness or competence is very important. On the other hand, superior competence may be irrelevant or even detrimental to a discussion. Let's imagine a group concerned primarily with establishing cohesiveness and openness in discussion, as is the case in group psychotherapy. Of crucial significance are social and emotional elements. Here the group is concerned with increasing mutual liking and attraction. In this case, perceptions of high trustworthiness are crucial. What seems to be important are factors of commonality which lead group members to identify with one another. If a member is perceived to be superior in competence, it could conceivably be a detriment. It may be looked upon as a barrier separating him from other members of the group.

Before leaving this section we should stress that credibility is but a single construct and typically operates in combination with other elements or variables to produce its effects. As illustrated in the previous paragraph, credibility is affected by the goal or purpose of the discussion. In addition, perceived similarities and dissimilarities affect attraction among members, and this, in turn, influences the effects of credibility within a group. Still other variables might be mentioned. So the picture of credibility we've painted isn't quite finished; the completed picture is more complex. The material we've introduced, however, does represent fundamental notions about the nature and effects of credibility. Just keep in mind that other factors combine with credibility to affect communicative behavior within the group. (For a current review of the interaction of credibility with other variables, see Simons, 1973.)

exercise 1

Form a leaderless group. What kinds of prior determinants of credibility are perceived as significant for members of the group? Why are they significant? What kinds of ongoing determinants are perceived as significant? Why? Compare the relative importance of prior versus ongoing determinants. What kinds of behaviors are group members likely to exhibit toward those who exhibit these characteristics?

Attitudes

As pointed out in chapter 1, attitudes are tendencies to evaluate a symbol, person, object, or behavior in a favorable or unfavorable manner. These predispositions have a very strong influence upon a group member's behavior, especially in his role as receiver. Attitudes play a major role in the processing and ultimate acceptance of information. Our first task is to try to get a better handle on what an attitude is.

The nature of attitudes

In practical terms, an attitude can be conceived of as a point on a continuum ranging from favorable to unfavorable response options. For example this might be Vera's response to the message topic:

Use of the contraceptive pill by unmarried women

good ____ _X_ ____ ____ ____ ____ ____ bad.

Let's add one more person to the picture. Tom's response might look like this:

Use of the contraceptive pill by unmarried women

good ____ _X_ ____ ____ ____ ____ ____ bad.

It seems that Vera and Tom have similar attitudes toward the topic.

More recently, however, Sherif, Sherif, and Nebergall (1965) have rejected the notion that an attitude is merely a point on a continuum. They assert that an attitude consists also of latitudes of acceptance, rejection, and noncommitment. How can we conceive of these latitudes? We can use the letter A to indicate those positions on the continuum which are acceptable, the letter U to stand for those positions which are unacceptable, and the letter N to represent the latitude of noncommitment.

If we turn again to the attitude response of Vera and Tom, adding indications of latitudes, we might get a picture like this:

Use of the contraceptive pill by unmarried women

Vera good __A__ __X__ __U__ __U__ __U__ __U__ __U__ bad

Tom   good __A__ __X__ __A__ __N__ __N__ __U__ __U__ bad

We can now see that Vera and Tom do not have similar attitudes. Although both have identical most-acceptable positions (X), they differ on their latitudes. Looking at Vera's responses, we can see that she rejects most positions on the continuum aside from her most acceptable position and finds only the one position more extreme than her X to be acceptable. Tom, on the other hand, has a very small latitude of rejection and relatively large latitudes of acceptance and noncommitment. What can we derive from these two attitude configurations?

Ego involvement

Vera is said to be highly ego-involved in her position. This involvement is manifested by a large latitude of rejection and relatively small latitudes of acceptance and noncommitment. Tom, unlike Vera, is lowly involved. He finds few positions on the continuum unacceptable while simultaneously finding more acceptable and noncommittal positions. Of what value are these notions of high and low involvement in understanding communication processes within the small group?

First, we must understand tendencies of highly and lowly involved persons. Of primary importance is the fact that highly ego-involved persons are not readily susceptible to changing their most acceptable positions. Numerous studies have demonstrated that highly involved subjects tend to retain their most-acceptable stands when exposed to messages espousing a contrary position. Lowly involved individuals, on the other hand, tend more readily to change their most-acceptable attitude position to conform more closely to the positions advocated in a counter-attitudinal or belief-discrepant message. (Sherif, Sherif, and Nebergall, 1965)

What kinds of topics are people more likely to be highly involved with? Although this varies, most people are highly involved with personal matters. Most college students seem to be involved with such issues as V.D. control, a particular class they're taking, pot, the next football game or party, their car, and the opposite sex. What kinds of behaviors are likely when the business of the group concerns issues or topics of great involvement to the members?

In a small group, one would not have much chance of having a position he's advocated as being acceptable, if the group perceived the position as falling within their latitude of rejection. Recall that the highly involved person tends to have a latitude of rejection that takes up most of the attitude continuum. That means it's nearly impossible to get him to accept any position other than the one he currently holds. The lowly involved group member, on the other hand, having a larger attitude of acceptance and noncommitment, is more likely to be receptive to stands discrepant from his own most acceptable one.

In addition, members highly involved in their positions are not likely to work harmoniously with others espousing contrary views. There is likely to be conflict. In a study of conflict resolution, for example, pairs of highly and lowly involved individuals espousing opposing stands on an issue were given the task of negotiating to see if they could come to an agreement concerning positions on the issue. There was a strong trend for opposed, highly involved individuals not to achieve consensus, while opposed lowly involved individuals readily reached agreement. (Sereno and Mortensen, 1969) In this final case, since they were not involved in the issue and consequently didn't really care one way or the other about the topic, they tended to give in, modify, and compromise their stands. The hassle with the other person wasn't worth it.

---

exercise 2

Form a leaderless group of five to eight classmates. List the topics about which members are highly involved, topics that are especially meaningful, significant, and relevant to them. Probe the reasons for involvement on these topics. Analyze the nature and motivation for involvement on these issues. Discuss the possible impact of high involvement in these issues upon various dimensions of group communication such as cohesiveness, attraction, conflict, acceptance of differing opinions, resistance to group conformity pressures, and so forth.

Sex

Sex is a readily noted characteristic of group members. But is it of importance? In a word, yes. Why? Because in our culture

Categories of communicator characteristics

AUTHORITARIANISM SOCIAL SENSITIVITY ASCENDANT TENDENCIES

sex roles are shaped from infancy and childhood, roles often "requiring" different behaviors from men and women.

Men are taught to be more aggressive, self-assertive, and fearless than women. As communicators, men are likely to display more roughness of manner and language in a group than women. In many all-male groups, members often call each other by the vilest of names, such expressions being indications of affection. To fail to call a fellow member by a term of abuse may indicate a lack of closeness or group cohesiveness. Men traditionally have readier access to positions of leadership within a group. Groups in industry, government, and education, among others, more often than not have men as leaders. And typically, most groups have women as secretaries. On the whole men tend to be more quarrelsome and engage in conflict behaviors more often than women. (Ort, 1950) In addition, men are more likely to exhibit competitive rather than cooperative tendencies. In small groups, women are more likely than men to adopt systems and methods in which everyone will benefit. (Uesugi and Vinacke, 1963)

Women tend to conform to different norms than do men. (Shaw, 1971) Women, more particularly, conform because of social norms —they do not want to appear peculiar. Men, by way of contrast, tend to conform if in doing so they can accomplish the group task more quickly. (Tuddenham, MacBride, and Zahn, 1958) Among college students, women tend to be more concerned with establishing harmonious interpersonal relationships with others, while men seem more involved with task requirements—getting

SELF-RELIANCE UNCONVENTIONALITY EMOTIONAL STABILITY

the job done. (Berg and Bass, 1961) Women, more so than men, tend to express themselves in a compassionate, sympathetic, fastidious, and emotional manner. (Terman and Miles, 1936) Women also tend to demonstrate higher susceptibility to influence attempts than do males. In our culture, an aggressive, strong woman is looked upon as manifesting male tendencies—a definitely uncool thing. A man who gives in is likely to be looked upon as weak—and therefore feminine.

It's probable that these differences in sexual behavior will diminish in time. The developing and increasing impact of Women's Liberation upon the thinking of our culture will probably have a beneficial influence in this regard.

Before we leave this section, we should stress that sex is important primarily because our culture prescribes different role behaviors for men and women. Culturally determined sex roles have a large bearing upon personality characteristics we develop as communicators—the topic we'll examine more closely in the next section.

Personality

Personality is a fascinating communicator characteristic, fascinating because of the role it plays in social behavior. It is unlike attitude, which is a tendency to behave in consistent ways toward a particular person, object, and so on. Rather, a personality trait is considered to be a predisposition to behave in consistent ways in many different situations. Thus, to the degree that a personality trait is present, there should be regularity in behavior. Personality traits are important in group communication, since they manifest themselves as consistent behaviors in different groups, with varying purposes, and in dissimilar settings.

An extremely large number of personality attributes have been identified. Theorists and researchers give varied names to similar attributes and sometimes similar names to different attributes. Of the multitude of characteristics, six broad categories or classes may be identified. They are Authoritarianism and Dogmatism, Social Sensitivity, Ascendant Tendencies, Self-Reliance and Dependability, Unconventionality, and Emotional Stability. We will consider each of these as they affect the group participant. But first a word of caution. Personality attributes are not typified by their presence or absence. All people exhibit them to greater or lesser degrees.

Authoritarianism and dogmatism

The authoritarian or dogmatic person believes there should be status and power differences between people. As a group member, he is likely to use his power if he's in a position of leadership. As a leader, he is likely to be firm, demanding, and directive. He is not likely to accept ideas of others. He is particularly loathe to accept ideas when they go against group norms, for he believes that norms and roles should be strictly adhered to. (Shaw, 1971) Thus, somewhat paradoxically, the high authoritarian, although he may exhibit strength when he is in a position of leadership, will also exhibit behaviors that may be called weak. He shows weakness by his lack of independence. He conforms very closely to norms of the group when compared with the behavior of nonauthoritarians.

When in a subordinate group position the group member with authoritarian tendencies tends to be submissive and compliant. He tends to agree with what the group leader says, even if it goes against what he favors. As a group member he accepts his submissive behavior as natural and appropriate. (Adorno, Frenkel-Brunswik, Levinson, and Sanford, 1950) One of the interesting characteristics of the authoritarian is that he has trouble distinguishing between who the leader is and what he says (Rokeach,

1960). He tends to accept ideas of the leader not because of their intrinsic merit but because of his belief that leaders should be followed. The nonauthoritarian, on the other hand, rejects both the superior and subordinate role. He is not likely to accept the ideas of the leader without examining them critically. He is able to distinguish between what someone says and who he is.

Social sensitivity

This trait is exhibited by insight into the feelings of others. It is the ability to look at what's happening from inside the other person's skin. The group member who has this capacity to put himself in the other guy's shoes has what is called the ability to empathize. This trait seems to be moderately related to leadership success (Bell and Hall, 1954), acceptance by the group (Cattell and Stice, 1960), amount of participation (Bass, McGehee, Hawkins, Young, and Gebel, 1953), and group effectiveness (Greer, 1955). The person with low sensitivity to others tends to lack the requisites for social-emotional leadership within a group. His insensitivity to the feelings of others may contribute to his lack of acceptance by members of the group. This, in turn, diminishes his potential for participation because other group members may try to limit the extent of his contributions. This ultimately will affect his potential for increasing group productivity and efficiency.

Ascendant tendencies

Group members high in this characteristic wish to assert themselves and exert dominance over others. Thus, it's not surprising that they tend to emerge as leaders and influence group decisions (Borg, 1960). But all is not sunshine and light; there is a dark side too. Dominance also exhibits itself by harmful social behavior. The ascendant personality tends to make remarks that build himself up at the expense of others (Cattell and Stice, 1960). He also tends to exhibit rigid behavior (Borg, 1960), which would seem to work against success in dealing with others, especially in terms of engendering social support. These contradictory effects demonstrate the inconsistency still present in terms of research relevant to this personality characteristic.

Self-reliance and dependability

These group members demonstrate a sense of responsibility. They manifest such characteristics as integrity, self-esteem, self-reliance, and self-control. Not surprisingly, these individuals are likely to emerge as leaders and to be successful in helping the group accomplish its task. (Stogdill, 1948; Haythorn, 1953) Can we see why the member high on this trait also is likely to be more attractive to others, more popular, more active, and so forth?

Persons with low self-esteem tend to be highly susceptible to influence attempts by others (Hovland and Janis, 1959). This is especially true when the communicator attempting the influence has higher self-esteem. Members with low self-esteem are especially susceptible to appeals employing threat. And as might be expected, high self-esteem is associated with resistance to influence attempts by others and resistance to threatening appeals.

Unconventionality

This trait is exhibited by a lack of behavioral stability and control. The unconventional group member—to put it simply—does not behave in expected ways. He seems to be disinterested in the group's task. This tends to result in lowered group productivity, primarily because his behavior seems to irritate and distract the group from its task (Haythorn, 1953). Needless to say, he does not tend to emerge as a group leader.

Emotional stability

Of all personality characteristics, this trait has been studied more than any other. All behaviors associated with emotional or mental well-being are included here.

The most extensively studied index of emotional stability is the trait of *anxiety*. It is characterized by a general concern or worry about some uncertain or future event. The anxious person feels a vague unease, a nagging worry and concern. Yet curiously, he typically cannot point to a specific cause of his worry. Anxiety generally shows itself by inadequacy in relations with others and to the group. As a group member, the anxious person is unusually dependent upon the group. Yet, at the same time, he expects less of the group. Research tends to indicate that anxious members exhibit no behaviors having a positive effect upon the group. (Shaw, 1971)

A second trait related to emotional stability is that of *adjustment*. This personality characteristic refers to the degree to which the individual seems to relate in an adequate way to his environment, including people. He seems to have emotional control and emotional stability. Adjustment seems to be related to group effectiveness, development of cohesiveness, high morale, and group motivation. (Shaw, 1971)

---

exercise 3

Form a small leaderless group. Of the six broad classes of personality attributes—Authoritarianism and Dogmatism, Social Sensitivity, Ascendant Tendencies, Self-Reliance and Dependability, Unconventionality, and Emotional Stability—discuss those which seem most relevant to *task* and *social-emotional* behaviors within the group. What personality traits seem necessary for getting the job done? What aspects of task accomplishment are likely to be positively affected by these characteristics? Why? What personality attributes are likely to hurt task fulfillment? Why? What personality attributes seem most necessary for maintaining effective social-emotional relationships within the group? What personality factors seem vital for the maintenance of a cooperative, comfortable, and relaxed atmosphere? Why? What personality variables are likely to disrupt a cooperative, comfortable, and relaxed atmosphere among group members? Why? To what extent do specific attributes improve *both* task and social-emotional aspects of group life? To what extent do particular attributes help one aspect while hurting the other? What means might be taken to handle disruptive personalities?

Intelligence

The final communicator factor we'll consider is intelligence. Whereas attitudes and personality characteristics may determine what a person is predisposed to do, intelligence may determine what a group member is capable of doing. No matter what his attitude may be, there's no way an unintelligent group member can analyze and comprehend a difficult, abstract problem—let's say one involving symbolic logic.

Intelligence is a capacity to deal with a variety of situations and problems. It shows itself through an ability to analyze and solve problems, see relationships, evaluate critically, reach sound conclusions, and so on. The highly intelligent individual seems to participate more and be more active in the dynamic workings of the group. (Bass, McGehee, Hawkins, Young, and Gebel, 1953) Not surprisingly, leaders tend to be more intelligent than the average group member (Stogdill, 1948). Studies also indicate that intelligence seems to be associated with group popularity, although the correlation is very low (Mann, 1959).

Intelligence also seems to be negatively correlated with conformity (Nakamura, 1958). The highly intelligent group member tends not to conform to group norms as closely as his less endowed brother. This may create problems for him in the group. In addition, he seems less likely to accept influence attempts by leaders and other group members. However, the group member with low intelligence may also resist attempts at influencing him to change his ideas or behavior. Apparently his low intelligence makes him resistant to normal appeals using logic, evidence, and so forth. His behavior seems to be characterized by the expression, "Don't confuse me with the facts, I've already made up my mind."

As members of small groups we should be conscious of the important role that communicator characteristics play in shaping group processes. *Credibility*—the perception of competence and trustworthiness—is perhaps the most significant communicator variable influencing group behavior. *Attitudes* that we bring to a discussion determine to a great extent the potential conflict as well as the potential productivity. Cultural influences come to bear most strongly in the *sex* characteristic. Differing role behaviors are expected of men and women, behaviors that are unfortunately often discriminatory against women. *Personality* characteristics have a wide range of relationships to amount of participation, conformity and competition, leadership, and group productivity. Finally, *intelligence* plays an especially dominant role in task-related activities and in group leadership.

Before we leave our consideration of communicator characteristics, a few words of moderation seem in order. We have examined some major communicator characteristics influencing small group processes. We have not examined all of them—our selection was guided to a great extent by the availability of research.

We discussed characteristics in their extreme forms. We must remember that all the factors we examined are typically exhibited by all communicators to a greater or lesser extent and that all these communicator qualities are operating simultaneously. They are meshing constantly with changes in message, situational context, and interaction variables. This complexity should be unraveled as we proceed in our study. Nevertheless, we have at this point a handle on some of the major variables influencing communication behavior in the small group.

ADDITIONAL READINGS

Mortensen, C. David. *Communication: The Study of Human Interaction* (New York: McGraw-Hill, 1972). Chapter 4, "Psychological Orientation, discusses fundamental psychological processes operating within communicators. The chapter includes an examination of the nature and role of credibility and ego-involvement in communication.

Shaw, Marvin E. *Group Dynamics: The Psychology of Small Group Behavior* (New York: McGraw-Hill, 1971). Chapter 6, "The Personal Environment of Groups," surveys the experimental literature on characteristics persons bring with them to a group and the influence these exert upon group process.

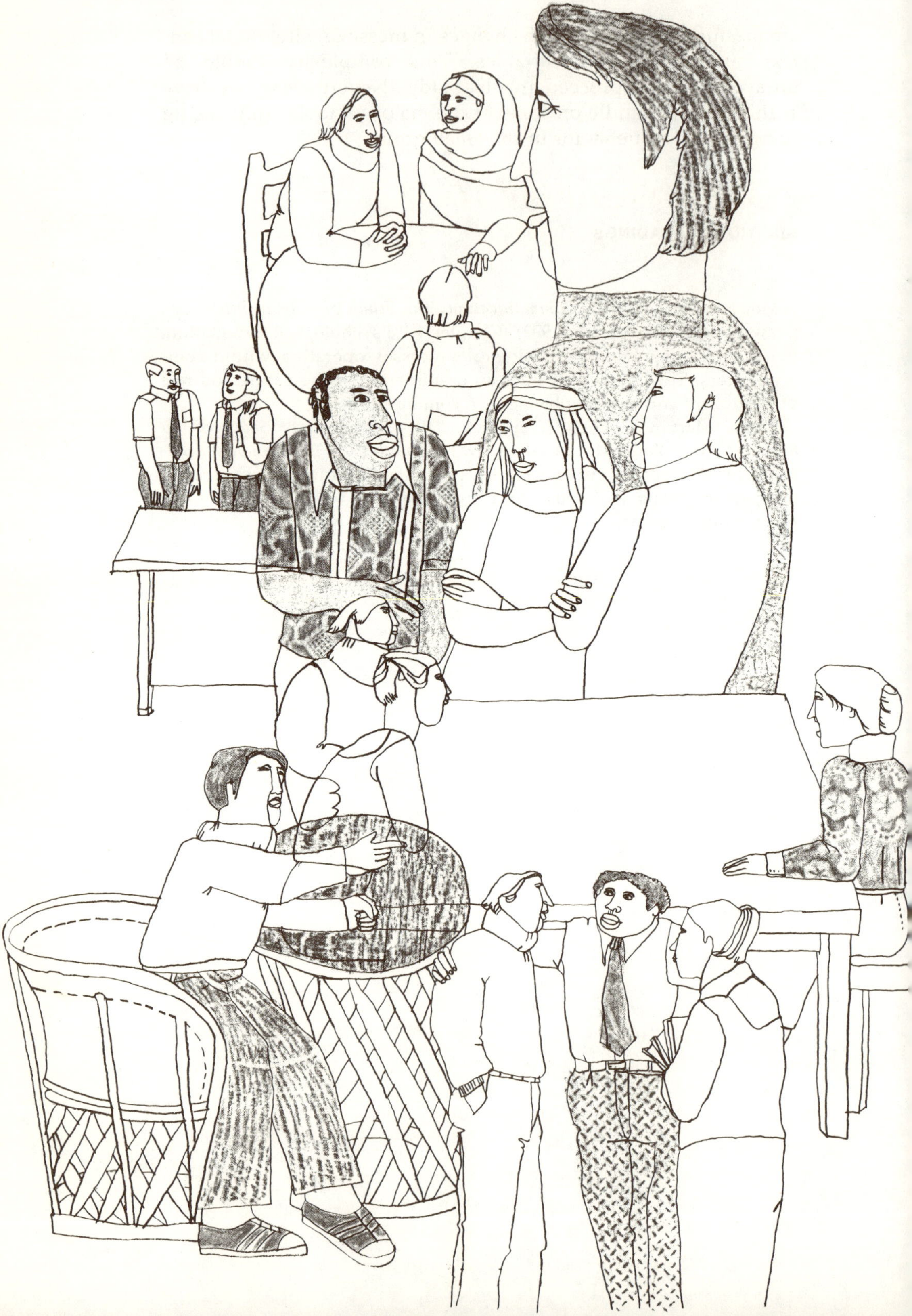

3. Verbal messages in small-group communication

PREVIEW

The nature, function, and pathological points of verbal messages are discussed.

What is the nature of language?
   Verbal messages consist of word labels arbitrarily assigned, and reflect our biases.

What are the functions of verbal messages in groups?
   Verbal messages furnish information, serve to initiate, strengthen and modify programs, motivate group members, provide feedback, and promote strategies.

What message strategies influence group members?
   Praise
   Criticism and censure
   Giving effective instructions

What causes pathological points in message sharing?
   Distortion
   Filtering
   Message overload
   Lack of acceptance

What is group member behavior in the verbal message environment?

Communication in the small group involves the process of sending messages in order to exchange ideas, impressions, suggestions, directives, requests, queries, and commands. Through this exchange, senders or sources attempt to create understanding on the part of those who receive these messages. *Understanding* is an important factor among members of the small group for it is through an understanding of objectives and issues that goals are achieved. Goal-oriented behavior is influenced through effective communication.

An understanding of goals, objectives, and issues depends on the interrelation between four basic components of the communication process:

1. Sources or senders to give out information.
2. Vehicles (symbols, messages, language) to carry information.
3. Communication networks to deliver information to various persons, or work stations.
4. Receivers to gather, interpret, and respond to the information.

In the previous chapter we discussed several aspects of the source in groups; in this chapter we shall discuss various aspects of messages.

In the first chapter, we noted that messages may be studied under two broad categories—their verbal and nonverbal features. In this chapter, we shall discuss the form, structure, interaction, and effects of verbal messages. Nonverbal messages will be discussed in the next chapter.

The term *verbal* refers to the use of printed or spoken words to evoke meaning or understanding. When we work together in a small group, we are required to perceive and receive a constant flow of incoming stimulus—data or messages. Our knowledge of the group's goals, and our feelings and attitudes toward ourselves and the group in general, will be determined by the way in which we perceive the messages. More important, the character of our knowledge, feelings, and attitudes will influence the type of messages or "vibrations" that we ourselves send out, and also the meanings or understandings that those messages evoke. Unfortunately, verbal messages do not always tell it like it is.

Consider the following dilemma. A lot of things are going on around me—all at once. The buzzing confusion of events never lets up. However, I cannot afford to be concerned with nor interested in *all* that's going on. Thus my problem is: How shall I extract that which interests me from all that's going on? What kinds of mental filters do I use? What do I say to myself and to others about the things that interest me? How shall I interpret? How shall I describe? Our interpretations and descriptions are detailed through language; first, (covertly) to classify and organize the sensory impressions that are coming in; second, (overtly) to inform our fellow group members of these impressions. Remember, however, that our language or messages may not tell it like it is. We shall see why this is so when we look at the nature of language.

The nature of language

Verbal messages consist of word-labels, which are arbitrarily assigned and reflect our biased responses to events and objects. In some parts of the United States, individuals who live on welfare are called chiselers by those who are opposed to government aid to the poor. Are they really chiselers? The problem is that in our description of events or objects or behaviors, we do not always call 'em as we see 'em; sometimes we call 'em as we feel when we see 'em; and sometimes we call 'em as we see 'em without realizing that we are not really seeing things as they are.

We see those things that we habitually pay attention to, or things that will facilitate our objectives at any given moment, or things that we can use as ammunition-data to justify our claims concerning someone in the group, and we overlook everything else. Thus the word-labels or verbal messages we use are susceptible to much personal bias and contamination. If our word-labels are tainted, then what may be the nature of the meanings we evoke in others?

How would you report or describe the following incident which occurred consistently in a group discussion class? On each occasion that his discussion group met to discuss a topic, Edgar sat silently, his chin in his hands, never speaking even when invited to do so.

In reporting, we have several choices. Here are a few:

1. "Edgar sits through the entire discussion and never comments. He has behaved in this manner on several occasions."

2. "I have never seen a more looney s.o.b. than Edgar. Those kinds of guys could go off the deep end any moment."
3. "Edgar is trying to make our group look bad. He knows that our grade depends on total participation and that's why he clams up."

Notice the changing character of our word-labels and messages as we moved from our first statement to the two succeeding statements. In our first statement we were *describing* as much of an event as we were able to perceive. In the succeeding statements we were allowing *guesses* to overcome us. In descriptions (2) and (3) we were running the risk of evoking the improper meanings from other members concerning the event. This is due to the extremely great amount of *abstracting* that we allowed ourselves. It should be apparent that the verbal behavior generated in statements (2) and (3) will not succeed in bringing about that "higher level" of understanding that we strive to achieve in group communication.

Total understanding depends on the message sender and message receiver having similar experiences with objects or *referents* conveyed in the message through word-labels. The words have no meanings in and of themselves. Rather words act as triggers to stimulate meanings in us. These meanings are brought along through our past experiences. Having had no experience with a group member who sits in silence, we conjured up word-labels to fit referents that seemed similar in behavior, and Edgar became some sort of lunatic.

We should understand that words are not mandated to us from on High; there is nothing magical about words. Words are arbitrarily assigned to things and events by the people who use them. Such arbitrariness gives us the facility to call a certain tool a lugwrench at one moment and a gizmo at another. But notice the escalation of the human problem when one discussant advocates "total, immediate disbanding of all of our military units in Europe and Asia," and an opposing discussant labels him "unpatriotic and lacking in dignity as befits a red-blooded American."

Here is another example: a few members of a policymaking group advocate the teaching of sex education in schools, in response to which the majority of the group members label them "a bunch of Commie freaks and weirdos." Are they really? Does the label "Commie freak and weirdo" bring about a correspondence between the person and the label, or between a thing and a label? No. The word is not the thing. A word is a stand-in for talking about a thing; and when used, it may constitute a reasonably good representation or a horrendously poor one.

Though potentially both useful and useless, harmful and harmless, orienting and disorienting, words are the stuff of which verbal messages are made. Verbal messages, in turn, are the vehicles through which the group controls its locomotion toward achieving the task, and its harmony among members. So, if and when we use words—let's be careful how we use them. Later in the chapter, we will focus on a few worthwhile suggestions. For the moment, let us shift our emphasis away from the nature of language; let us discuss a few aspects of the function, form, and structure of verbal messages.

The function of verbal messages in small groups

Verbal messages in the small group may be viewed as fulfilling the following functions:

1. Verbal messages furnish information for nonprogrammed or informal activities in the group. Such activities include the grapevine, scuttlebutt, gossip, and phatic communication or social chitchat. Though nonprogrammed, such activities are vital to the social fabric of a group.
2. Verbal messages serve to launch programs, strengthen on-going programs, and also aid in the adjustment of agenda.
3. Verbal messages aid us in the choice of strategy or arguments. Strategy is involved in decision-making and verbal messages are the substance of its implementation.
4. Verbal messages are used for motivating individuals in the group. The nature of the messages used in this setting is of vital importance to all groups, for success in motivation depends on the effectiveness of the message.
5. Verbal messages furnish information on the results of group activity. Such messages detail feedback of control information needed by decision makers, group leaders, bosses, and so on.

Since it is necessary that these five aforementioned functions be served, the structure and form of verbal messages assume great importance for the student of small-group communication. Regardless of the function or group situation, any group member who transmits information expects to have his ideas or impressions assimilated by certain "targets," or responsive individuals in the group. On the other hand, the receiver of that verbal message expects the message to meet his or her needs and demands in the group. However, we should recall that verbal messages consist of no more than a set of symbols in a patterned or structured arrangement, and that our senses are titilated or depressed by the meanings that we attach to those symbols. From these symbols structure is formed, content is manifested, and meanings are attached.

Those of us who serve as members of groups must realize that our every act in a group constitutes a behavior. Behavior communicates. Messages are constantly being emitted. Consequently *content* is always present in a group situation. A fundamental point to note is that most communication settings are often hazy because of the inherent inability of words or symbols to serve as adequate representations of events or situations. This haziness or unclarity creates tension between senders and receivers; and whenever there is tension or strain between group members, an increased need to communicate and to be communicated with is aroused (Fearing 1953–1954). At this point, verbal messages are exchanged in greater quantity and frequency in order to remove or reduce the tension, and success depends on our ability to vary our message strategies.

We should note, also, that the increase in communication through verbal messages must respond to two basic group needs in order to reduce tension. First an increase in verbal messages may be needed to clear up uncertainties concerning the task. Second, an increase in verbal messages may be needed to provide members with reasons for their need to participate in the group's activity. The first provides method; the second provides motivation. The study of message strategies becomes more important when we consider that the method- or motivation-inducing messages are invariably tainted by the sender's perceptions of things, persons, and events. The receiver, too, listens to or reads these messages and modifies them in terms of prior experiences, perceptions, and sensations. We must seek means of bringing verbal messages into closer correspondence with the meanings of several group members simultaneously.

Message strategies

We use message strategies in order to change the behaviors of group participants. In order to change behaviors we must resort to *persuasion* rather than coercion if our relationship with the group is to continue in an atmosphere of friendliness and goodwill. Persuasion depends on our ability to structure verbal messages and fashion strategies. Much of our attempts at persuasion in the group is channeled through: (1) *praise*, (2) *criticism* or censure, and (3) *giving instructions*. Unfortunately, we all tend to fail at these chores in crucial situations. Let us look at some of the verbal pitfalls, and a few ways to correct our verbal messages in each of the three acts of praising, criticizing, and giving instructions.

Praise

Praise, used effectively, improves the quality of a group; used ineffectively, it may insult the person being praised, and alienate the other members of the group. The proper use of praise calls for qualities of leadership—tact, fairness, sensitivity, objectivity, and an ability to explain. Praise should be reserved for praiseworthy events. Specifically, praise should be used to boost better-than-average performance into outstanding performance into outstanding achievement. On the other hand, we should use simply acknowledgment for satisfactory performance.

How should we use praise? Are there certain key strategies to be kept in mind? We believe that three basic principles would serve us well.

1. Keep praise appropriate to the achievement.

However you put it, praise should convey the message: "I am proud of you." If your verbal message does not reflect justifiable pride, it belittles the receiver and belies or depreciates the value of his accomplishment. Statements such as "That was an excellent suggestion, Elmer" and "You took care of that assignment in excellent fashion" are ample praise the first time around. But repeated over and over again whenever Elmer "performs," they become monotonous, hollow, and worthless. Moreover, the other group members may soon be alienated by your condescending manner. It is also possible that through wanton and indiscriminating praise, Elmer would be put on the spot in front of his fellow group members, especially if Elmer knows (or feels) darn well that the other members are performing just as well. Look, if Elmer turns you on that much, we suggest that you tell him so privately—don't gush on the group's time.

2. Combine praise with recognition.

What we have said thus far should not lead us into thinking that public commendation in the group should be minimized. We insist that when a member has made an outstanding contribution, he or she should be praised publicly. However, we must realize that lavish praise for a noteworthy achievement will be interpreted as a hollow gesture unless such praise is combined with some form of recognition. Recognition (or reward) varies according to the group situation. For some high-achieving group member, recognition may be manifested through promotion; in another group, recognition may be a delegation of more authority; and in some cases, some type of special award may suffice.

We emphasize the point of recognition in this chapter because of the word-weariness that has overtaken our society. Words are so much with us that we can no longer feel their weight or their warmth when they stand alone. We have heard "Atta boy, Harry" so often that we no longer feel a sense of uplift when it is said to us. As group leaders or people who profess an understanding of group dynamics, we must seek ways to enrich our verbal messages.

Praise should accomplish the dual purpose of informing and inspiring the group. Consequently the verbal content of the message should help to achieve these objectives. When we praise others, we should be prepared to give them opportunities to demonstrate that their performance was not just a fluke; moreover, we should give them other assignments to show that we have confidence that they can continue to do outstanding work. If you were on the receiving end, we believe that this is exactly the way you'd want to be treated.

3. Use praise as an incentive, not as a billy club.

Do not resort to the gimmick of verbally praising one member's performance in order to stampede other members into better performance. "Fantastic work there, Seymour baby! That's really showing these miserable hammerheads how to do it! Hey everybody, look at old Seymour flip those tin sheets!" You can bet that they'll look at Seymour, and that they'll be looking at him for a long time. They will not be likely to see Seymour with the same amount of "admiration" as you do.

The lesson is simple: If other group members feel that your praise is nothing but camouflaged criticism of them, the group performance will deteriorate instead of improving. Instead of insinuating or hinting that everyone else should imitate Seymour, it would be far better to just let them see that Seymour's flipping talent (or energy?) is both recognized and appreciated. They'll catch on.

One other word of advice. In most groups performance of the majority is rarely good enough to merit praise. Yet their performance is seldom poor enough to warrant outright criticism. You *cannot* afford to ignore these members. They are entitled to know just where they stand, and it is your duty to tell them. In the group, silence is not golden—at least, not the leader's silence. Keep your mouth shut, and you will be misinterpreted: some will misconstrue your silence for praise; others will misconstrue it as criticism.

The level and the quality of performance in your group—whether it is a work group, discussion group, case-study group, or troubleshooting team—can be increased if you tell members *frequently* that they are doing all right, while encouraging

Persuasion by praise, criticism, and giving instructions

them to do better. *Don't* give the impression that you are thoroughly satisfied. Let them know that you feel they have the ability to do even better work and you are confident that, with their help, the entire group can improve its standing.

The use of praise, or at least the considerations involved in using praise, should remind us that verbal messages are not only good supervisory and motivational tools; they are also delicate tools. To use verbal messages well entails more than a mere ability to speak or write. If giving praise demands so much consideration, we must wonder at the tremendous taxation that *making criticisms* requires. This next section on message strategies deals with the issue of criticism.

Criticism and censure

Criticism and censure sometimes act as lubricants to set the wheels of the group in faster motion. Fortunately, there are some leaders who, inclined to feelings of discomfort when "chewing out" others, refrain from criticizing. Unfortunately, there are others who think it necessary to criticize constantly in order to keep "my workers honest and on the ball." Somewhere between these extremes there is a balance that we must attain. Criticism and censure can be effective if we use words wisely. Here is an anecdote that shows what can happen if words are not chosen wisely:

Boom-Boom Branigan has been assistant production supervisor of a die-casting group for about four years. Boom-Boom is always on the run, checking on supplies, adjusting defects, working on schedules with the production people, explaining reasons for substandard parts to the white-shirt guys in quality control. The problem is that whenever Boom-Boom has to leave his group, it means that supervision is interrupted. This situation really annoys the manager, J. Mortimer McNasty. He is further annoyed because he is not always aware of where Boom-Boom is or why he is not in the assembly area. One day, the manager calls Boom-Boom in, and tells him that henceforth he must check with him (McNasty) whenever he intends to leave the assembly area. Here's a transcript of that confrontation:

MCNASTY: Look here, Boom-Boom. You are spending a helluva lotta time outside your area. Now, as far as I'm concerned, that's bad. It's not the way I want things to go around here. From now on this is how it's going to be: You make sure that you check with me first whenever you have to go on some crazy mission anywhere in this plant. You got me?

BOOM-BOOM: Well, you're the boss, Mr. McNasty... but I don't know why you want me to report to you every time. I'd have to come to you pretty near fifty times a day. You know that I'm on the run most of the time.

MCNASTY: Never mind that. Just do as I say. I don't have time to go into all of the reasons. As a matter of fact, I think the reasons are obvious enough. Tomorrow, you report to me. Okay?

BOOM-BOOM: (sighing loudly as he prepares to leave) Mr. McNasty, this is unreasonable. You *are* unreasonable. Furthermore, you are crazier than I think you are if you really believe that I'm going to come running to you to *beg* for permission every time I have to go down the line. Do you know what? I quit. I sure as hell quit!

Now there is reason to believe that Mortimer McNasty had legitimate reasons to be concerned about what happens whenever

Boom-Boom left his group unsupervised. Why else would he want to see Boom-Boom's face fifty times a day? However, Boom-Boom Branigan was not entirely unreasonable in responding the way he did. Let's examine the situation.

The manager's verbal message seemed to convey only the idea that a *change* was necessary. Unfortunately, that message did not state *why* a change was required. Boom-Boom, on the receiving end, perceived the manager's message as casting aspersions on his ability and trustworthiness as assistant production supervisor. He was flabbergasted and got defensive. "I quit," he said. But don't believe him. Those two words should not be taken literally because of the intense emotional context in which they were uttered. Let us reconstruct the confrontation to see what happens when verbal messages are carefully and thoughtfully put together:

MCNASTY: I realize that you've got a helluva lot of running around to do every day. And quite frankly, Boom-Boom, I don't know how you can do it day after day. But when you are not there, supervision really suffers. It *really* breaks down. You know, I think that both of us will have to work something out here.

BOOM-BOOM: I'll tell you something, Mr. McNasty. I've been worried about that too. I lie awake nights thinking about that. I get to thinking that maybe we need one or two more group leaders to give me a hand whenever I've got to go down the line.

MCNASTY: I think you've got a good idea there, Boom-Boom. But I have a feeling that it will take us quite some time to look into the leadership problem. Let me look into it, and I'll try to get some data to back up my request for more leaders. Those guys upstairs like to see hard data before they talk with me. *In the meantime, I think it would help if you look around for me before you go down the line.* In that way I can keep my eyes open for any problems until you get back. If you'd remember to do that from now on, it should help you and me to keep things going right on schedule.

BOOM-BOOM: As you say, Mr. McNasty. I'll remember to give you the old on-the-road sign whenever I've got to hit the trail.

In the first dialogue, the manager had failed to supply the *why* to his request or criticism. In the second dialogue, the supervisor gives the assistant a good reason for the request, and he did not belittle or minimize the suggested solution advanced. In the end, it is Boom-Boom who says: "I'll remember to give you the old on-the-road sign...." The result is goodwill, cooperation, and a feeling of accomplishment.

There are, of course, other occasions when a more deliberate type of criticism must be directed at group members. Our example, in the two dialogues, presented more observation or request verbal messages than outright criticism messages. When criticism is warranted, we should also be mindful of the way we tailor verbal messages.

First of all, if you have to criticize, be constructive. This usually turns out to be an effective way to inspire better performance. What reaction can you expect to "You are doing this thing all wrong. Don't be a jackass, Henry. Come on, you know better than that." You'll stand a chance of getting a better reaction if you say: "You know something, Henry? I really think that you can improve on this work, with just a few minor adjustments. Look, try doing it this way and let me know if it works any better. I have a hunch we may be able to do it."

One may contend that publicly reprimanding a group member may be better than allowing him or her to get away with shabby work; however, we cannot recommend this as good group maintenance behavior where it can be avoided. Your criticism will be more effective if you recognize that the individual under censure has certain rights. The most obvious are:

1. The right to privacy during criticism or reprimand.
2. The right to tell his side of the story and to explain any extenuating circumstances.
3. The right to hear specific charges for specific instances of poor performance, misbehavior, or misconduct.
4. The right to consistent treatment for particular offenses and not be singled out (and made a special example) of a group of fellow offenders.
5. The right to make an honest unintentional mistake without receiving scathing rebukes and severe tongue lashings.

Remember that if you prejudge a situation and think that you know the answers before you ask questions, you can alienate not only the member directly involved but the rest of the group as well. Making sure that a group member is given the opportunity to explain his side of the story involves more than just courtesy; it also involves a chance for you to prevent considerable self-embarrassment, especially if there were indeed extenuating circumstances that led to the violation of or deviation from procedure. The obtaining of facts may also enable us to deal with the situation in a logical point-by-point manner. Resist the temptation to argue. Don't get into verbal shouting matches. Talk about the member's performance in terms of "more" or "less," rather than "good" or "bad." And remember, the more private the confrontation, the better the outcome.

Thus far, we have discussed the verbal message strategies involved in issuing praise and censure. These are vital tasks in group maintenance, and we have pointed out the care and forethought that should be exercised. There is one other task that conjures much difficulty for leaders and members of groups: *giving effective instructions*. Let us examine the verbal message strategies demanded in this instance.

Giving effective instructions

Most of us, when giving instructions to others, often overlook the fact that the guy at the receiving end brings his own unique meaning system to the situation. Whatever is said is often interpreted in terms of his perceptions, memories, expectations, needs, and so on. It is tough to give instructions in such a way that the requests or directives would be carried out fully. Here are a couple of examples.

An office supervisor notices water on the floor, apparently spilled by the secretary as she carried water to the coffee percolator. As she walks by she calls out to a secretary nearby: "Hey, what's the matter with you people? Don't you know we're supposed to keep this office clean? Take care of that water; it's a mess!"

The secretary, Vicki Twinklefingers, nods and turns back to her IBM wonder machine. A few minutes later, the accounts receivable girl, Gladys Gains, slips and falls on the very same water puddle. She's badly hurt and misses several days of work.

When the office supervisor tries to reprimand Vicki, she replies, "I didn't know what you meant. I thought you said something about water on the percolator table. Besides I was busy and thought you'd want me to finish the memos before I did anything else. You told me to put a rush on the memos."

Here's how the misunderstanding and an accident could have been prevented.

The office supervisor sees the water on the floor and approaches the nearest secretary:

"Do you see that water on the floor, Vicki? That's really dangerous. You or one of the other girls could have a bad fall. I'd appreciate it if you'd dry it up right now. Forget the memos for the time being. This shouldn't take much time. We've got to prevent accidents, you know. O.K.?"

One of the most obvious differences in the two versions is that the second one used enough words to get the message across. The office supervisor made her message as *redundant* as possible so that even if some information was lost, its vital meaning content would still remain. There were some other good principles of effective message sharing exhibited in the latter version. You would notice that:

1. The instructions were put in the form of a request instead of an order.
2. The instructions included verbal messages giving the *reason* for the extra task and letting the group member know that her own personal welfare was at stake.

Someone may argue that these principles are all well and good in getting our point across in such simple tasks as drying up a puddle of water, covering paint cans, wearing safety goggles, and so on, but what about more complicated instructions? Does this task call for a difference in verbal message strategies? Here are some guidelines to be followed:

1. Whenever you are giving complicated or lengthy instructions, try to get the receiver to ask questions.

This will provide you with feedback and will alert you to existing problems. For example, some group members may reasonably feel that there is a conflict between the new instructions and certain standard procedures if the instructions were not carefully explained. If the receiver does not take the initiative in asking questions, you should exert some effort in trying to draw out these questions.

2. Make it a point to repeat basic instructions.

We are not suggesting that we resort to needless repetition by way of a lot of unnecessary words. You don't want to bore people to indifference or death. We are suggesting that you review the instructions at certain key junctures, not only at the time of giving the instructions, but also later on while the group member is actually carrying out the task.

You should attempt to achieve these three basic requirements of successful verbal communication:

1. That people listen to you.
2. That they understand you.
3. That they react to what you say as you want them to.

The first point is the most important. Our failure to meet these fundamental requirements is responsible for most blunders in oral communication. Too many of us assume that just because other people have ears, they will or should listen to what we have to say.

People don't always listen, and this is often because they are not interested in what we are trying to tell them. They may appear to be listening, but their thoughts are elsewhere. How do we solve this problem?

The key to making your spoken communication, or verbal messages, more successful resides in a knowledge or awareness of your listener and his interests. Here are three basic guidelines:

1. Know your listener; try to be aware of his needs, how he reacts, what makes him tick.
2. Talk with him, or direct your remarks to him in terms of his own interests.
3. Let him know by your attitude and behavior of your interest in him.

Failure to follow these guidelines may result in a monologue. You will merely be expressing yourself, discussing your own interests; consequently, your words may never register in the mind you are trying to reach. Remember that every member of the group wants to be recognized as a person.

Strategies notwithstanding, we should realize that what works well in one situation may not work as well in another similar situation. No matter how skillful we may be with messages, breakdowns in communication will inevitably occur. In this next section we will look at some of those crucial pathologies or dysfunctions that beset senders and receivers in their responses to verbal messages.

Dysfunctional or pathological points in message sharing

Difficulties with verbal messages often arise from one or a combination of the following factors:

1. the nature and functions of language
2. deliberate misrepresentation
3. size and complexity of the group
4. lack of acceptance of inductions, suggestions, norms, and deviations

These four factors, in turn, lead to several pathologies or dysfunctions in the operation of the group. Some of these are:

1. distortion
2. filtering
3. message overload
4. lack of acceptance

Let us examine each of these separately.

Distortion

Distortion results from semantic breakdowns: (1) the efficiency or inefficiency of a language to convey a point of view, (2) the kind of language being used, (3) the similarity or dissimilarity of experiences or referents shared by senders and receivers.

Distortion often happens because a language is sometimes inadequate to carry a person's expressions. Sometimes we cannot find words to describe our feelings. At such times, we do the best we can. However, there are times when we do not perform with our best verbal behaviors; sometimes we tend to frame our references inadequately and distortions occur.

Overhearing a conversation in which the name "Henrietta" was being mentioned frequently, I asked of my buddy Al: 'Who is Henrietta?" Replied Al calmly, 'Henrietta is a pig who lives down on Pacific Avenue."
"Oh," said I.
Is she, or isn't she? And if she isn't, then what is she? Either way, Henrietta loses. I wish that Al would be more precise with his answers. As far as I know, Henrietta lives in either a sty or a brothel on Pacific. Henrietta?

Well, we can't do very much about the structure of our language—we are stuck with it. But we can certainly improve on the manner in which we string messages together. We must realize that messages traveling around from person to person in a group have to be *translated* to suit the various authoritative and mental levels at which they are received. Engineers tend to speak a different language from farmers, farmers from doctors, doctors from lawyers, and students are in a class by themselves. Person to person, much is lost in translation.

What may we do to minimize distortions? One effective way would be to constantly ask for feedback from our listeners to make sure that they have really grasped the intent and content of our message. Or we may make use of redundancy, particularly if we are passing on technical information in the group. The repetition that goes on between pilot and copilot as they go through a checklist before takeoff is a good example of the *redundancy principle*. (Guetzkow, 1956)

Filtering

Filtering is mainly a subconscious mental process of misinterpreting, misperceiving, or misrepresenting facts or situations. In most instances this filtering occurs without malice or mischief on our part. It's simply that we all tend to view facts, statements, situations and so on, through the filters of our own expectations, whether optimistic or pessimistic, biased or unbiased. If members of a group prejudge a given member as a "no good, conniving, power-grabbing swine," they may run the risk of filtering even the most well-intentioned comment made by the suspect into an understanding that matches their expectation.

Filtering flows both ways; we tend to filter incoming messages and outgoing messages. In the first instance, messages from people we like tend to sound good, and messages from people we dislike sound bad. Outgoing messages emanate from us, and even here filtering occurs. Here's how it may occur: One day during the Annual Fraternity Cook-Out, Lucius Fibbergab saunters off in search of firewood and stumbles upon an eight inch long garter snake asleep on the trail. The snake scares the living daylights out of old Fibbergab, but he musters enough adrenalin to pick up a stout branch from the underbrush and with about fifty strokes reduces the reptile to a ribbon. The snake, fortunately, was fast asleep and never knew what hit him.

Fibbergab fetches the firewood, and later that night while everyone swaps stories around the campfire, he rather modestly tells the group about the python that attacked him while he was out searching for wood. He relates that he stood his ground—that being the best way to respond to a "killer snake"—and after parrying and thrusting with his scouting knife, he slew the mighty python.

We should not judge Lucius Fibbergab too severely; we are all guilty of telling our suped-up fish (and snake) stories. We all tend to strain reality through our mental filters. A friend of mine repeatedly tells me about the date he had last summer "with this gorgeous chick—she was last year's Homecoming Queen at Bad-Axe Agricultural Institute." Actually, he ran into (not literally) Knap-Sack Katie while she was thumbing a ride on I-69. She wanted a ride to Omaha where she worked in the stockyard as a hog-caller. Why the filtering? One reason is that people have a desire to look good in the esteem of their peers.

Remember that filtering is likely to occur with most of the verbal messages that we transmit in criticism, communications, requests, orders, directives, casual comments, and instructions in the group. Whatever the circumstance, we should be aware of the tendency to filter. It may not be a bad idea to run audits on the information sent and received in the group. Insisting on feedback of meaning and understanding may be a way to accomplish the audit.

Distortion, filtering, message overload, or lack of acceptance may cause dysfunctions in the group

Message overload

Some group leaders, coordinators, and managers find themselves bombarded with data, information, reports, requests, and complaints. When this saturation occurs, we say that the channel is overloaded. Dubin (1959) argues in favor of establishing a monitoring effect. This monitoring effect is used by a college president, for example, who surrounds himself with assistants who clear all incoming messages in order of priority and importance and condense the content before passing it up the line.

In small groups that depend on a free flow of information, this may not be a good plan. However, as a group increases in complexity, measures must be taken to ensure that saturation with messages and information does not occur.

Lack of acceptance

Lack of acceptance of message constitutes another cause of failure in group task accomplishment. The fact that a member receives information does not guarantee acceptance. Acceptance depends on the needs, motives, experience, and education of the receiver, plus the social milieu in which he exists.

We realize that acceptance of a message is not a necessary criterion for doing what the message requests. But people tend to be happier when they find themselves performing behaviors that they *can* accept. Morale is better in such instances. On the other hand, when group members perform tasks efficiently even though they do not agree with the requested performance, acceptance would be low and morale would be weakened. Fear appeals are sometimes used to compel individuals into performance.

Some of the factors which determine acceptance of messages are as follows:

Reality. Reality to an individual is that which he derives from his personal definition of the environment. Individuals differ and reality varies. What I see as realistic may not be realistic to you. Problems emerge in the group when we attach our own definitions of reality to the contents of a message. Consequently, some messages are accepted and some are rejected.

Ambiguity. Messages are susceptible to many shades of interpretation. To compound the problem, it is quite possible that an individual may not have a clear picture of reality at a given moment; or the messages themselves may be hazy. Ambiguity results from this confusion, and the messages are less likely to be accepted.

Credibility. Messages are accepted if a receiver believes a sender. Where trust is lacking, acceptance will be hindered.

Congruency. Congruency relates to the perception that a member has concerning the correspondence of the message to his or her needs, motives, and values. Does the message conflict with, or does it enhance, those values, motives, and needs? If there is a positive correspondence, then congruency will be great, and acceptance will be high. With negative correspondence, the opposite occurs. (Fearing, 1953–54; and Zajonc, 1959)

These factors, reality, ambiguity, credibility, and congruency, are all interrelated. As these stresses impinge on the human system, let us look at some of the concrete things that group members do with the messages that they receive. Much of the following discussion is derived from Collins and Guetzkow's review (1964) of work done by Campbell (1958).

Group member behavior in the verbal message environment

1. A group member's understanding of the message is generally abbreviated. For instance, conference members retain and assimilate only a small portion of the information that is held collectively by the group. (Campbell, p. 342)
2. Group members remember the middle portion of messages least. (Campbell, p. 348) We suggest that speakers seek ways to heighten the retention capability of the middle portion of the messages. Repetition and redundancy may be useful techniques. Summaries at the end of a presentation may also be useful.
3. Group members tend to break down the entities in a message and consign them to clear-cut categories. Seemingly, it's easier to pretend that things exist in extremes, and by such pretense, one need not bother with all of the facts in the middle. We tend to exaggerate some differences, and we tend to blend others.
4. What a group member listens to will be packaged in with all of his past experiences—those that were rewarding; those that were punishing. We are constantly attempting to maximize rewards and minimize punishments. Thus we approach each message with a what's-in-it-for-me attitude. If a message seems to threaten, we tend to avoid the message and reject the sender.

5. We tend to handcuff senders onto their messages. Consequently if we are impressed with what is frequently said by one individual, we tend to expect that verbal behavior from him consistently. The problem emerges when we associate an individual with consistently offending messages. We tune him out, at times, and run the risk of missing vital inputs that he may occasionally bring to the group.
6. Conformity pressures sometimes exist in great proportions in small groups. When this occurs in a message environment there is a tendency toward ganging up. We sometimes tend to *distort* our impressions to fit the impressions of the majority in a group. This, of course, is beneficial to consensus, but it sometimes contributes toward selling out one's better judgments.

We should find ways to increase our efficiency as senders and receivers in order that the group process may be beneficial and effective. McCroskey, Larson, and Knapp (1971) provide some helpful hints that are definitely worthy of attention. They suggest that a communicator who wishes to achieve greater accuracy in his message environment will analyze his listener(s), situation(s), himself, and the special conditions that surround him. That communicator should be mindful of—

1. The degree of accuracy that can be achieved realistically in a given context.
2. The interference of our own attitudes toward one another and toward messages exchanged among us.
3. Our own limitations as senders and receivers—our mental filters.
4. An empathy with our receivers' socio-cultural background.
5. The effect of certain loaded words on certain receivers.
6. How to structure our messages in order to give clearer reports to those around us.

There is a hope that if we become seriously concerned with the operations of language—its nature, form, function, and messages—we may be able to heighten our efficiency in small groups. More important, there is the hope that we will become more mindful of our fellowmen and spare others the tyranny of ill-chosen or ill-fitting words. Beyond that, we can teach others and ourselves, as well, that words don't mean; people mean.

ADDITIONAL READINGS

Collins, B., and Guetzkow, H. *A Social Psychology of Group Processes for Decision-making* (New York: John Wiley, 1964). Chapter 9 contains a helpful discussion of the issues involved in group communication and interaction. The discussion on pages 183–87 deals with the manner in which group members respond to messages.

McCroskey, J.; Larson, C.; and Knapp, M. *An Introduction to Interpersonal Communication* (Englewood Cliffs, N.J.: Prentice-Hall, 1971). Chapter 8 deals with verbal message variables in interpersonal influence. This chapter gives a good review of scientific findings.

Mortensen, C. D. *Communication: The Study of Human Interaction* (New York: McGraw-Hill, 1972). Chapter 5 details an extensive review of studies of the dynamics of verbal interaction. Students will find this material most helpful.

Scheidel, T. M. *Speech Communication and Human Interaction* (Glenview, Illinois: Scott, Foresman, 1972). See chapter 6 for a discussion of the interaction between language and perception. Chapter 6 also presents ample coverage of the nature of language.

Scott, Wm. G., and Mitchell, T. *Organization Theory: A Structural and Behavioral Analysis* (Homewood, Illinois: Richard D. Irwin, Inc., and The Dorsey Press, 1972). Chapter 8 discusses communication processes in the organization. The section entitled, "Appendix: Notes on Communication Dysfunctions" (pp. 157–64) is valuable reading material.

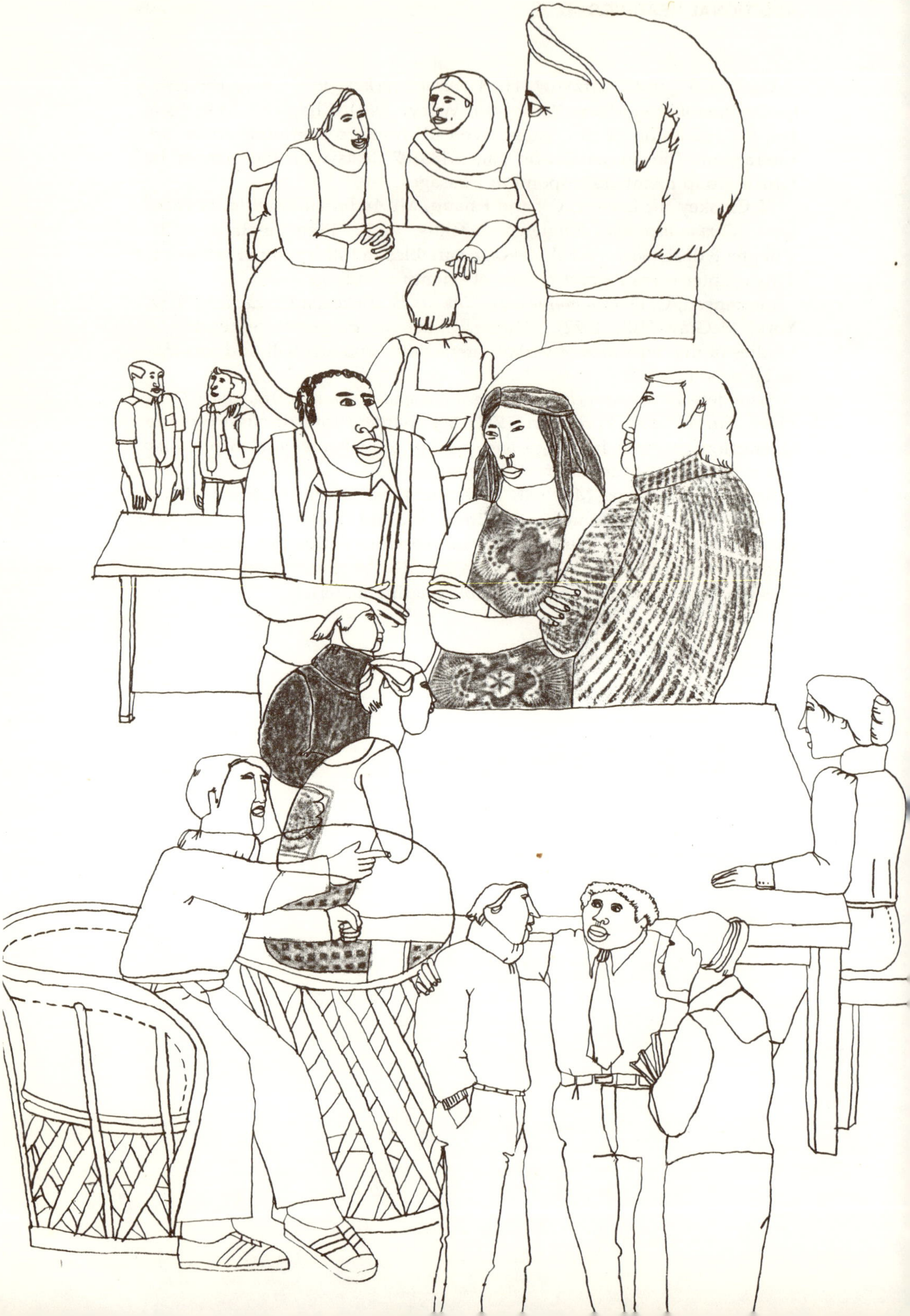

4. Nonverbal messages in small-group communication

PREVIEW

What is the significance of nonverbal message cues?
　The major portion of messages is understood largely through nonverbal cues accompanying them.
　A list of these nonverbal cues might include
　　body motion or kinesic behavior
　　paralanguage or metacommunication
　　proxemics—that is, the effects of spatial factors on communicators

What are the signals of nonverbal language?
　Certain features of nonverbal language provide an index of emotions, intentions, feelings, and desires. These features are studied under the following terms:
　　signals of emotions
　　signals for control and direction
　　signals of interpersonal orientation
　　signals for clarification

How do spatial arrangements and social distance influence the quality and quantity of group communication?
　Frequently, the seating arrangement exerts considerable influence on the flow of communication in the group.
　The amount of social distance between communicators is frequently influenced by the kinds of messages being exchanged.
　The personalities of the communicators, and also the prevailing cultural norms, will influence the distance maintained between them.
　The violation of personal space may lead to defensiveness and aggression.

Spoken and written words—verbal message cues—constitute only a minor portion of the messages that trigger communication in the small group. The major portion is derived from what we are sometimes unaware of—nonverbal cues. Nonverbal cues are those communication triggers that spring from our behavior in the presence of others. They are present even when we behave unintentionally. Every glance, every twitch of the eyebrows, every nod of the head, or movement of the hand is a nonverbal message cue that can be interpreted by others. The people around us tend to put a meaning to the various changes of our behavior. Since we are always behaving, either consciously or unconsciously, it follows that we cannot really keep from communicating as long as we are under the scrutiny of others. Weird Waldo, seated impassively at the discussion table with a guppylike gaze while everyone else is jabbering, is "communicating" as much as Motor-mouth Morton, who advances an asinine opinion on every issue. Both are a bother to the group because we attach meaning to their behavior.

---

exercise 1

To heighten our appreciation of the effect of nonverbal message cues:

1. Select seven individuals from another class to discuss a particular topic (chosen on the basis of relevance or importance). Make sure that the group goes through the normal process of researching and preparing in advance of the actual presentation.

2. Assign the following roles to each of two participants, making sure that the remaining five participants are unaware of the roles.

3. Situation: During the entire discussion (approximately 25 minutes), Role-player A gazes vacantly and wordlessly, refusing (silently) to be drawn into the interaction. Role-player B constantly interrupts, cutting off other speakers in the midst of conversation and disagreeing with almost everything that's said.

4. Immediately following the discussion, let the five "naive" group members answer the following questions:
   a. Were you adversely affected by the behaviors of any of the group members?
   b. What particular effects were you conscious of?
   c. What did you think of Mr. A's silence while everyone else was involved in the discussion?
   d. What did you think of Mr. B's performance?
   e. How would you interpret Mr. A's behavior?

Researchers have discovered that we obtain approximately 35 percent of meaning from the verbal messages that we read or hear, while approximately 65 percent is triggered by nonverbal messages. In short, it is not what one says that's of major importance; rather it's what one does, or what one does while saying something. In order to be effective group communicators—that is, senders and receivers of messages—we should be as concerned with nonverbal message cues as with verbal ones. Nonverbal messages communicate the desires, intentions, attitudes, orientations, roles, responses, and feelings of group members. As participants in group activities, we cannot afford to misread, misunderstand, or misperceive these vital signs.

Since an understanding of nonverbal messages is crucial to the success of small group interaction, we should try to identify the several cues to which we frequently give meaning. A list of nonverbal message cues might include: (a) *body motion or kinesic behavior*—gestures, various shifts and movements of the body, facial expressions, eye movement, and posture; (b) *paralanguage or metacommunication*—various voice qualities, laughing, smiling, and yawning; and (c) *proxemics*—the effects of spatial factors on communicators.

Other nonverbal message cues may include smell, touch, manner of dress. However, we intend to focus on the three categories—body motion, paralanguage, and proxemics—in this chapter. Particularly, we shall study the cues which we have listed in the previous paragraph in terms of their usefulness in helping us to understand (1) how they portray various emotional states, (2) how they serve to control the interactions between group members, (3) how they point up the orientations shared by members, and (4) how they assist us in clarifying the verbal language we hear.

In the remainder of the chapter we will discuss the effects of interpersonal use of the space around us; the nonverbal language

*Body motion,
or kinesic behavior*

aspects of power or authority; and status difference. For the moment, let us discuss the features of nonverbal language that may give us an index of the emotions being expressed or felt by members of the group as it seeks to accomplish its goal.

Nonverbal language: the signals of emotions and feelings

In order to learn what a person is really saying, we should do more than listen to his words. We should look for the giveaway signs in behavior, or—to put it another way—we should attempt to read the nonverbal language cues which he may intentionally or unintentionally display. We can remember occasions when we seemed unable to find words to express an emotion, or when we deliberately attempted to camouflage how we really felt about something. Recall, for instance, finding yourself in a social group for the first time, and the effort you made to show that you "really" did not feel awkward in that situation. Or the time when you were hurt by some snide remark thrown your way and tried not to show it. How successful were you? If you were not successful, what signs betrayed your façade?

How may we detect true messages in small group communication? What are some of the nonverbal cues that we should look for? For example, how can we know when a person is really interested in discussing a particular controversial issue? How may we tell when one of the members is angry concerning some misunderstanding that occurs? How do we know when someone is scared in spite of words to the contrary? Don't get hung up on the nouns and the verbs and the adjectives. Concentrate on the face and the various shifts and postures of the body. This does not suggest that we should go around staring people to death. We have to be tactful and diplomatic as we go about the task of reading the cues of nonverbal language. Certainly, psychiatrists, and some mothers and fathers, are most adept at this kind of observation.

So, the face and the body are the targets of observation whenever we find it necessary to pinpoint the way a person really feels. A face sticks out most of the time, and our bodies are impossible to hide. Faces in particular are good indices of emotional states, because they emit expressions that are relatively standard and conventional in any given culture. There are certain standard or conventional ways of "looking scared," or for "appearing to be really interested" in a task, or for feeling awkward. Certain psychologists (for example, Tomkins and McCarter, 1964) suggest that there are certain tell-tale signs that reliably reveal internal emotional states or responses. See how many of these nonverbal cues we can remember from our own experiences, or, perhaps, how many we can role-play.

---

exercise 2

How many of these nonverbal cues can you remember from your own experience? Let's do some acting—pantomime, perhaps. Use no words, just gestures and facial expressions. Notice the events described in no. 1. The emotion called for is interest—excitement. See how well you can pantomime this emotion before the class. Take turns with the pantomime for all of the events in this exercise.

1. EVENT: A member of the group is explaining an excellent plan for raising the necessary money quickly in order to build a swimming pool at the Student Union.
   EMOTION AROUSED: Interest—excitement

2. EVENT: Your committee has been awarded a monetary prize of one hundred dollars per member for being the most efficient activity group on campus.
   EMOTION AROUSED: Enjoyment—joy

3. EVENT: In the midst of the group discussion, the delicately prim and proper Hortensia Proudbody accidentally spills a glass of water on the table and blurts out a four-letter word.
   EMOTION AROUSED: Surprise—amazement

4. EVENT: A female member of the committee has been quizzed and grilled (to the point of breaking) concerning some mismanagement of a group activity.
   EMOTION AROUSED: Distress—anguish

5. EVENT: The gang is holding an initiating ceremony down in Merrou's Grotto. There is a legend that the damned cave is haunted, but none of the guys believe in "that kinda stuff." While everyone is sitting around reciting the fraternity oath, a big hairy nurd is sneaking out of the shadows right behind big Al who is sitting there reciting his heart out, oblivious to his impending predicament.
   EMOTION AROUSED: Fear—terror

6. EVENT: A buddy on whom you had been depending for a vote on a vital issue now cops out and casts the deciding vote for the opposition.
   EMOTION AROUSED: Contempt—disgust

7. EVENT: During a rather hectic argument on some issue, your opponent has impugned your honesty, goodwill, and integrity.
   EMOTION AROUSED: Anger—rage

All the emotions or states that we role-played were displayed largely on the face or generally in the head area. According to Tomkins and McCarter, when we feel excitement or interest, our eyebrows tend to move downward, our eyes track with a kind of intent looking and listening attitude; enjoyment is manifested by broad smiles and smiling eyes; surprise or startle sends the eyebrows upward, and our eyes blink momentarily as if attempting to focus; in distress or anguish, our eyebrows arch, mouths turn down at the corners, we sob or cry tearfully; fear or terror does remarkable things to the countenance—eyes fix into a frozen stare, the face grows pale and sweaty, the body trembles, and the hair bristles on the head; a feeling of contempt or disgust brings on a sneer with upper lip tightened and upward; when angry or enraged, we frown, clench our jaw, narrow our eyes, and our face becomes flushed or red.

As Mortensen (1972) puts it: "The face is a visible source of (emotional) leakage." He reports some research conducted by Huenegardt and Finando (1969) in which a subject, watching a film designed to arouse emotional stress, was instructed not to show any emotion. When the subject was interviewed later, he expressed great certainty that he had been able to conceal his feelings or reactions concerning the events in the film. Photographs, taken without his knowledge, revealed that the subject did, indeed, reveal several emotions. In spite of his efforts, there were changes in his facial expression which portrayed his responses and inner feelings.

What can we say about body movement and its tendency to reveal emotions? Researchers contend that body movement tends to give hints of *response to feelings* rather than hints of feelings themselves. Body movement gives us clues as to how a person is dealing with his feelings at a given moment. The face or head may inform us about the feelings of a person; the body movement informs us about *how* the person is responding to his feelings. (Ekman and Friesen, 1967) The face displays the nature of the emotion; the body displays the intensity of the emotion.

Body movement furnishes us with vital signs that should be recognized by those of us who participate in or supervise group activities. Sometimes, it is very important that we know when to ease the pressure that is being exerted on a member of the group. For example, how may we tell when stress or tension is really mounting in a particular person? The evidence is that when stress becomes too intense, the person tends to fidget, shift, or change his posture quite frequently (Dittman, 1962; Sainsbury, 1955). However, while the body grows restless, we would observe that the person's hands tend to display a consistent pattern of movement, for example, a consistent rubbing of the palms. Edman and Friesen (1969) give us a few other valuable pointers: When a person feels uncertain about an issue, decision, or event, he or she resorts to a hand shrug; a person who is signaling an intent to answer a direct question tends to demonstrate a sort of open hand reach.

We can also read nonverbal message cues in order to assess the quality of the interaction in a discussion group as a whole. A good rule of thumb is that when individuals feel knowledgeable and comfortable about a topic, their body movements tend to be frequent, vigorous, zestful, or enthusiastic. When the topic is unfamiliar or tension-provoking, body movements tend to be more inhibited or uptight. We can even estimate the amount of camaraderie and cohesion that exists in a group. When group members feel friendly toward one another, we should see a general relaxed posture during the discussion—there will be much eye contact between individuals; rather than being aloof, members will be seen as reaching forward or drawing closer to one another. Conversely, when there is friction among members, postures will be tense, and members will be seen as leaning away from one another. (Baxter, Winter, and Hammer, 1968; Mehrabian, 1971)

Various body movements and facial interactions offer nonverbal language cues which may be interpreted with great accuracy. But we should realize that our ability to interpret them depends on our sensitivity to how *we* have generally behaved when angry, elated, fearful, insecure, and so on.

This concludes our discussion of the nonverbal cues which tell us how people feel within themselves and toward others. We will discuss now the manner in which certain nonverbal language cues act to control the flow of communication in the group process.

Nonverbal language: the signals for control and direction

Have you ever noticed how group discussion sometimes appears to proceed in an orderly fashion even though the leader minimizes obvious control over the group? We may have noticed that only one individual speaks at a time, others seem to be able to anticipate when a speaker is in the process of concluding a statement, and individuals seem to begin speaking as if on cue. In this section, we will focus on a few of the nonverbal message cues that help to control or direct the flow of communication in the group.

Recall our example at the beginning of this chapter: Motor-mouth Morton. He talks a lot. How do we get him to shut up? This problem demands considerable tact. It would not be wise to say: "All right, super yap—button up and give someone else a chance!" Whatever you do, you don't want to antagonize old Motor-mouth! Yet there is a way to stifle him without resorting to a direct verbal confrontation. We can deny him the customary eye contact by shifting our gaze deliberately for a prolonged period in the direction of another group member. In this way we are actually withholding the feedback of approval that a communicator generally needs.

There are, of course, several other situations that may warrant control and direction in the process of small group communication. We may want to encourage a group member to continue speaking—particularly when he or she is in the process of presenting information that facilitates goal achievement. In such instances, a few quick nods of the head can serve as an effective signal of encouragement. On the other hand, there may be the situation in which we may wish to give Siggy Torkbutt an opportunity to have his say as soon as Mary Hassler has made her point. In this case, we would motion toward Siggy with an open-palm gesture of the hand and a quick upward lift of the eyebrows.

We may recall some of the nonverbal message cues that we use habitually to slow down someone who is proceeding too fast with a spurious argument, or to force a rambling speaker to get to the point. In such situations, we use hand movements to convey our message. The fact that group members respond to these signals and modify their activities gives ample evidence that many nonverbal message cues are culturally shared and understood.

The commonest controlling nonverbal cues consist of eyebrow motions, shift of posture, eye contact, hand movement, and head nodding. The effective group communicator attempts to familiarize himself with the nonverbal behavior that people use in various situations. Such a communicator develops an "instinct" for knowing when to shift from one person to another, when antagonism is mounting, when group members are unable to understand instructions, and so on. In addition, he may also need to gain insights into the orientations that exist between the members. The next section explores this important subject.

Nonverbal messages: signals of interpersonal orientation

In most instances, group members tend to position themselves so as to maximize eye contact during interaction. However, as group interaction progresses, we may notice that eye contact may decrease in certain situations and may persist in other situations. The frequency and type of eye contact generally signal the kind of orientation that members desire to maintain among themselves.

We would notice that eye contact is generally avoided when members become highly ego-involved in a situation or when members find themselves being "crowded." Weisbrod (1967) studied the various aspects of eye contact as signals of interpersonal orientation in groups. He discovered that power coalitions which developed in the groups tended to exert great influence on the amount of eye contact that was shared. Group members who spent the most time looking at their fellow discussants (i.e., looking and listening while the person was speaking) saw themselves as having more influence than those individuals who spent less time looking at the speakers. Apparently, people tend to increase eye contact with others when they desire to seek approval or recognition. (Efran and Broughton, 1966)

What are the most prevalent kinds of eye contact? What meanings do others attach to them? There are eyes that look at us with a penetrating or piercing glare, eyes that blaze with the fire of

indignation, eyes that look sheepishly, eyes with a vacant stare, and eyes that seem determined not to look at all. Exline and Winter (1965) found that those who suffer from emotional problems or from strong guilt feelings tend to maintain or encourage very little eye contact. Researchers also tell us that people who think in abstract terms engage others in more eye contact than those who think concretely. Also, members who are dependent on others for reinforcement tend to maintain more eye contact than those who feel less need for reinforcement. (Argyle and Kendon, 1967)

Aside from basic individual differences in the manner in which various group members maintain eye contact, we should also be aware of unison eye contact. For example, as individuals discuss together frequently, their involvement with the group should increase, and so should the mutual eye contact among them. Should we detect very little mutual eye contact in such a group, we may conclude that certain dysfunctions or difficulties may be occurring, and that effective group interaction is being hindered. Maybe they are not listening to one another, because if they were, they would spend more time in eye contact and less time looking away. (Argyle, 1967)

We should note, too, that the type of issue being discussed in the group has an influence on the interpersonal orientation among members. In discussions where issues are highly personal, or threatening and embarrassing, group members are given to more silence and less eye contact than when the issues are non-threatening. Overall, the eyes serve as a dependable index of the health of the group; they tell us when people are motivated to work together as a cohesive organization, and when they feel the need to avoid interaction. Aside from body movement and eye contact, there are other nonverbal cues that may assist us in understanding the psychological climate that exists in the group. Vocal cues represent quite a category of nonverbal messages.

Nonverbal messages: signals for clarification of verbal messages

During a particularly hectic discussion over the issue of donating money from the general fund of the Student Association to a schol-

Paralanguage, or metacommunication, is various voice qualities such as pitch, drawling, or clipping

arship for needy students, Thaddeus Fish III delivered an impassionate argument against the proposal. When Fish III concluded, the floor was granted to Casper Smirkerman, who asked that the executive board of the S.A. pay tribute to Mr. Fish, "a man who is truly blessed with a sense of priorities, as can be witnessed from his having voted to donate five hundred dollars to the Annual Toilet Race just last week!" Fish III sprang to his feet complaining that his integrity was being questioned, to which charge the chairman informed him that Mr. Smirkerman had intended to pay tribute and not to impugn integrity. Mr. Fish perceived a different intent, and, livid with rage, he advised the chairman: "Sir, it isn't a question of what Smirkerman said; it is a question of *how* he said it."

We agree that how something is said does give a clue concerning the intention or the emotion of the speaker when he said it. There was something about the tone of Smirkerman's voice that had upset Fish III. Whatever the case, let us look at some of the vocal cues that furnish us with nonverbal message cues for clarifying verbal messages.

The tone of the voice assists us greatly in our attempt to interpret verbal messages. Certain tones are characterized by increasing loudness or increasing softness. Generally, increased loudness is a signal of mounting anger, hostility, or alarm. There are, of course, a variety of body movements and facial expressions that accompany these feelings. Increasing softening of the voice is often used to convey feelings of grief, frustration, helplessness, disappointment, and powerlessness.

Sometimes, we depend on the *pitch* of the voice for nonverbal language cues. A loud, high-pitched voice may indicate alarm, annoyance, anxiety, fear, threat; while lowered pitch may be used for purposes of giving emphasis to certain points or arguments. *Drawling* and *clipping* are also useful information-giving cues in small group communication. When someone says drawlingly, "Of course, Elsa is a nice girl," we often get the feeling that the person is making a deliberate attempt to contradict the verbal message. However, if he were to increase the tempo and change the tone, there would not seem to be such a contradiction. Pittenger and Smith (1967) suggest that when "Well," "Yep," and "Nope" are uttered in a sharp clipped manner, the person is generally attempting to signal, "It's my turn to talk now." They suggest, further, that "No" or "Nope" with a clip does not generally suggest negation because it is not uncommon to hear one member say to another: "No, you are damned right." Basic agreement is being signaled, along with an opinion that the previous speaker had not gone far enough with the argument.

Mortensen (1972) offers some additional suggestions concerning the value of vocal cues. He suggests that if an air of excitement and interest accompanies verbal statements, the vocal cues serve to promote the importance of what is being said. At other times, when a person's tone of voice exhibits confidence, he will be generally successful in increasing his credibility among the members of the group. It is important that we understand the manner in which others depend on our vocal cues for an understanding of our moods, personality, and feelings toward the task and fellow group members.

Let us shift emphasis, now, from the behaviors that are emitted intentionally or unintentionally and turn to a discussion of certain aspects in the physical environment that exert influences on behaviors in the group. Let us talk about spatial distance, seating arrangements, and the responses that are elicited.

Nonverbal messages: social distance and seating arrangement in the small group

The distance that group members maintain among themselves and the seating arrangements that are provided exert considerable influence on the flow of communication in the group. Speaking and listening are facilitated when group members feel that they are separated from one another by comfortable distances. The amount of distance that each of us needs in order to communicate comfortably is largely dictated by our personality and by the way that we feel toward those around us. Outgoing persons or extroverts seem to be more comfortable operating in close quarters than are withdrawing persons or introverts (Williams 1963). We also use distance to communicate feelings. When we increase the distance between ourselves and others in the group we may be intent on communicating feelings of dislike, detachment, avoidance, rejection, fear, contempt, anger. When we decrease social distance we communicate a willingness to be drawn into fellowship, or liking for those around us, and feelings of security concerning the issues being discussed.

It should be pointed out that there are factors other than feelings or personality which contribute to the amount of social distance that we maintain between ourselves and others. Hall (1959) suggests that social distance between communicators is sometimes dictated by the kinds of messages being exchanged. We would run the risk of violating social protocol if we were to stand fifty feet away from another person and blurt out private and confidential information. We would tend to stand closer. On the other hand, the exchanging of neutral and nonpersonal information does not warrant such encroachment or invasion. We would tend to stand further away. Above and beyond the nature of the message, we should also consider the familiarity that exists between the communicators in the group. We tend to maintain greater distance between us and people that we don't know. Flip Wilson's characterization of Geraldine demonstrates this relationship between proximity and acquaintance. Geraldine often says, "Don't come near me and don't you ever touch me—you don't know me that well!" Mortensen (1972, p. 233) states it aptly: The more established the friendship, the greater is the tolerance for proximity and physical contact.

Encroachment or invasion of one's personal space or territory by another generally evokes defensiveness and even aggression in certain situations. The manner of aggression depends on the person who is being invaded and the manner in which the invader intrudes. Sommer (1969, p. 35) reports some research that was conducted by Russo (1967):

> There were wide individual differences in the ways victims reacted—there is no single reaction to someone's sitting too close; there are defensive gestures, shifts in posture, and attempts to move away. If these fail or are ignored by the invader, or if he shifts position too, the victim eventually takes to flight.... There was a dearth of direct verbal response to the invasions.... Only one of the eighty students asked the invader to move over.

Some of the defensive gestures consisted of turning one's head away from the invader, using an elbow as a wall or barrier, placing books or other personal objects in the path of the person, ignoring the invader altogether, leaving the area, and even resorting to obscenities. If the situation does not facilitate any of these behaviors, the "victim" may seek retreat by avoiding eye contact.

One of the real problems of invasion of personal space is sometimes caused by crowding in small groups. Crowding forces us to limit our customary territorial behavior. There is evidence that crowding does have an effect on interpersonal orientations in the group. Some of the studies show that men expressed negative reactions to crowded situations in a mock jury trial. They liked other members less, considered them less friendly, gave more sentences to defendants in taped jury trials, and thought other members in the crowded room would make poor jury members. They found the experience unpleasant and became more suspicious and antagonistic. Women responded differently to the crowding. They were more lenient in the sentences handed down to defendants on the taped trial, considered others to be more friendly and likable. (Knapp, 1972)

The question of personal space should be understood by the student of small-group communication. We need to understand the dynamics of arranging people in such a way that effective group communication will occur. Also, our understanding of the need for maintaining comfortable social distance will ensure tactfulness and consideration as we work with others. Let us discuss another aspect of territoriality or space in the small group—*seating arrangement.* Where do individuals prefer to sit? Why do they manifest such preferences? Seating arrangements in the small group determine who will be drawn into communication and interaction patterns, the amount of interaction that occurs, and the emergence of leadership.

As early as 1961, Robert Sommer conducted research to find out where people tend to sit in discussion groups. He found that individuals prefer to sit across from others (obliquely opposite) as opposed to sitting side by side. However, when the distance across is too far for comfortable conversation, side by side seating is used. One possible explanation for sitting opposite may be found in a study of eye contact conducted by Argyle and Dean (1965). They found that the closer people sat to each other, the less eye contact took place. Since individuals sitting side by side found themselves too close, they were unable to study one another as much as they would have liked. Argyle and Dean also found that tension increased when close proximity and eye contact were increased.

Hare and Bales (1963) discovered not only that seating position influences the amount of interaction a person will give and receive, but also that persons who might be inclined to dominate the discussion tend to choose the more central seats. The central seats are generally the end and middle seats at a rectangular table.

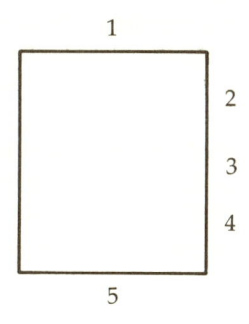

```
           1
       ┌───────┐
       │       │ 2
       │       │
       │       │ 3
       │       │
       │       │ 4
       └───────┘
           5
```

These are called high-talking seats. Seats 1, 3, and 5 in the diagram indicate the high-talking positions. It is also interesting to note that individuals who sat in these positions also tended to receive more communication from other group members. These seating positions are also identified with status, since individuals who do the most talking are likely to be perceived as being leaders by the other members of the group.

Since the leader is usually the one who directs interaction and sometimes makes decisions, it is understandable that he would seek out the most advantageous position from which to utilize eye contact for purposes of signaling, gaining feedback, exhibiting dominance or authority, and challenging the various positions or arguments that are advanced in the group. Steinzor (1950) points out that "if a person happens to be in a spatial position which increases the chances of his being more completely observed, the stimulus value of his ideas and statements increases by virtue of his greater physical and impressive impact on others." This very centrality of the high-talking seats tends to discourage those who suffer a high level of anxiety. Anxious individuals avoid these seats because they do not relish the increase in eye contact that is a consequence of occupying such positions.

Some of the findings that we have discussed should furnish us with vital information that could make us more effective in groups. Many stressful encounters could be avoided through proper spatial arrangement. Those who feel uncomfortable under the gaze of others should be seated in positions with less centrality.

If a high level of interaction and participation in a group situation is desirable, it might be advantageous to have an expressive individual sit opposite a quiet person in order to encourage the quiet person to speak more. Or the leader might find it helpful to have two people who tend to monopolize a discussion sit next to each other.

This chapter has touched on only a few of the vital components of nonverbal language signals in the small group. Communication involves more than the mere transmission of words, but unfortunately the emphasis is usually on the study of the verbal component much to the neglect of the vital nonverbal aspects. We hope that we have been successful in stimulating new awareness and insights. To the extent that we have been successful, we believe that our performance as group members will be enhanced.

ADDITIONAL READINGS

Brooks, William. *Speech Communication* (Dubuque, Iowa: W. C. Brown, 1971). Chapter 6 covers the various types of nonverbal communication and offers an excellent comparison between nonverbal and verbal communication.

Knapp, Mark. *Nonverbal Communication in Human Interaction* (New York: Holt, Rinehart & Winston, 1972). Chapters 2, 4, 5, and 6 offer excellent discussions of the influence of environmental factors on human communication, the effects of physical behavior on human communication, the effects of the face and eyes on human communication, and the effects of the vocal cues which accompany verbal communication.

Mehrabian, Albert. *Silent Messages* (Belmont, Calif.: Wadsworth, 1971). Chapter 2 describes the way in which power, status, and fearlessness are communicated through nonverbal messages.

Mortensen, C. David. *Communication: The Study of Human Interaction* (New York: McGraw-Hill, 1972). Chapter 6 represents a comprehensive discussion of the components of nonverbal interaction. The chapter details many research findings which should prove very helpful.

Sommer, Robert. *Personal Space: The Behavioral Basis of Design* (Englewood Cliffs, N.J.: Prentice-Hall, 1969). This is interesting reading on the effects of physical structure of the areas in which people work and live on human response behavior.

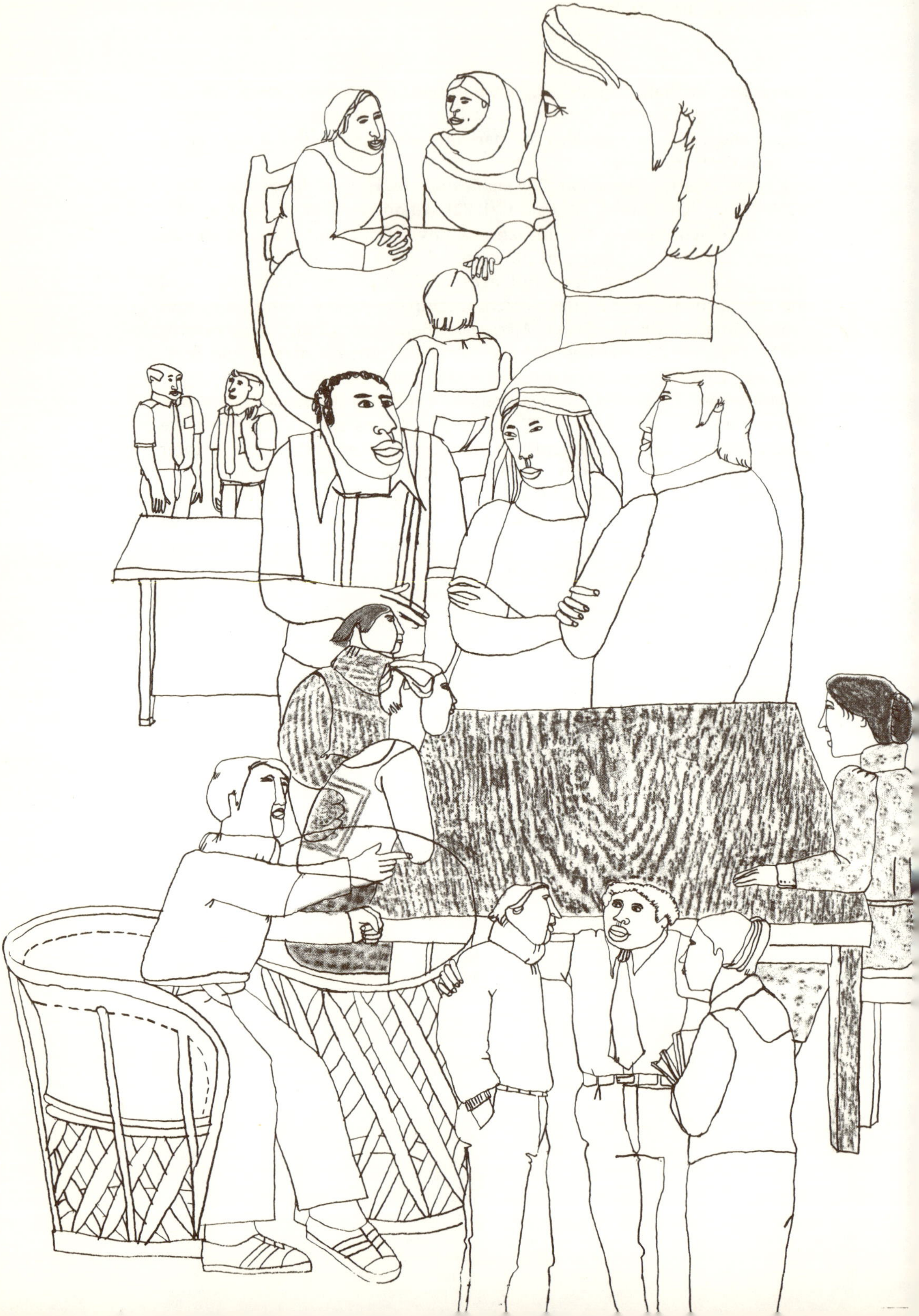

5. Problem solving

PREVIEW

What is problem solving?
Recognition and attempted alleviation of some relevant difficulty
A cause as well as an effect of group interaction

What are the key phases leading to an interactive group atmosphere?
Orientation
Deliberation

What are the basic problem-solving viewpoints or perspectives?
Group interaction
Thought processes
Group decision making

What is the interaction process analysis?
A means of classifying member interaction
A method of interaction analysis describing both task and social emotional dimensions of the group dynamic

What is the reflective-thinking process?
A procedure or set of stages training the mind to respond to problems
A way in which group members can identify the scope, specificity, limits, and alternate solutions to a problem

What are these problem-solving procedures?
Ideal-solution form
Single-question form
Reflective-thinking form

What is the decision-making problem-solving approach?
A task-oriented perspective to group problem solving
An identification of four phases in group problem-solving: orientation, conflict, emergence, and reinforcement

The local board of education meets to decide the best way to approach the voters for a bond issue to build a new high school. A fraternity committee gets together to discuss plans for a weekend party. Members of the student government and representatives of the university administration convene to create a new governance system. The United Nations General Assembly meets to agree on the best way to collect delinquent dues from member nations.

At first glance these four examples of group deliberations may appear to have little in common. There is, however, one common denominator: a problem in need of solution. As we indicated in chapter 1, most groups can be viewed as problem-solving groups. When we speak of problem solving, we are referring to that task of the small group which involves the *recognition and attempted alleviation of some relevant difficulty*. The key concept in identifying the problem-solving group is the term *relevant*. Members of the group should perceive that the problem and their attempts to solve it are important to *them*. In one sense, virtually every day is filled with situations that call for decision-making behavior on our part. It may concern the food we eat, the class we attend, the people we talk to, or the groups we join.

Generally, we go about this day-to-day decision making without consulting other people. There are, of course, many circumstances in which we must make decisions as a group. In this chapter we want to deal with the group as it engages in problem-solving communication. First, we want to describe various approaches to the solution of problems faced by groups. Then we want to discuss the kinds of communication networks that groups employ in the resolution of problems. Before that, though, we want to take a look at this group process as it relates to the rest of our group communication model. Recall that in chapter 1 we spoke of the interaction component. We said then that interaction can be thought of as the *dynamics of communication*. It is the action of the group. Imagine a collection of people who do not interact. Funny, isn't it? Because if you do think of such a group, what comes to mind is a group of sullen commuters, an audience of people not speaking to each other, or the collection of people in your most boring lecture class. In other words, when we speak of group interaction, we are talking about the verbal and nonverbal give-and-take of the group members. In no circumstance is this exchange more crucial than during problem-solving deliberations. How does problem-solving behavior fit in with the systems model? What are some methods of problem solving? How do groups organize for purposes of problem solving?

Interaction as a system component

We want to consider here the general relationship between the interaction component of our group communication system and the other components. We want to think of problem solving as one factor of our interaction component. One principle that we might note at this point goes something like this: *A group's ability to develop a dynamic interaction will be directly related to its problem-solving behavior*. A related principle—"the other side of the coin"—could be stated like this: *A group's problem-solving ability is directly related to its ability to develop a dynamic interaction*. What do we have here? It is an example of our contention that variables affect and are affected by each other in the group communication system. The point that we are trying to make right now is that as a small group goes about its business of solving problems, making decisions, or committing itself to action, it must realize that its success depends directly on its interaction. Okay, let's take a look at our interaction component before we get into the business of problem-solving patterns and procedures.

We think that Phillips and Erickson (1970) have a pretty good approach to the notion of interaction when they call it "an exchange of meanings or communications." It boils down to the strength of relationships within the group. As we said earlier, group interaction is related to the system components of message, situational context, and communicators. We can think of the group interaction as the group's *activity*—its business. This interactive behavior serves as the vehicle for every task that the group faces.

Of course it would be foolish to think that this interactive relationship is an easy one to achieve. By now you probably enjoy a healthy dynamic in the groups to which you belong. Yet if you were to look back on your experience in the early stages of that group's life, you would probably find that there were some trying times. Let's see if we can describe the various phases leading to the establishment of an acceptable interactive atmosphere in the typical group. Here we assume that all individuals are strangers to each other.

There is always the *orientation* in group life. This period is typified by unsure communication—a kind of "chicken dancing" stage in which participants feel each other out for an identification of various attitudes and feelings toward certain objects or events. Think of your first day in this class. You might have known a few of your classmates but, for the most part, your peers and the instructor were probably strangers to you. What was your reaction? What was the nature of your communication? Guarded? Innocuous? Safe? Of course one keeps his mouth shut to find out where everyone else is on certain issues. You made tentative judgments about classmates and the instructor—judgments that by now you have confirmed or rejected. The point is that you entered this group and existed in it for some time at a very low level of interaction.

Think for a moment about your group's ability to solve problems at this orientation stage. Limited? Sure it was because member give-and-take was restricted. Much of your behavior was random—without pattern or system. That is to be expected.

Have you ever joined a group during its organizational meeting and elected officers? What happened? Very simply, the individuals who talked the most were elected. Why? Because the group was merely a collection and not an interactive or dynamic body. Thus, the individuals' ability to solve the problem of carrying out meaningful elections was severely limited. Okay, what are we getting at? Just this: at the *orientation* stage of group life members are disoriented and lack the ability to meaningfully solve problems. They may be interacting, but the nature of the communications that they are exchanging are not substantive enough to allow them to address complex issues.

Once the members have become oriented toward the group and its goals, they enter a phase of interaction that we can refer to as the *deliberation* stage in the group's life. This stage is identified by an emergence of interpersonal *trust* among members. You take chances, you know the others, you identify with the group's functions. The sharing, the interaction, is more complete and represents a more honest exchange of communications among group members. Often, members can enter this stage simply because they have spent considerable time with each other on some common task. The point is that they are able to take communicative risks that were impossible at the earlier stage of group life. It is at this stage in the group's existence that interaction is at its fullest and that problem-solving behavior is most productive.

Regardless of the group to which we belong, we probably experience these two stages in the development of group interaction. It may happen when we pledge a fraternity or when we enter a class; we may experience such stages when we marry or when we begin a new job. At any rate, the development of group interaction is not something that simply happens when we get people together. Rather, it is that dimension of the group that occurs as a result of active and purposeful communication. We should understand that problem solving can occur in either stage, but that it is probably more productive when members have progressed into the deliberation stage of group life.

Problem solving as a group task

It is a good idea to be able to approach a problem from as many different perspectives as one can. Therefore, we want to suggest that you look at a problem-solving task from at least three different viewpoints. Specifically, we want to discuss problem-solving patterns that focus on the nature of the *group interaction*, the *thought processes* that are employed in solving a problem, and in the various phases of *group decision making* in solving a problem.

---

exercise 1

Compile a list of the difficulties that you have encountered during the past twenty-four-hour period. No matter how trivial the issues may be, list them. Now ask yourself the following questions:

1. Do my problems generally involve the same individual(s)?
2. Do my difficulties come about as a result of interaction with others? Do they lead to interaction with others?
3. What is my most common method of problem solving when I interact with others? Do I withdraw? Do I work it out at the time? Do I postpone the problem?

Group interaction and problem solving

We have discussed at length the necessity for a group to establish a significant level of interaction. This "cement" which holds the members together is the single most important feature in effective problem solving. But, more importantly, we ought to have some way to analyze or classify the group interaction. Bales (1950) devised a method of analyzing the content of small group communication that he called the *Interaction Process Analysis (IPA)*. In a nutshell, the IPA is a way of categorizing member behavior in small group problem-solving deliberations.

Bales' model is predicated on the notion that individuals recognize two types of orientation: task and social-emotional. Stated another way, we think of the job that we have to do, task orientation, and the personal relationships with the other group members, social-emotional orientation.

Group members have basic reactions for the social-emotional area and task area. Specifically, in the social-emotional area, there are *positive* and *negative* reactions. Thus, if we are more concerned with this dimension, we spend most of our time positively or negatively evaluating information or people.

On the other hand, since the task area is more identifiable by the informational content of the communication, the task reactions consist of two categories: *questions* and *attempted answers*. For example, if we are preoccupied with the task dimension of our group, we spend most of our time asking and answering questions. True, we may be making eloquent speeches along the way but these are generally in response to some question by another group member.

Bales proposed six problems that are logically applicable to any interaction system. These are problems of orientation, evaluation, control, decision, tension-management, and integration. Actually, it is probably easier to think of these problems in terms of stages through which the problem-solving group moves. Thus, you would see a group at its earliest meetings interacting about orientation matters. Later on, the group would focus its attention on matters of control or decision.

But let us tie the IPA to our system model. If we define communication as a process in which messages act as a linkage between people, then we ought to know as much as we can about the linkage. The IPA affords us the opportunity to examine the nature of the linking messages. What are the characteristics of the messages? How are they originated? What types of feedback do they elicit? These are the kinds of questions approached by interaction analysis. Later in this chapter we will examine the other components (communicator, message, situational context) as they relate to the interaction component. For now, however, we should remember that interaction can be analyzed according to the communicative acts that occur within the group. Moreover, we should keep in mind that knowing more about the nature of the interaction *per se* will help us to know more about the other components of our communicative system. The Bales Interaction Process Analysis gives us the opportunity to do just that.

Let us move now to a consideration of the exact nature of the communication exchanged by problem-solving group members. Bales found that generally the type of communication was similar to that in figure 1.

The first thing that you see as you read this figure from left to right is the major category of the communicative act. The message will be identified as social-emotional positive reaction, task attempted answers, task questions, or social-emotional negative reactions.

The next column of figure 1 identifies typical statements or behaviors that illustrate the major problems we noted earlier. Finally, the lines joining the statements or behaviors are identified with either an a, b, c, d, e, or f, indicating the exact problem classification. So you can see that if an individual asks for information (statement 7) and another group member gives it to him (statement 6), the interaction is identified as a problem of orientation.

As you examine figure 1 more closely you will see how this method is designed to analyze the communicative process within the problem-solving group by examining the various communicative acts.

Why should we be concerned about some scheme to analyze group processes that, admittedly, involves some pretty arbitrary judgments? Remember earlier when we talked of the dynamic quality of group interaction and its importance in problem-solving communication? Well, analyzing the interaction process of a small group should give us some insights into a group's problem-solving capability. We think that some of Bales' findings employing the IPA are more significant than the method. For example, more time was spent in category 5 (Gives Opinions) than in any other single category. It makes sense, doesn't it? In many groups we spend a great deal of time evaluating messages, analyzing information, and expressing our feelings about some issue. At the other end of the continuum, the least amount of time was spent in category 9 (Asks for Suggestion). This may be a bit difficult for us to understand. Why are individuals reluctant to ask for direction or possible ways of acting in a certain situation? Could it be that we become so involved in our own approaches to the problem that we think that others have little to offer? Other questions can be asked about the various percen-

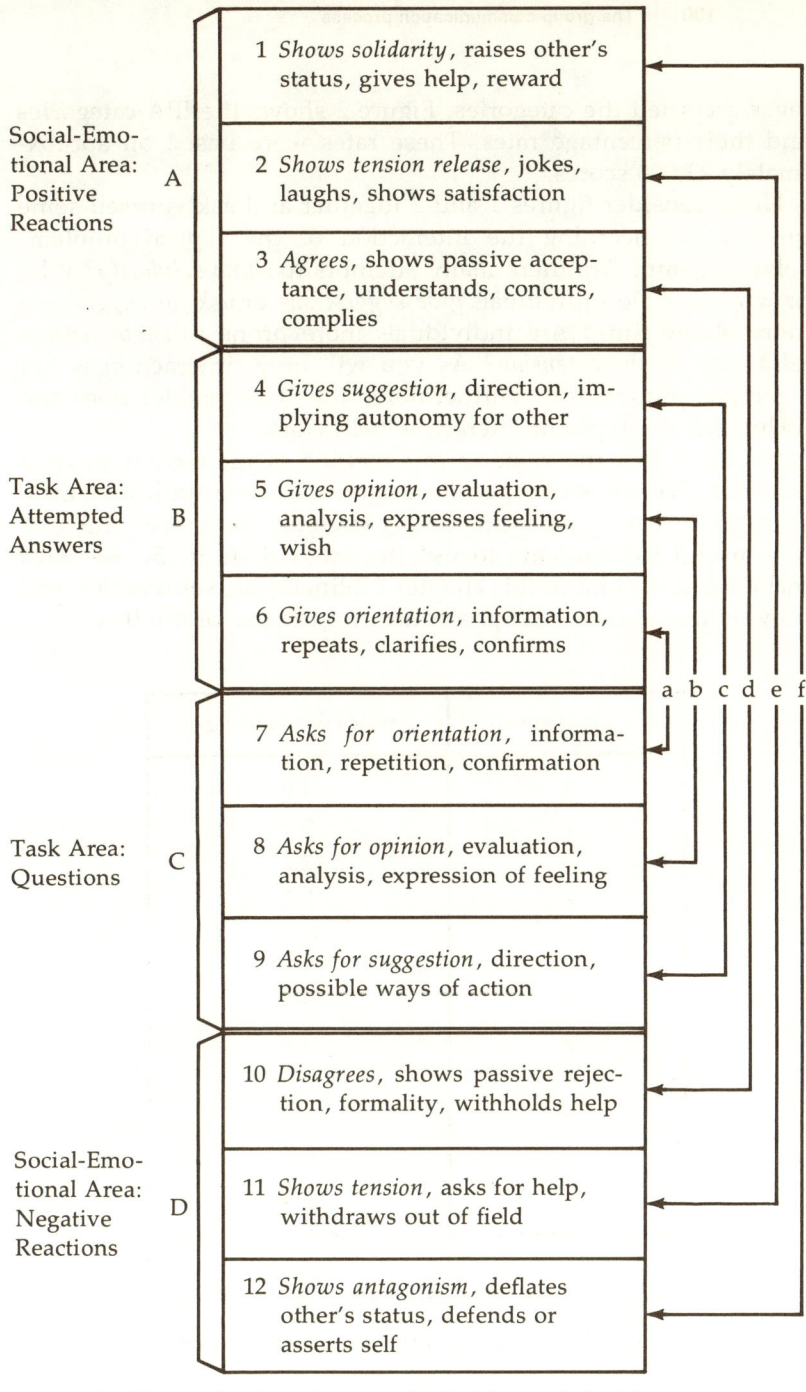

Social-Emotional Area: Positive Reactions	A	1 *Shows solidarity*, raises other's status, gives help, reward
		2 *Shows tension release*, jokes, laughs, shows satisfaction
		3 *Agrees*, shows passive acceptance, understands, concurs, complies
Task Area: Attempted Answers	B	4 *Gives suggestion*, direction, implying autonomy for other
		5 *Gives opinion*, evaluation, analysis, expresses feeling, wish
		6 *Gives orientation*, information, repeats, clarifies, confirms
Task Area: Questions	C	7 *Asks for orientation*, information, repetition, confirmation
		8 *Asks for opinion*, evaluation, analysis, expression of feeling
		9 *Asks for suggestion*, direction, possible ways of action
Social-Emotional Area: Negative Reactions	D	10 *Disagrees*, shows passive rejection, formality, withholds help
		11 *Shows tension*, asks for help, withdraws out of field
		12 *Shows antagonism*, deflates other's status, defends or asserts self

a. Problems of orientation
b. Problems of evaluation
c. Problems of control
d. Problems of decision
e. Problems of tension management
f. Problems of integration

Figure 1. Interaction process analysis: Categories and major problems (Bales)

tages accorded the categories. Figure 2 shows the IPA categories and their percentage rates. These rates were based on approximately 23,000 scores.

Now, consider figures 1 and 2 together and ask yourself some questions concerning the interaction of the typical problem-solving group. Are there many attempts to *show solidarity*? Why or why not? Do individuals *give suggestions* or *ask for suggestions* more of the time? Are individuals more prone to *show tension release* or to *show tension*? As you will note, interaction is not a simple proposition. Furthermore, the Bales model does not include all the types of interactive behaviors.

We think that the value in this method of interaction analysis is that it gives us some specific categories of communicative messages in the group problem-solving circumstances. We think that it is useful for students to use the method itself. So we have included at the end of this chapter bibliographic sources that will provide instructions and procedures for the use of the IPA.

CATEGORIES	PERCENTAGE RATES
1	1.0
2	7.3
3	12.2
4	5.2
5	30.0
6	21.2
7	5.4
8	3.5
9	.8
10	6.6
11	4.4
12	2.4
	100.0

Figure 2. IPA categories and percentage rates

exercise 2

Observe a permanent small group in operation over several days. Using the twelve categories developed by Bales, answer the following questions:

1. What is the relationship between task-oriented and social-emotional oriented behaviors? Specify.
2. Can you identify leadership on the basis of the behaviors?
3. Can you identify the factor of cohesiveness within the group? What behaviors have you observed that lead you to your conclusion that cohesiveness does or does not exist?
4. Can you identify obstructionists within the group? Which of the categories that you have observed lead you to your conclusion?

Thought processes and problem solving

If one were to look at all the books that deal with small group communication, he would be left with the impression that John Dewey's (1910) reflective thinking process is the most popular pattern for problem-solving discussions. It is. What Dewey gave us was a pretty elegant set of procedures for "training the mind" to respond to problems. In essence, his argument is that in our attempts to support some belief, the mind goes through a testing process that examines the belief (problem), analyzes it, and selects some meaningful solution. We want to discuss it here but before we do, a few words ought to be said about the logic or rationale for using this procedure. Too many individuals think of the reflective thinking process as a procedure. Others think of the process as an organizing model for small group discussions. While the reflective thinking process may contain elements that would lead one to conclude that it is a set of procedures for organizing a problem, it would be naive to conceive of the Dewey model in such mechanical terms. For while it is true that the process is a method, it is also true that it is a type of theory. As such it has a very close relationship to both our thought processes *and* our group behavior. It is especially useful in predicting and describing group problem-solving behavior. So let's take a look at it.

Reflective thinking involves the recognition of the following "logically distinct steps" (Dewey's language) in the resolution of some problem: (1) a felt difficulty; (2) its location and definition; (3) suggestion of possible solutions; (4) development of the suggestion solutions; and (5) further observation and experimentation leading to acceptance or rejection of some solution. There is, of course, a danger in trying to think of the reflective thinking steps in process terms. This is very natural, since every time we number or order items, there is always the feeling that they are sequential. That is, we must think of them in discrete, separate terms. For the record, we are not abandoning our process orientation to the study of small-group communication. Moving through one phase, or step, of the reflective thinking process should not be taken to imply that the step is no longer experienced or employed once we have passed it. These steps interact with each other in a very systematic manner. The phases are dynamic and our interpretation constantly changes depending on the material under discussion. Our point here is simply this: ordering the phases in the reflective thinking approach should not be taken to be in contradiction to a process orientation.

Let's examine each phase in the reflective thinking process as Dewey outlined them. Then let's see if we can apply these steps to some problem that might be similar to one that we have experienced. Keep in mind that our example is simplified—perhaps oversimplified—so that we can take a detailed look at the process, *not* so that we can observe the sequential "happening" of each of the phases.

Recognizing a felt difficulty is of course crucial to the problem-solving group's existence. After all, there must be recognition of some difficulty or important issue before the group begins deliberations. Of course we can handle the problem that hits us square in the face. The fact that our group is broke, or that we are under attack by some outside force, or that we must make some decision regarding applicants into our group—all these contain elements that immediately define themselves for our group deliberations. But there is another kind of problem that we face and this is one that is more difficult for us to come to grips with. That is the problem that may be felt by *some* members of the group and not by others. The Jewish student who feels some discrimination by other members, the woman who feels that she is not able to move up through her organization because of male chauvinistic attitudes, the faculty member who feels that his department is going to hell in a hand basket but cannot convince others of the problem. These are the types of problems that are not so easy to identify. Yet they are problems nevertheless. Have you ever experienced a situation that makes you feel uneasy, but you are at a loss to explain it to other members of your group? Such feelings are termed by Dewey to be "undefined uneasiness." The point here is simply that the *group* must come to some agreement as to the nature of the problem facing it and this must be done before the group members can settle down to the task of problem solving. Thus the first step in the reflective thinking process involves some degree of group consensus about the problem facing the group.

Once the group has identified the problem, it is faced with the task of defining and delimiting the problem. It may be that this second step and the recognition of the felt difficulty are about the same. For example, the recognition of a problem that may be faced by a student group seeking to bring to campus some speaker of a radical cause may serve to point up the difficulty per se and the location of the difficulty. Let us assume for the moment that such a group in its "Great Issues" series has pretty well adhered to establishment speakers and now desires more diversity in presentation of views. You can see that the felt difficulty (lack of diversity) and the definition of the problem (too many establishment speakers) are virtually inseparable. Such problem and problem-definition circumstances are not always faced by the problem-solving group. While many group members seek to move right past the definition stage and into the solution period, it often happens that the location and specific delimitation of the problem is the most crucial step in the entire problem-solving sequence. It is at the definition stage that the systematic powers of the group are called into action. For if the group cannot logically define and delimit its problem, later discussions will be random at best.

This step calls for a clear definition of terms, location of the problem, attempts to delineate the exact *nature* of the problem. What is establishment? What is discrimination? What is the historical genesis or pattern of the problem? Many other questions that probe the complexity of the felt difficulty are necessarily asked. The key terms in defining the problem are to determine its *scope*, its *specificity*, and its *limits*.

We cannot overemphasize the importance of the definitional stage of the reflective thinking process. This is the area in which most groups fall far short of the demands of the Dewey model. Since the reflective thinking process is an individual process that is applied to small group settings, ask yourself the following question: When I am faced with a problem do I pay more attention to finding out what the problem is or how to solve it? Failure to thoroughly engage in problem definition before moving on to probing alternatives and solving the problem is just another way of hampering yourself. Problem solving is hard enough without making it more difficult by failing to know as much as you can about the problem that you are trying to solve.

The third step in the reflective thinking process calls for suggestion of possible solutions. To hear most problem-solving groups one would think that this is the first step in their agenda. How many times do we jump right into what ought to be done? Probably more than we care to admit. Presumably, by the time that we arrive at this step we have analyzed and explored the problem so that we know what the nature and limitations of the problem are. Now we must make the difficult step of hypothesizing on the basis of this information what we ought to do. At this stage we do everything we can to offer as many alternatives to the issue at hand that we can. Our analysis of the problem, step 2, has armed us with some direction. This step specifies the many directions that we can take. At this stage we are dealing with *ideas* or *guesses* for the solution of the problem. Actually, little evaluation ought to be done. The group's primary task is to get some courses of action out on the table for later evaluation and examination.

Once the group has proposed several alternatives to the problem, the primary task is to develop the solutions and test their adequacy. Thus, step 4 in the reflective thinking process calls for a thorough examination of the proposed solutions and analysis of those solutions according to criteria that the group has developed through its deliberations. This criteria, of course, has been established as the group moved through its analysis and exploration of the problem under consideration. Dewey argued that it is at this step that the *implications* of the solutions are tested and here that the true *reasoning capability* of the group is called into play. Think for a moment of the complexity of this stage in the problem-solving agenda. The group has determined that it has some relevant difficulty, it has located that problem through complex analysis and exploration, and members have proposed various alternatives that are perceived as answering the problem. Now, the group faces its most crucial behavior to date, it must come up with a decision that will justify its prior thorough handling of the problem. It's risky and it involves a great deal of member activity. For at this stage the members are faced with some *action* that they must commit themselves to. Actually, some groups cease to exist at this stage. Such groups as special committees, task forces, and others may exist for the sole purpose of gathering information and then proposing to some other group several feasible alternatives. But usually, groups are expected to come up with some specific solution to a problem. The development of the suggested solutions phase implies that we will analyze the solutions and select the solution most suited to our needs. Criteria that we have developed earlier in the group deliberations might have included cost, feasibility, practicality, and time. Often, groups tend to forget that they have developed such criteria. In the heat of discussion, it is imperative that members remember such criteria, for logical decision making calls for such a plan.

The final step in the reflective thinking process demands that the group seek some verification of the suitability of the suggested solution. Up to this point the conclusions of the group are hypothetical and need some kind of testing. In a way, we are *observing* as we did in steps 1 and 2. We are seeing if it works. It may be possible to run a pilot program. In our example of the speakers committee, it would be possible to narrow the selected speakers down to one and to hold some interview. But as you know, it is not always so easy to test such solutions. What of the fund-raising decision made by the group? In such cases, it might be wise to make such judgments tentative and for some designated period of time. We do such things with elections and membership on certain university committees. At any rate, whatever the method of observation or verification procedure used, it is necessary that the suggested solution be tested.

It might be wise at this point to take a problem experienced by a group and to briefly examine the difficulty in terms of the Dewey model of reflective thinking. Let us say, for example, that the students of a particular university are required to take two years of a foreign language in order to meet minimum requirements for an undergraduate degree. Further, let us assume that the university's scholarship-standards committee, which is charged with degree requirements, is composed of both faculty and students. Over the years, students have enrolled in the two-year language requirement—occasionally complaining but offering no unified reaction against the requirement. Now, petitions are circulated by undergraduate students indicating that there is some unfavorable sentiment toward the requirement. The petitions are presented to the committee. The committee meets to discuss proper disposition of the complaint. Now what is the felt difficulty—the problem? Members of the committee perceive the problem differently. Some members see the problem in question form: "What can we do to justify the requirement?" Others say, "How can we best handle these troublemakers?"

The committee members agree that the problem facing them is multifaceted for it includes justifying the requirement, handling the troublemakers, and examining the logic of further requiring the language. In a political tour de force, the committee agrees that the problem for discussion ought to be an examination of the logic and rationale of the requirement. Such a problem might be worded, "What ought to be the university's policy toward the two-year language requirement?" At this point there ought to be minimal ambiguity on the part of the members as to what the issue of discussion is. We now move on to a consideration of a delimitation of the problem.

The committee decides that there ought to be some uniformity as to the definition of terms of the problem. What is the exact nature of the current requirement? What does the university catalog have to say about the requirement? What is the nature of the university policy as it is now enforced? Why was the requirement enacted in the first place? How long has it been on the books? These and many more questions must be answered by the group before they can pretend to have more than surface knowledge of the problem. Of course, it is understood that there is some degree of legitimacy on the part of those raising the issue in the first place. The point is that the problem is assaulted from as many different perspectives as possible. At no time does the group address itself to the issue of whether or not the problem can be solved or whether it will be solved. At this stage, the group is concerned with knowing just what the problem is. It is important to note that discussion of the issue should not be taken as a rejection of the status quo. Retaining the requirement can always remain as a viable alternative. What the group should be doing at this stage is analyzing and exploring the problem completely without the distraction of suggested solutions.

The group has moved through this step after several days or months of discussion and is ready to run some ideas. At this point, subcommittees may be formed if the group is large enough. The important thing to remember here is that the membership has agreed that they will now entertain some thoughts as to what the future course of action ought to be. Members meet and get the ideas out on the floor. The solutions are not rejected or accepted here. Of course it may happen that some solutions obviously are at odds with criteria developed by the group during earlier sessions. For example, if the group decided during the second stage that the solution—whatever it is—is to be enacted the next academic year, then a solution that calls for long-range implementation would be inappropriate. Also, if the group decided that the language department personnel were irrelevant to the solution, then a solution that called for a position from that group would be inappropriate. The point here is that, barring examples like these, evaluative judgments about the solutions are not made.

During the development stage, step 4, the group members sift through the proposed solutions. Each is evaluated in terms of the criteria, advantages, and disadvantages. In our example, let us assume that three specific solutions have been advanced: (1) the requirement be dropped completely; (2) the requirement be reduced to one year; (3) the present two-year requirement remain in effect. Solution 1 is evaluated and after lengthy discussion, it is rejected because it would mean that several graduate teaching assistants would be unemployed. Moreover, the requirement has been in existence for forty years and the objection has just recently been proposed. Thus, to capitulate to the dissidents would be a very harmful precedent. Solution 3 is rejected because most committee members really cannot see the practicality of requiring two years of a language when there are other subjects that deserve as much attention. In addition, a committee is hardly credible when it meets for an extended period of time only to reaffirm the status quo. (Don't laugh. By such logic are some committees formed and maintained.) Solution 2 is the chosen alternative. True, it is a compromise, but it does have all the benefits of the two other solutions. Also, committee members really see the advantage of that required year.

Our example may seem trivial, but the principle isn't. Reserving judgment about the solutions until *all* have been proposed will ensure a more logical treatment of the merits of each.

Finally, the committee is ready to test and verify its chosen solution. The decision is made to try this system for a limited period of time and, more importantly, to charge a group with formal monitoring of the new requirement. This new group will be expected to report to the main committee regularly over the next two years.

Through the use of the reflective thinking process, the committee has moved systematically and logically through the cumbersome process of formulating and resolving a problem issue. There is no doubt that this could have been achieved without the Dewey model. But we question whether it would have been as satisfying to the participants. The use of this process has treated each phase of the problem-solving deliberations as a system made up of interrelated components. The group was not able to speak of solutions to the problem until they had specifically defined its scope. They were not able to speak of the scope and nature of the problem until they were in agreement as to what the problem was. Finally, they did not simply choose a solution and hope that it would take care of itself. They plugged in a vital verification step which allowed them to test the adequacy of the solution to their problem.

How does this all fit in with our group system model and our earlier discussion of the Bales Interaction Process Analysis? As we will demonstrate later, the workings of the reflective-thinking model directly affect the way that the interaction component of our system model relates to the other components. Whereas the IPA identifies specific categories of communicative behavior, the reflective thinking process allows us to view these interaction behaviors in broad context. Stated another way, the Dewey model gives us some idea of the *overall process* involved in problem solving, while the IPA provides us some specifics regarding communication behavior *during* the problem solving.

In the next section, we will consider three different procedures that can be used by groups to solve particular problems. These procedures are preselected patterns for solving the problem.

exercise 3

Break your class into five- to eight-member groups. Select some campus problem for which group members have a high level of involvement. Discuss the issue using Dewey's method of reflective thinking. The exercise should run over several days so that each step of the process is adequately examined. At the end of each stage of the process conduct a group evaluation of the deliberations. The following questions should be used as guides for this evaluation:

1. Did one individual "take charge" of the group?
2. Which member(s) was most task-oriented; which was most social-emotional oriented during each stage?
3. Was the problem well formulated for each stage of the process?
4. Were assertions supported during each stage?

Procedures for problem solving

Many groups never solve their problems systematically. Many group members become frustrated, dissatisfied, and bored when their group's approach to problem solving is unsystematic or even irrational.

When we have to select a particular class to take during a semester, or a life-mate "for better or for worse," or a job that we might be stuck in for the next thirty years, we usually have some preconceived notion of how we will go about solving our particular problem. We tend to follow certain personal patterns of problem-solving that have been successful in our prior attempts. While the plan of action we select may appear to others unsystematic or irrational, it may very well be quite systematic and rational within our own realm of experience.

Groups can follow preselected plans for solving problems. Their problem-solving activities need not be unsystematic or confusing to either the group members or outside observers. In this section, we will examine three patterns of problem solving which appear appropriate and desirable for success in certain situations. Specifically, we will discuss the *Ideal Solution Form*, the *Single Question Form*, and the *Reflective-Thinking Form*. Brainstorming, which we describe in the last chapter, is sometimes included as a pattern for problem solving; however, rather than repeat that description we would ask that you read that section in chapter 11.

In order to investigate how each pattern operates in a problem-solving discussion, we offer the following problem-solving situation. We will illustrate how the three patterns can be used to solve this problem.

THE CAMPUS PARKING CRISIS

Suppose you are eating lunch with a group of students from your group-discussion class. You mention that you were late for the mid-term.

"Why were you late?" one friend asks, "Did your car break down?"
"No, I just couldn't find a damn parking place!"
"You're kidding," another friend adds, "I couldn't find one yesterday."
"Neither could I," a third friend points out, "In fact, I haven't been able to park on campus the last three days."

Each group member adds that he or she was unable to find a place to park at least once within the last week. Realizing that your failure to find a parking spot is not unique, you suggest that your friends meet later that day to attempt to solve the parking problem. All agree to form a committee. It is suggested that more students be added to the committee to make it more representative of the student body. You also seek out assistance from several faculty members. All students and faculty meet that afternoon in the student union. Interest is high. You have a worthy goal: How can we guarantee parking spots for students on campus?

Before we begin to use this problem situation to illustrate the three problem-solving patterns, we might notice that the problem—failure to find parking space on campus—has been put into the form of a question, *how can we guarantee parking spots for students on campus?*

```
┌─────────────────────────────────────────────┐
│              QUESTIONS OF FACT              │
│         Do college graduates make more money│
│           than non-college graduates?       │
│                                             │
│          ┌──────────────────────────┐       │
│          │    QUESTION OF VALUE     │       │
│          │ Is a college degree worthwhile?  │
│          └──────────────────────────┘       │
│                                             │
│         What proportion of business executives│
│              have college degrees?          │
└─────────────────────────────────────────────┘
```

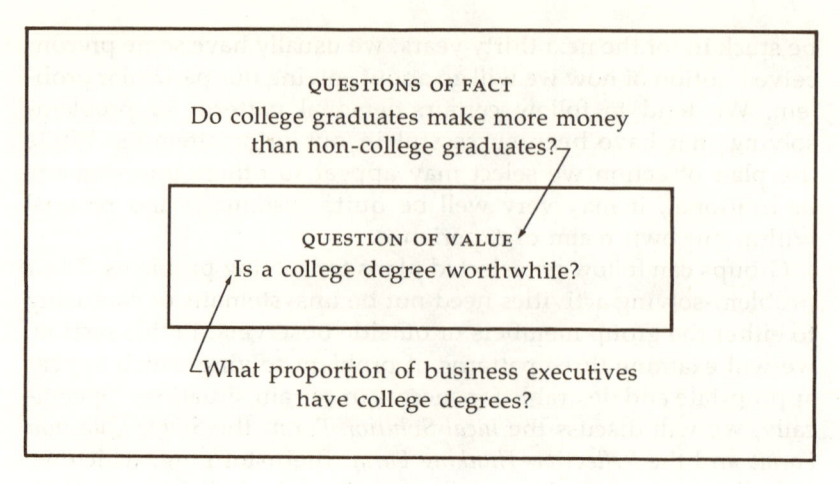

Figure 3

Problem questions used in problem-solving patterns consist of three kinds: (1) fact, (2) value, and (3) policy. Many discussions are completely concerned with questions of fact. Among these problems are such questions as: "Who is teaching this course?" "Does a college degree mean more income for individuals over a lifetime?" "Is discrimination still prevalent in our society?" Educational groups are usually concerned with problems of fact. Group and individual research in the library or laboratory are best for providing the answers to questions of fact. Spontaneous discussion groups whose purpose is to solve a question of fact may be at a disadvantage. Such groups may lack the necessary first-hand information to provide an adequate solution to the problem. In our parking problem the students may need to gather information from fellow students, faculty, and staff prior to any intelligent discussion of the problem situation.

Questions of value require the group to assess the worth of some object, idea, concept, or person; for example, "Who is the best teacher of group discussion?" "Is college worthwhile?" "Is discrimination bad?" Questions of value call for weighing and evaluating a problem against certain practical or ideal standards. If the standards are unclear, it will be difficult to resolve the problem. If we examine a question of value closely, we will notice that questions of fact must be answered prior to solving a question of value. Figure 3 illustrates this point.

A question of policy requires that the group arrive at a specific course of action in order to solve the problem. "How can we guarantee each student a parking place on campus?" "What can the students do to clean up our environment?" "How can we

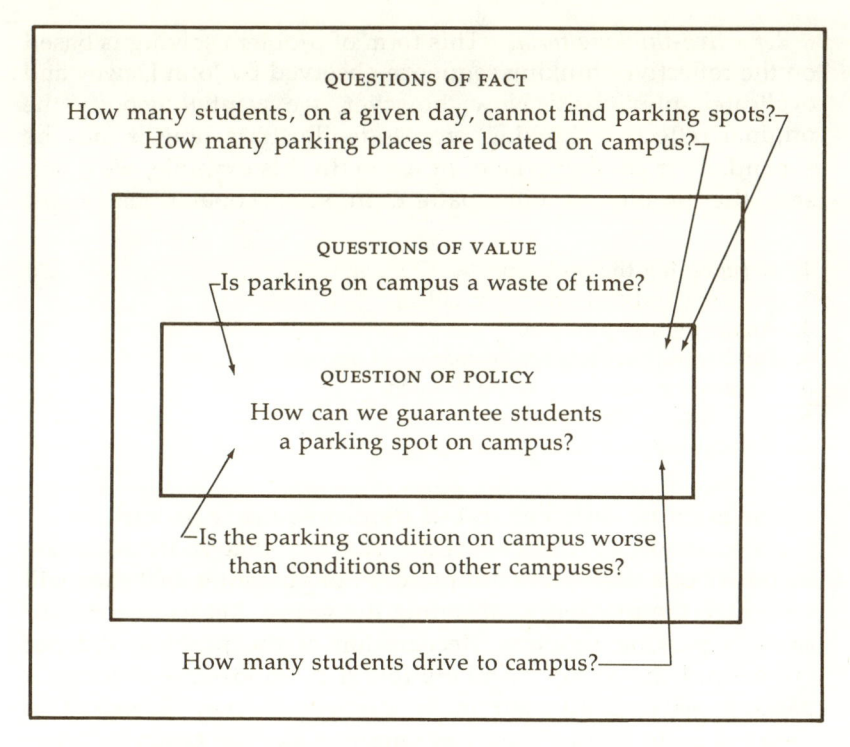

```
                      QUESTIONS OF FACT
       How many students, on a given day, cannot find parking spots?
          How many parking places are located on campus?

                    ┌─────────────────────────────────────┐
                    │        QUESTIONS OF VALUE           │
                    │   Is parking on campus a waste of time?
                    │                                     │
                    │    ┌────────────────────────────┐   │
                    │    │    QUESTION OF POLICY      │   │
                    │    │  How can we guarantee students │
                    │    │   a parking spot on campus?   │
                    │    └────────────────────────────┘   │
                    │                                     │
                    │   Is the parking condition on campus worse
                    │      than conditions on other campuses?
                    └─────────────────────────────────────┘

              How many students drive to campus?
```

Figure 4

guarantee peace in the world?" A discussion involving a question of policy must also consider questions of fact and value prior to their own solution. Figure 4 illustrates this point.

Having stated our problem in the form of a question, let us now proceed to view how the reflective thinking pattern is implemented in a problem-solving discussion.

exercise 4

Select four of the subject areas listed below and phrase three problem-solving questions for each area. Make one a problem of fact, one of value, and one of policy.

Women's Rights	Foreign Aid
School Busing	College Costs
Teaching Methods	Marriage
Income Tax	Drugs
Olympic Games	Football

Reflective-thinking form. This form of problem solving is based on the reflective-thinking sequence observed by John Dewey and explicated previously. Now, however, we want to modify the original reflective-thinking process to illustrate how it may be expanded for another type of problem. In this example, we'll present the problem-solving pattern in seven operational steps:

1. Recognizing the problem
2. Locating and defining the problem
3. Analyzing the problem
4. Establishing criteria for evaluation of solutions
5. Suggesting solutions to the problem
6. Selecting the final solution
7. Testing the solution

Let us examine each step in this problem-solving pattern.

RECOGNITION OF THE PROBLEM. The fact that individuals are members of a discussion group does not guarantee that they will recognize the problem confronting the group. Let us refer to our campus parking problem. Recognition of the problem did not occur until the group members found it impossible to locate a parking place. Until their initial discussion, they thought that their failure to find parking was unique. Once the group becomes aware of the problem, a goal emerges. Our group of students would attempt to find some way to guarantee each student a parking place on campus.

In this stage of problem solving, group members consider the significance and urgency of the problem, its affect upon the group and individuals. If you've ever driven to a campus and were unable to locate a parking place or one within a short distance of your next class, the problem of parking becomes significant and urgent.

DEFINITION OF THE PROBLEM. Group members must not only recognize that a problem exists, but they should determine the exact nature of their problem. Group members must define and clarify terms, recognize possible limitations, and establish the extent of the problem. Before group members propose solutions to any problem, they should attempt to clarify the meaning of words and ideas in the problem question. It may be necessary to rephrase the problem question, so that it can be understood. The question, "How can we guarantee each student easy access to classes?" can be interpreted as attempting to deal with parking problems, position of buildings on campus, congestion of students on campus walks, and so on. Obviously, a question so worded could present difficulties, if your group's only intent is to study campus parking problems. The question might be worded, "How can all students be guaranteed a parking spot on campus?" This question is more specific and restrictive in meaning. Its intent clearly identifies the group's purpose.

The group also must recognize any limitations inherent in a discussion of the problem. If a problem is too broad in scope to be discussed at one meeting, it may be divided into subproblems to be handled at separate meetings. If the group can meet only one time, it behooves the group to limit the scope of their problem. Classroom discussions, for instance, have a relatively short time to work with a problem and, consequently, should be limited.

Groups, particularly classroom groups, attempt to solve problems that are outside their span of control. As a classroom exercise this is acceptable; however, in real life, group members must attempt to deal with problems that they can control. The problem, "How can all students be guaranteed a parking spot on campus?" is a problem that group members can have some power to solve and can work with other legitimate campus groups to implement proposals. We have seen a number of problems on our campuses settled in this manner.

The group must also be able to gather the materials needed to solve the problem. For example, little in the way of factual materials can be gathered for the problem, "What does God look like?" However, if we change the problem to, "What characteristics do individuals ascribe to God?" then we may be able to gather data which may be applied and utilized in solving the problem-question.

ANALYZING THE PROBLEM. Every group must be able to locate the important facts concerning their problem. Group members must find the information that will indicate the following: How serious is the problem? Who is being affected? Where is the problem occurring? Why does the problem exist? Referring to our parking problem example, we might ask: How many students can't find parking? Are we talking about ten percent or seventy-five percent of the student population? Are students affected only after 9:00 A.M.? Is parking difficult all over campus or in specific locations? All of the above questions attempt to provide an answer to the most important question of all: Why can't students find parking spaces on campus? We are attempting to locate the cause(s) of the problem.

Locating the exact cause of a problem is sometimes a difficult task for the group. Ask yourself the question: Is abortion the cause or effect of birth control? If we give this question some thought, we will notice that it is not easy to answer. Abortion can be the

REFLECTIVE THINKING — 1. RECOGNIZING 2. LOCATING & DEFINING 3. ANALYZING

effect of relaxing birth control laws, or the cause of relaxed birth control laws because of the danger involved in illegal abortions.

Many times groups are so superficial in their analysis of problems that they fail to differentiate between the causes and symptoms. There is a very sad story of a young girl who began tripping out on drugs. Her friends were able to persuade her to give up using drugs, but soon after she began drinking excessively. They cajoled her into giving up liquor. Finally, she killed herself. The point of this example is that treating the symptoms of a problem will not resolve or eliminate the causes.

It is at this stage of the problem-solving sequence that the group seeks to provide itself with enough information to evaluate the problem. Fact finding consists of pooling the information resources of all group members. If group members possess little of the needed information, the problem-solving session will be relatively unprofitable. Before proceeding to the next step in our problem-solving sequence, we must test our information. Phillips (1966) has set forth an excellent set of standards for testing factual materials in a problem-solving discussion:

1. Is the information factual, inferential, or evaluative?

An inference is a statement about the past or future based on present information. For example, the statement, "parking places will become scarcer as student population increases," is an inferential statement based on present facts. A statement like "the present campus parking situation is poor" is an evaluative statement. Evaluative statements are constructed from factual statements, but such statements ask a group member only to agree or disagree with its intent. For example, the statement "the present parking situation is poor" could be derived from the following factual statements: "50 percent of the student population can't find campus parking" "Students must arrive on campus by 8:00 A.M. to be assured a parking spot close to a classroom." Evaluations and inferences should not be treated as factual information in problem solving.

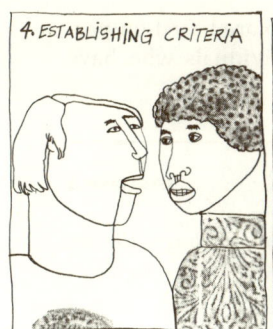

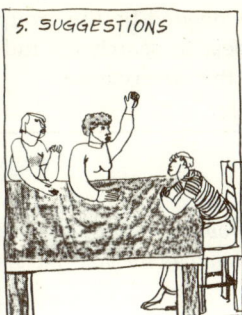

2. Are the facts current?

If the student parking on campus had doubled since 1965, the number of students driving to campus in 1965 would be of little help in attempting to find the actual need for parking. However, college students sometimes fail to search for the most recent information applying to a problem area. Using facts that are outdated can lead to erroneous conclusions on the part of the group. This will affect the quality of the group's decision or final solution to the problem.

3. Are the facts drawn from acceptable authorities?

The qualification of authorities is sometimes difficult to ascertain. We all have individuals on whom we depend for guidance; however, they are not always qualified to present information we need. An authority is a qualified person in a specific field. He applies his authority only to his own field. Benjamin Spock is a man who is well qualified to speak on child care, but can we say he is an expert on foreign policy? In our original problem, we might ask the advice of campus police who control the selection of parking areas on campus. Their suggestions on the extent of the parking problem would be viewed as authority based information.

4. Are the statistical statements biased?

Statistics are commonly used to represent large amounts of data because they provide a concise form in which to present the facts. However, statistical data can be manipulated to provide a specific interpretation to the data. Laymen cannot always be expected to have the knowledge needed for a correct statistical interpretation. The group may be forced to call on an expert for assistance.

5. Are eyewitness statements confirmed?

Each person views the same experience differently. Ask any three people in your class to describe the same event and you will find three different views of the same phenomena. We are all different psychologically and physiologically. If facts needed by the group are based on personal experience, it might be best to search for individuals who have had similar experience to verify the observation.

---

exercise 5

If you were to participate in a problem-solving discussion dealing with the following three areas, where would you go for your facts? What specific references would you use?

Socialized medicine
Birth control
Innovations in education

Ask yourself if your information is:

1. current
2. drawn from authoritative sources

ESTABLISHING CRITERIA FOR EVALUATING SOLUTIONS. In this step the group establishes certain standards for judging each problem solution. The ultimate question each group must ask is, "What standards or criteria must be met before a solution can become acceptable to us?" In attempting to solve our parking problem the group might ask: "Is the solution practical? Will it cost too much? Will the people who have the power to implement the solution do so?" The criteria established by the group narrows the range of solutions that will be acceptable and considered later. Once the facts have been accumulated and tested and the criteria established for evaluating the solutions, the group can begin to suggest possible solutions to the problem. Sometimes groups use the brainstorming technique to draw out many possible solutions. The solutions proposed should be realistic and based on the factual information provided by group members.

SELECTING AND TESTING THE FINAL SOLUTION. In most problem solving, discussion steps 5 and 6 are combined. After determining the advantages and disadvantages of each solution, the group selects the one that provides the greatest number of advantages and least disadvantages. This step involves the examination of each solution against the criteria established above, and a final comparison and weighing of the most acceptable solutions. In classroom discussions, the group rarely has time to test their selected solutions. However, if a group can put their final solution into effect, they may find that it is unworkable or impractical.

[1. ALL AGREE] [2. IDEAL SOLUTION] [3. CHANGE CONDITIONS] [4. BEST APPROXIMATION]

In this case, the group may go back to the previous step to examine new solutions.

Let us now move on to investigate our last two problem-solving patterns.

Ideal-solution form This problem-solving pattern emerged from practical experience with managerial groups (Kepner and Tregoe, 1965). It consists of four steps:
1. Are we all agreed on the nature of the problem?
2. What would be the ideal solution from the point of view of all parties involved in the problem?
3. What conditions within the problem could be changed so that the ideal solution might be achieved?
4. Of the solutions available to us, which one best approximates the ideal solution?

Let us examine how this pattern can be used with our original problem-solving example—the campus parking crisis.

Remember that our students in their initial discussion had discovered that they were unable to find parking spaces on campus. The intent of their meeting in the student union was absolutely clear—they were searching for a means to improve student parking. They had all agreed on the nature of the problem.

If we can imagine ourselves at that meeting, we can see how the group might proceed through steps 2, 3, and 4. Initially, the groups would state the ideal solution. In this case, the solution would guarantee every college student driving to campus a parking spot at the time desired by that student (step 2).

The group would then examine the problem-cause(s) to identify conditions that must be changed to implement the ideal solution. In this step the group collects the facts needed for determining not only what is occurring, but what can be done in the future to resolve the dilemma. For example, let us hypothetically state that our students found that the campus has 3,000 parking places and 10,000 different students drove cars to campus during a period of one week. Furthermore, during peak class hours, 3,500 students attempted to park on campus. By examining these facts, we can discover that the campus needs an additional 500 parking places to meet student demands (step 3).

We all realize, however, that groups cannot always implement the ideal solution. External and internal constraints operate against implementation of the best solution. In our example, the college administrators may not have the space needed for 500 additional parking spaces or they may have land but no money to make it suitable for parking. The group would then examine alternative solutions to the problem: (1) providing tram service from off-campus parking zones, or (2) asking students to share rides to campus, thus reducing the total number of cars driven to campus.

The first alternative does not fulfill our ideal solution. It does not solve our basic problem. However, the second alternative does address itself to the crux of the problem. It provides a means for alleviating the campus traffic congestion and provides each student with a parking space. The second alternative also operates within the constraints of the situation. No new parking places will have to be found on campus and there will be no cost to the college. Since the ideal solution cannot be implemented, the group would adopt the second alternative as their solution to the problem.

Single-question form. This pattern was developed by Carl E. Larson from the works of Harris and Schwahn (1961). Harris and Schwahn attempted to describe the reasoning process of successful and unsuccessful problem solvers. The pattern for successful problem solvers consists of five steps:

1. What single question provides the group with the answer that is needed to accomplish its purpose?
2. What subquestions must be answered before we can answer the single question we have formulated?
3. Do we have sufficient information to answer confidently the subquestions?
4. What are the most reasonable answers to the subquestions?
5. Assuming that our answers to the subquestions are correct, what is the best solution to the problem?

We will illustrate this pattern with the use of our original parking problem. Let us again place ourselves in the problem-solving situation. The pattern begins when we state the problem question, "How can we guarantee every student on campus a parking spot?" We would then list all questions that must be answered to give us the answer to our problem question. Questions such as, "How many students drive to campus?" and "How many parking places are on campus?" would have to be answered prior to our making an intelligent answer on the problem question. To answer the subquestions we would engage in a fact-finding activity. We apply the information gained from our research to the subquestions. We might find, for example, that 3,500 students drive to campus and that there are 3,000 parking places on campus. This information would answer our two subquestions. Unfortunately, we cannot always find all the information necessary to completely answer a particular subquestion. In this case, we must apply what materials we have available to developing the most justifiable answers to our subquestions. After answering our subquestions, we use this information to answer our initial question. The answer to the initial question will constitute our problem solution. From the limited information we possess on this problem, it would appear that one answer would be to increase the number of parking spaces.

We have attempted to detail three patterns of problem solving. Realize, however, that these are not the only patterns that have been developed. We have selected these three because of their frequency of use or their success in problem-solving situations.

---

exercise 6

Divide the class into three groups. Each group is given a specific problem-solving pattern: (1) ideal solution; (2) single question; (3) reflective thinking. Each group is given the same problem and asked to arrive at a solution to that problem.

After the groups have solved the problem ask each other the following questions:

1. Which pattern produced the best solution?
2. Which pattern was easiest to operate within the group?
3. Which pattern produced the greatest group-member satisfaction?

The final question we must ask ourselves is, "Does one problem-solving pattern operate more effectively than another?" Brilhart and Jochem (1964) compared three different patterns:

brainstorming; a form of reflective thinking; and a pattern based on Bales' phase movements. The brainstorming pattern tended to produce more and better solutions than did the other two patterns. The value of the reflective-thinking pattern was termed "dubious at best, and harmful at worst."

Ovid Bayless (1967) noted that the earlier study of problem-solving patterns failed to examine that which really counted, the *final solution*. In an attempt to find which pattern produced the best final product, Bayless examined three patterns of problem solving, including reflective thinking. The results provided no evidence that the pattern had a significant effect upon the quality of the final product. In addition, the quantity of ideas seems to bear no relationship to the quality of the final solution.

This study did indicate that the *problem* the group deals with does affect the effectiveness of the discussion. A group of students trying to select the best method for teaching college courses would fare much better than the same group attempting to formulate policy for the United States prison system. Familiarity with a problem would appear to provide a more secure group environment. Insufficient information on a particular problem may make the members feel inadequate in their task. In turn, this feeling of inadequacy may cause frustration, leaving group members unsatisfied with the group's decisions, and inhibiting their ability to communicate. Obviously, students would be more familiar with and would have more information on teaching methods in college classes than on the present state of the United States prison system. Lack of information and familiarity with a problem does not always stop a particular group from attempting to solve the problem, but it does lend serious doubts to the solution that is finally selected. Typically, students in a group discussion class are the worst perpetrators of this problem-solving crime. Required to present a number of artificial problem-solving discussions, they are sometimes forced to select problems in areas in which they have little expertise or information.

Group members using the reflective-thinking pattern generally perceive their leaders to be very effective. Brainstorming, on the other hand, allows for leadership too permissive to fit many individuals' perception of effective leadership.

More recently, Larson (1969) investigated the ability of groups to solve a problem accurately. The accuracy of three patterns was compared: single question; ideal solution; and reflective thinking. In keeping with the findings of earlier studies, the reflective thinking pattern was the least productive of the problem-solving forms. The single-question and ideal-solution forms, on the other hand, did not differ significantly from each other in their accuracy in solving problems.

It would appear that successful group problem solving can be facilitated by the selection of the proper method for the particular problem with specific group members. We can no longer assume that the reflective thinking pattern, taught in most group-discussion classes and used most frequently by groups, is the most appropriate and desirable method for successful problem solving. If a problem-solving pattern fits, we should use it. We should not be forced into an inflexible pattern for solving all problems that confront us.

Next, we want to briefly consider another model—this one concerned primarily with decision-making behavior during problem-solving group communication.

Decision making and problem solving

Wouldn't you like to have a penny for each decision that you make in the average day? From choosing what to wear in the morning, to the type of entertainment to enjoy in the evening, we are constantly bombarded with circumstances that call for some decision. The same principle holds true for the problem-solving small group. Every step of the way, members are placed in positions that call for judgments about the next course of action. Generally, when we thought of small-group problem solving in the past, we tended to avoid or neglect the decision-making process. You know the syndrome: Avoid something long enough and either it will go away or someone else will handle it. Not so with the problem-solving group's decision-making behavior.

It seems foolish and quite presumptive of us to prescribe some way or method that group members ought to follow for ease in decision making. In the first place, no such prescription exists. And, secondly, the types of problem-solving circumstances are simply too numerous and varied for any one method. What we want to do is to spend some time discussing a descriptive model of decision making. As we attempted with the IPA, we want to illustrate what appears to happen in small-group problem solving. Whereas in the reflective-thinking section we were able to do a modest bit of prescribing, Fisher's research (1970) does not lend itself to such a presentation.

In essence, Fisher argues that problem-solving groups move through four interrelated phases in their deliberations: orientation, conflict, emergence, and reinforcement. What makes this model interesting to us is that the social-emotional characteristics of problem solving were not considered. In other words, only task-oriented behaviors were of interest. Let's briefly discuss the four phases and try to relate them to our earlier discussion of the IPA and reflective thinking models as interesting ways of observing and analyzing small-group interaction.

The first phase of problem-solving discussion—*orientation*—was typified by the amount of clarification and agreement on the part of group members. Individuals would make assertions in attempts to test the other group members. Remember, our earlier model of interaction development refers to this as a period of "chicken dancing"—a period of unsure social-emotional relationships. Group members have a tendency to agree with ambiguous comments. By the same token, the orientation phase is noted for the statement of ambiguous comments. What it boils down to is that individuals make a lot of low-information statements. But it's still interaction, isn't it? It allows us to know where the other guy's head is. There is little reinforcement during this period. Apparently, individuals are too busy carving out their communicative territory.

Thus the orientation phase is not typified by a great deal of task accomplishment. It is a period of loosening up and getting to know others. Does it match your experiences?

The second phase—*conflict*—moves into a dramatically different direction. Individuals have formulated their position on certain issues and certainly are not afraid to voice those positions. Unfavorable comments are numerous and responses are, too. Ambiguity has been significantly reduced and group members are ready to make decisions about the positions of others. Attitudes are polarized, the group direction is solidified, and members are aware of the kinds of decisions that are being made. In a nutshell, the individuals have moved from a highly ambiguous state to one of specificity. It is interesting to note that there is a tendency to disagree more with unfavorable than with favorable comments. In other words, all hell breaks loose with some members of the group. Yet it does seem natural, doesn't it? After all, we probably have experienced some similar situations in which we were very polite in the earlier stages of the discussion only to be vehement in our position once we found out what the game was. Your early interaction was very safe, innocuous, nonthreatening. As you moved into circumstances with more information, you became more entrenched in a position, and at that point conflict ensued. We'll speak more about conflict in chapter 6, but it is well to note here that the existence of conflict should not be taken as a negative characteristic.

The third phase—*emergence*—is characterized by a reduction in the amount of conflict and argument. This reduction occurs gradually through communication and interaction. There are fewer unfavorable communicative units and members generally tend to avoid conflict. Fisher acknowledges that the most crucial characteristic of this phase is that group members do not appear to defend contrary or unfavorable attitudes as much as they did earlier. At any rate, ambiguity tends to reoccur. We may explain this as a result of more information bombarding the group. On the other hand, we can say that the individuals are more ambiguous because they are replowing old ground. They may have said all there was to say in the earlier phases of the deliberations. But, the ambiguity present in the emergence phase is useful. Fisher claims that it serves as modified dissent. In other words, group members use ambiguous messages and interaction to facilitate their attitude change from unfavorable to favorable positions.

Actually, ambiguity can be a useful factor in the development of a dynamic group interaction. It does not polarize individuals; rather, it gives them room to think and to accommodate if they care to. While it is impossible to say all things to all people, the use of ambiguity may allow group members to affect more attitude change than a strategy that depends on telling it like it is.

The final phase is identified as the *reinforcement* stage. Argument is virtually irrelevant here as members become aware of the decisions that they are to make. Conflict is all but gone and individuals are more cohesive in their attempts to resolve the problem and reach consensus. Interaction regarding the proposals is marked by positive reinforcement and support from all quarters. Ambiguity tends to dissipate and individuals seem to be unified in their task.

This model describes small-group problem solving and pays

particular attention to the decision-making behavior performed by group members. Whereas the IPA and the reflective-thinking model take account of both task and social-emotional orientations, Fisher's model specifically discounts the latter. By paying special attention to the task dimensions, he speaks directly to the communicative behaviors individuals perform when they are concerned about the task per se.

exercise 7

Using the discussion of exercise 3, identify the various stages in terms of Fisher's phases of decision making.

1. Were the phases—orientation, conflict, emergence, and reinforcement—present?
2. Were there any behaviors suggested by the IPA that were present during the deliberations? How did they affect the decision making?
3. Did the decision-making phases affect any of the behaviors identified by the IPA?

Group problem solving and the communication system

Thus far, our discussion has been restricted to problem solving per se. We have discussed interaction as a crucial component of our communication system. But we have said little regarding the relationship that may exist between the interaction component of our model and the other three components: communicator, message, situational context. Perhaps with an understanding now of how groups engage in problem-solving behavior, it might be profitable for us to spend some time relating this dimension of our model to the other components. Recall that we prefer to speak of group communication operating as a system in which each factor affects and is affected by every other factor? Let us see if a case can be made for this dynamic relationship with regards to our component of interaction and group problem solving. Is problem solving affected by the activity of other communication factors? How do other system components affect the group's problem-solving capability? Perhaps an overview will help us put things in proper perspective.

First, we turn to a brief consideration of the communicator factor in our model and examine its relationship with problem solving. Regardless of the elaborate model that one employs, the success of the group's problem-solving venture will ultimately rest on the individuals who are involved in the group. It doesn't make any difference how much financial support a group may receive or how much moral support it may have behind it. The communicator characteristics inherent in the group will significantly affect the manner in which the group approaches its problems.

The attitudes that the group members have toward the issue, toward other group members, toward the group structure will influence the group's problem-solving behavior. The amount of information that individuals bring to the situation will similarly serve as an influencing cause. Finally, personality characteristics of the communicators can serve as causes of changes in problem-solving behavior of the group.

A group member's level of dogmatism, his credibility as a group member, and his self-esteem will all contribute to changes in the problem-solving nature of the small group.

On the other hand, the problem-solving interaction carried on by the group members will lead to changes in their communicator characteristics. Interaction will lead individuals to change their attitudes, the level of their involvement, or the information they have regarding the issue. In a similar manner, individuals can be reeducated and thus have their levels of dogmatism changed as a result of problem-solving interaction.

Our point here is simply that the communicator component of our model will *affect* and *be affected by* characteristics of the interaction component, more specifically problem-solving behavior. But let us consider the other components of the group-system model.

The message factor can easily be seen to influence and be influenced by the problem-solving activity of the group. Bales' IPA and Fisher's model point up the differences in messages during certain phases of problem-solving behavior. But our point here is even more basic. It is simply that as individuals go through some problem-solving scheme—whether it is similar to Dewey's, Fisher's, or some other—they are constantly modifying their messages. The use of more intense language, the nonverbal responses that are elicited, and the way in which arguments are ordered and structured are all message factors that can both cause and be caused by problem-solving interaction.

What effect does a raised voice have during your problem-solving deliberations? Are there individuals in your groups who constantly treat each point as some issue to be won in a debate? Are there individuals in your groups who must have the spotlight during most group sessions? These questions and others like them tend to point out the importance of message factors in the successful resolution of problems. More important, a recognition of them is crucial to the group's functioning. For how can your group hope to solve some relevant problem without taking into account the many communicative messages that will be exchanged over the period of deliberations?

The physical characteristics, the group's function, the group's norms and roles all serve as factors defining the *situational context* of the problem-solving communication. How does the arrangement of the room affect problem-solving behavior? Does the way in which a group goes about the task of problem-solving reinforce or violate existing group norms? Does group leadership grow out of or lead to effective problem solving? The answer to these questions is a simple, "It all depends." Why? Factors of the situational context can be manipulated to cause changes in the group's problem-solving activity; *or* these factors can evolve out of the group's communication. Are the roles that individuals play independent of group problem solving? Hardly.

Our point throughout these last few paragraphs is not to develop a lengthy treatise on the interrelationship among all elements. Rather, we want to call your attention to some principles that individuals involved in group problem solving often overlook. Principles that tell us, for example, that changes in communicator attitudes will surely lead to changes in the manner in which individuals will handle some problem. Another principle warns us that the way in which we establish group norms will determine in large part the methods that we use in problem-solving deliberations.

But the list of principles is infinite. Remember that we are not dealing with some isolated component of the group communication system every time we sit down to solve some problem. The factor of interaction distinguishes one group from another. But this factor is influenced by communicator, message, and situational context variables.

In this chapter we have tried to consider some of the more crucial elements of the problem-solving small group. We began with a definition of problem-solving groups and moved into a consideration of the part that interaction plays in the identification of successful groups. We talked about interaction as a system component in our group communication model and identified two stages in the development of interaction within the group: orientation and deliberation.

Next, we moved on to discuss three approaches to the problem-solving group: Bales' Interaction Process Analysis, Dewey's

Reflective Thinking Process, and Fisher's Decision-Making Model.

We have investigated a number of problem-solving patterns. The procedures for utilizing each pattern were illustrated using a single discussion problem. We have pointed out, however, that problem-solving patterns are not always equally effective. If our purpose as a group is to produce a large number of solutions, we should use a brainstorming pattern. The group members' perception of leadership is also related to the problem-solving format: If the group expects more restrictive leadership, the reflective-thinking pattern should be used; if the group expects a more permissive leadership, one should use brainstorming. We might suggest that the selection of a problem-solving pattern be weighed against: (1) number of solutions, criteria, ideas, and so on, desired by the group; (2) accuracy in the solution of problems; (3) leadership expectations on the part of group members; and (4) the group's knowledge of the problem.

Finally, we recalled the concept of system and restated the point that no one component of the system can exist without affecting and being affected by other components.

Are you now armed with sufficient information to be a problem solver par excellence? Will your small-group experiences be a little more pleasant now when before they might have been troublesome at best? Obviously, these questions, while sounding facetious, do have some logical basis. Instead of trying to provide clear-cut answers we might be wise at this time to speculate on the implications of these various models of problem solving.

For one thing, these various approaches suggest that to the extent we can systematically pattern our problem-solving tasks, we will increase the *predictability* of group behavior. When deliberative time is a crucial variable, the ability to predict interactive behavior may be most important.

Another implication of our discussion is concerned with the nature and extent of group leadership. We will be addressing ourselves specifically to leadership behaviors in chapter 9, but it is relevant at this time to consider the relationship between the style of leadership used and the pattern of problem solving employed. Can an authoritarian leader dominate during a reflective-thinking procedure? Does Fisher's model lend itself to a leader who is primarily social-emotional oriented? Does Bales' analysis lead one to conclude that the individual who interacts the most will be the group leader? These questions give us some idea of the implication for leadership that problem-solving interaction models suggest.

Problem-solving patterns are not "cookie cutters" to be used in the same manner that we would interchange tools or cars. Rather, they are facilitative mechanisms that aid the group in its various goals. As members of problem-solving small groups, we ought to be keenly aware of our behavior in such groups. Knowledge of problem-solving factors, discussed in this chapter, may aid us in modifying our group behavior and becoming more effective in problem-solving tasks.

ADDITIONAL READINGS

Davis, James H. *Group Performance* (Menlo Park, Calif.: Addison-Wesley Publishing Co., 1969). While many of the research studies cited may appear to be complex and impossible to read, you will find Davis' treatment of person, environmental and task variables excellent for an analysis of problem-solving circumstances. Of particular interest is his discussion of interactive effects in groups.

Mortensen, C. David. *Communication: The Study of Human Interaction* (New York: McGraw-Hill Book Co., 1972). Mortensen's treatment of communication networks (chapter 9) describes the way in which messages flow within a group. These interactive channels provide insight into means of analyzing problem-solving behavior. Of particular interest is his discussion of information transmission in a variety of network settings.

Psychology Today: An Introduction (Del Mar, Calif.: CRM, 1970). Chapter 32 ("Small Groups") is an easy-to-read overview of several facets of small-group behavior. Of particular interest to our discussion of problem-solving activity is the treatment of various issues beginning on page 603. You will find the discussion of Bales' model, for example, to be clear and graphically impressive.

Gulley, H. E. *Discussion, Conference, and Group Process* (New York: Holt, Rinehart & Winston, 1968), pp. 57–92. Provides some clear guidelines on preparing for the more formalized group discussion presentation.

Brilhart, J. K. *Effective Group Discussion* (Dubuque, Iowa: Wm. C. Brown, 1967), pp. 22–44. A simple and clear description of the overall organization of a group discussion. A Creative Problem-Solving Pattern is also presented.

Phillips, G. M. *Communication and the Small Group* (Indianapolis: Bobbs-Merrill, 1966), pp. 72–89. An excellent description of the role of the standard agenda in a problem-solving discussion.

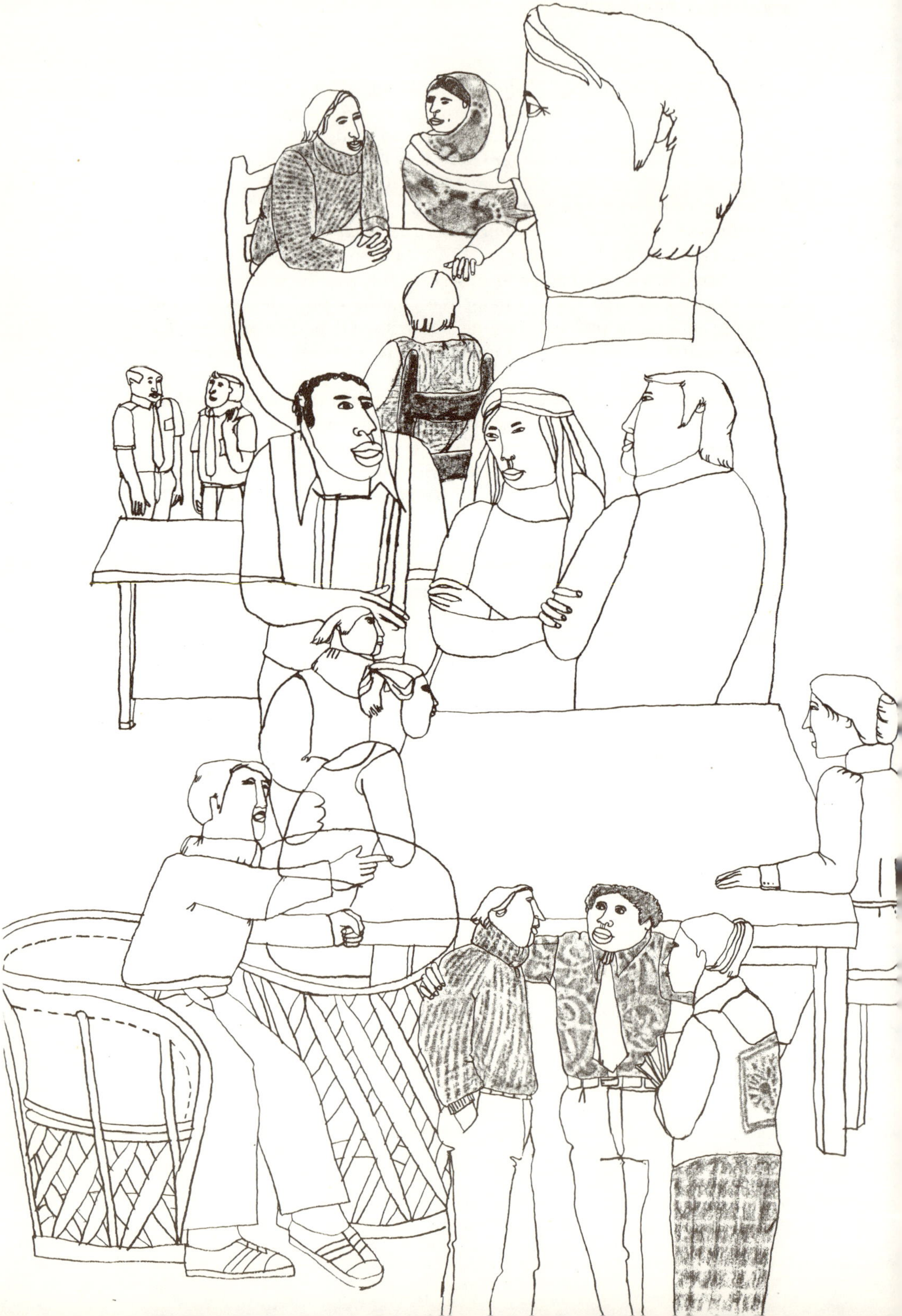

6. Norms and roles

PREVIEW

What are norms?
Norms are group standards specifying what behaviors are encouraged, allowed, or forbidden within a group.

Why do norms develop within small groups?
Norms develop because they are perceived as helping task and social-emotional goals.

What is the relation between norms and small-group behavior?
Norms tend to produce conformity.
Norms influence communicators, meanings given to messages, and important aspects of group interaction.

What are roles?
Roles refer to the many positions a person occupies and the variety of behaviors tied to each of them.

Why are roles developed within small groups?
As with norms, roles develop to enable the group to accomplish its task and social-emotional activities.

What is the relation between roles and small-group behavior?
As with norms, roles influence communicators, messages, and elements of group interaction.

Picture a small group. Imagine that each member of our group decided independently of the others how he was going to act. Consider the consequences. Coordinated activity within the group would be difficult if not impossible. Forget efficient task accomplishment. Forget the development of cohesiveness. All we reasonably could be sure of is that chaos would reign.

Most of us don't realize how much we depend upon social structure to help us in our day-to-day communication. We have learned what is appropriate and inappropriate communicative behavior in various settings. We know that certain messages considered acceptable at a veterans club meeting to organize a beer bust are out of place at a meeting of the campus planning committee. We know pretty well how we should act when we discuss a business matter with our boss as opposed to how we, as coaches, should talk with our Little League charges at a half-time meeting.

Perhaps we can sum up what we're trying to say so far this way: communication can't be studied apart from its context. We can't study people and their messages without regard for the social system in which they exist. Likewise we can't study social systems such as small groups without considering the people who comprise them. *Communication is impossible without some semblance of structure.* We need structure to be able to predict the behavior of others in our group. We need structure to prepare and provide appropriate responses. We need structure to achieve group goals. We need structure to maintain harmonious relations between group members. We need structure to promote individual well-being.

Norms and roles probably provide the most important sources of social structure within the small group. They provide the clearest means for predicting behavior within the group. Of all the dimensions of our group communication model, norms and roles have the greatest potential for promoting task accomplishment and personal satisfaction.

What we'd like to do for the remainder of this chapter is discuss norms and roles and the part they play in group communication processes. We're going to be somewhat arbitrary in what we select. As with most other topics, we couldn't cover everything about norms and roles as they relate to small-group communication even if we wished to—the content is too vast. We do believe, however, that the material we present will provide a sound, clear, and useful understanding of these extremely significant constructs of the situational context dimension.

Norms

Norms defined

Groups that have achieved some measure of permanence or stability develop norms. A norm is a group standard. It is a "rule" that is accepted at least to some degree by most members of the group. Norms are guidelines that define personal relationships, prescribe forms of interaction, and influence the meanings that emerge. They are standards of conduct of the group providing a means for determining what is appropriate behavior in what would otherwise be a chaotic situation. Homans (1950) tends to reflect these notions in his statement: "A norm, then, is an idea in the minds of the members of a group, an idea that can be put in the form of a statement specifying what the members-. . . should do, ought to do, are expected to do, under given circumstances" (p. 123). Norms, in essence, suggest what should be done within a group. They embody values concerning behaviors encouraged, allowed, or forbidden within a group.

Norms can be thought of as existing only if departure of member behavior from a norm is followed by some punishment. This implies that the group has means for applying sanctions for norm deviation. The handling of deviation and punishment, though, is a somewhat complex affair. For instance, norms may differ in the range of permissible departure allowed. Some norms may not apply to the whole group, but only to selected members. A few members of the group may be allowed greater freedom than others to deviate from norms.

Development of norms

Some factors seem to be especially relevant in forming norms. Of primary significance is the extent to which members find that conformity to norms is rewarding or costly to the group's goals. Another condition is the degree to which the norm behavior fits in with basic values of the group members. An additional factor is the degree to which group behavior is being observed. And, finally, the extent to which punishment may be imposed strongly influences whether a norm will develop. We can tie these conditions affecting norm formation into a neatly packaged conclusion: *norms develop because conformity in values and behavior is perceived as improving the outcomes experienced by members of the group*. Thus the elementary school community council (comprised of students, faculty, and parents) in attempting to solve educational problems confronting the children, may place a high value on insuring that contributions from all representative subgroups of the council are received equally. For example, the group may develop the norm of using "Mr.," "Mrs.," and "Miss" before everyone's last name (including the students') to prevent status differences from unduly influencing reception of ideas. Or the group may decide to call everyone by his first name in order to lessen the potential negative effect of status upon the group's deliberations. Other norms, such as agreeing not to speak for more than ten minutes, restraint from the use of obscenity, avoidance of attacking personalities, and so on might be adhered to in particular groups if the members felt that these standards increased productivity or helped maintain desired social-emotional conditions within the group.

Characteristics of norms in discussion groups

Groups exist for a reason. They may exist to share information, to maintain themselves, or to solve problems. These purposes or tasks often can best be accomplished if certain standards of behavior are exhibited within the group and others restrained. In addition, groups consist of individuals with personal needs and wants. Many of these needs are social or emotional in nature. Certain standards of behavior pave the way for harmonious relationships, while others lead to strained associations between group members. Consequently, norms are typically developed dealing with both task and social dimensions of the group.

Norms and small-group behavior

The most general statement that can be made concerning norms and small-group behavior is that *norms tend to produce conformity*. Let's look at the nature of conformity. Conformity may be of two types. A person may conform with the majority simply for the sake of agreement; to avoid their displeasure and the possible

*Norms are standards of conduct that provide a means
for determining appropriate behavior
in what would otherwise be a chaotic situation*

punishment they may mete out. But he may also conform because the group standard dovetails with his own attitudes and values.

Some people see conformity as a negative consequence. They view conforming as leading to loss of individuality, restriction of creativity, and reduction of all members to the level of mediocrity. In the main, though, there seem to be good and sufficient reasons for conformity to group norms. Norms provide order. They offer the means for the coordination of individual behaviors. As we've said earlier, effective group interaction would be impossible without some semblance of order within the group.

A few of the people holding negative views of conformity sometimes play word games. They call conforming to standards of behavior they approve of "cooperation," and compliance with standards of behavior they disapprove of "conformity." As we use the word, conformity basically refers to behavior complying with group standards—whether these be "good" or "bad."

To sum up so far, conformity to group norms can be either negative or positive. Conformity produces the undesirable negative effects so frequently attributed to it when group members comply only for the sake of conforming. On the other hand, some agreed-upon standards of conduct are essential for effective group action.

In moving to a consideration of the specific relation between norms and communication behavior within the small group, let's again refer to our model. We'll focus particularly on the relation between norms and communicator, between norms and message, and between norms and interaction dimensions within the small group. As is true of any attempt to break down the communication process into component parts, our categorization is arbitrary. For as we have observed, communication is a process occurring in a system, and all parts of the system relate to and bear upon the others. Thus when we talk about norms and messages, for instance, of necessity we'll also be discussing communicators and interaction. So keep in mind that our purpose is to try to place some of the many complex relationships in some kind of readily understood pattern.

Communicators. Let's look at a few communicator variables that bear upon normative behavior. Communicators with high intelligence seem to conform to norms less than individuals with lower intelligence. This relation is one we have probably experienced. Think, for example, of the discussions you've participated in or observed this term. Wasn't it usually the more intelligent member who would question or challenge the group's norms or decisions? Turning to personality, highly authoritarian individuals tend to conform more than those who do not have this personality trait. This really isn't a surprising finding. As we've noted in the chapter on the communicator, the highly authoritarian person tends to need structure. He believes in the necessity for rules. As in the soap commercial we can just hear him say, "I'm glad I follow the group's norms. Aren't you glad you follow them? Don't you wish everybody did?" A somewhat surprising finding is that people in power conform more closely to the norms of their groups in some respects. But not surprisingly, under some circumstances members with power are allowed to deviate from accepted norms more than their less influential associates. We allow our leaders to bend the rules a little at times to get the job done. A closely related variable is status, which is the prestige accompanying a group position such as that of leader. People with average status conform to a greater extent than those with high or low status. The high-status member (such as the leader) has certain powers and rights that allow him to break the rules while other group members wink at his behavior. The low-status member has nothing to lose, so he is also likely to break normative rules. Thus it is the communicator of average status who conforms most closely to group norms.

Messages. Norms play a fascinating role in message perception, evaluation, and production within a small group. A classic series of experiments have demonstrated that group norms have much to do with responses made to a variety of messages. This research asked people to do such things as judge apparent movement of a stimulus (Sherif and Sherif, 1956) and determine which of three vertical lines is the same length as a standard line which is presented at the same time (Asch, 1951). In these experiments, the individual is typically asked to make these judgments *in the presence of others, whose standards are openly declared*. The typical finding is that a substantial portion of individuals are consistently influenced by the norms of the group. They adjust their own judgments of message cues to conform to those of the group, even when the norms differ from their own. These judgments are more likely to conform to the group's standards if the stimulus is difficult to judge—that is, if the person has problems in making objective judgments of the stimulus. We can readily see, for example, how an engineering major might tend to conform to standards agreed upon by a group of English majors in a discussion evaluating the works of modern poets. Yet it must be admitted that some people will conform to standards made by the group even when they *know* the group's norms are *wrong*.

Another significant relation concerns the effect of norms upon positive or negative reactions to messages. The attitudinal response to praise and criticism is markedly influenced by the social context in which it occurs. The act is always interpreted in relation to some normative context. For example, norms in our culture are biased in favor of praise. There seems to be a strong norm toward saving face. Consequently, be *very careful* when you make negative evaluations in your groups, for you can easily rub people the wrong way. Furthermore, the status of the person giving the praise or criticism is a crucial factor. Evaluations made by a superior to a subordinate tend to be interpreted by group members most favorably, praise or criticism of a peer by another peer is judged next most favorably, and judgments by a subordinate of a superior least favorably. These findings seem to suggest: Don't mess with the leader, or at least be very diplomatic in criticizing a leader, if you want to maintain the goodwill of the group. All of this research supports the inference that the meaning actually communicated to group members depends on their norms. The meaning a group member intends to communicate depends on what he assumes their norms to be. Understanding and misunderstanding within a small group may reflect the accuracy with which norms have been perceived and the degree to which they are part of the message-sending and message-receiving behavior of the group communicators.

Some interesting studies have been conducted on the effects of deviation from group norms upon the pattern of messages sent within a group. Schacter (1951), for example, had three conditions in an experiment. In a small-group setting, confederates fulfilled three experimental conditions: the *deviate*, who took a stand at the opposite extreme from the mode of the group, the *mode*, who expressed the group's position, and the *slider*, who first took an opposed stand but later came around to the group's position. The first series of messages were directed primarily toward the deviates (deviates and sliders). The number of messages to the slider, however, decreased as he approached the modal group position. Messages to the deviate (who maintained his opposing stance) increased up to a point and then decreased dramatically. The general picture that emerged was one of increasing attempts to get the deviate to conform to the norms of the group, followed by complete acceptance if he did, and rejection and isolation if he maintained his deviant opinion.

Interaction. One of the most important aspects of the interaction dimension is cohesiveness (see chapter 7). When cohesiveness within the group is high, there is greater pressure exerted to maintain the group's norms. Members of highly cohesive groups are very sensitive to failure to act according to group norms. Religious orders, for instance, typically are very touchy about maintaining their norms. When norms are violated, overt pressure for conformity will arise.

Norms also have an influence upon accomplishing tasks such as problem solving. The relation is somewhat roundabout. The pattern goes something like this: when people form groups they develop group norms. This increases their attitudinal similarity. This similarity in value results in greater communication effectiveness within the group. Better communication helps in attaining group goals. Attainment of group goals increases interpersonal liking. This in turn increases the interaction rate over and above that required for the attainment of group goals. The higher communication rate leads to a further increase in value and attitudinal similarity among group members. And so on.

Norms affect task accomplishment in yet another way. Norms act as substitutes for the exercise of personal influence. Norms produce simpler and more efficient patterns of behavior, and save the wear-and-tear that would be necessary to produce these behaviors based upon personal persuasion alone.

---

communication diary

1. *Discuss your general tendencies and feelings about conformity to group standards.*

2. *Identify norms you believe to be important for improved social relations and task accomplishment.*
   Discuss the reasons for your choices.

3. *Identify norms you believe to be unimportant or detrimental to improved social relations and task accomplishment.*
   Discuss the reasons for your choices.

It should be said that the effects of norms upon group behavior are not restricted to laboratory research. Support has also been found in field settings. Studies have been done on whether people obeyed or violated traffic signals (Lefkowitz, Blake, and Mouton, 1955), whether they did or did not signal when driving (Barch, Trumbo, and Nangle, 1957), whether they did or did not exhibit volunteering behavior (Rosenbaum and Blake, 1955), whether they conformed to "Do Not Enter" signs (Freed, Chandler, Mouton, and Blake, 1955), and so forth. In these studies, what the individual perceived to be norms for the behavior strongly affected his own behavior. In the famous Bennington study, Newcomb (1943) showed that through their college years, students accepting the college community as a dominant reference group moved in the direction of commonly held liberal attitudes.

Roles

Norms and roles are not really separate topics; these two constructs overlap. Whereas some norms within a group apply to all members, others pertain only to certain individuals or subgroups of persons within the group. These subclasses provide a method for identifying different roles within a group. Group members are said to be in the same role if the same norms exist with respect to their behavior.

Roles refer to the many positions a person occupies and the variety of behaviors tied to each of them. Roles may be looked at in light of whether they are expected or enacted. The terms *role expectations* and *role performance* best characterize these distinctions. That is, role may be thought of either as a set of expectations people have about required behaviors or as the actual behavior engaged in by the person. Role behavior is generally agreed upon not only by the occupant of the position but also by other members of the group. To the degree that there are differences between role expectation and role performance, the likelihood of conflict and group dysfunction is increased.

Characteristics of roles

Roles are the organized patterns of social relationships into which the individual must fit. Each position within a group has many required role behaviors. The group task leader, for instance, may be required to assign jobs, draw inferences, test soundness of reasoning, and so on. The group social-emotional leader may have the functions of encouraging, harmonizing, and releasing tensions when conflicts among members arise.

An important point to understand regarding roles is that people play different roles in different groups. Some members of this class play the multiple roles of student, parent, provider, community leader, and so on. The quiet follower in a discussion class may be a team leader on the athletic field. The role that a person takes in various groups takes into account the part each member wants to play and the part the others expect him to play.

There are certain assumptions contained in the concept of roles. It is assumed that there is considerable agreement about what someone in a certain position should do. It is also assumed that most people within the group are inclined to play these roles.

A single role within a small group cannot be considered apart from its relation to other social roles in the group. Together, a group of related roles comprise a social system—in this case, a small group. Each position in a group has one or more counterpositions. To put this another way, roles require complementary functions. Rights and duties of one role tend to be the "other side" of those of associated roles. One can't be a husband without having a wife, a father without having children, a group leader without having group subordinates or followers, and so forth.

Whereas some roles encompass a small portion of a person's total behavior, others may be all-encompassing. Performing the behaviors required as president of the United States consumes much more of an individual's total behavior than acting as a den mother for the cub scouts. Behaviors associated with the role of male or female, or member of a religious order encompass nearly all of any particular individual's activities, no matter what the group may be. Males, females, and members of religious orders are expected to conform to certain norms of behavior regardless of the group.

Role formation

Roles tend to develop whenever a group continues to exist for some time with group activities to perform. To accomplish these activities, divisions of responsibility come about. Different members of the group are made regularly responsible for various group activities and tasks.

Many factors account for the formation of roles within small groups. Perhaps the most important is the group task. Some roles are designed to achieve group tasks, such as those of information exchange, solution formation, and answer exchange. Not to be neglected, though, are roles that have as their purpose the development and continuation of a harmonious group atmosphere. Such roles include tension releaser, encourager, and harmonizer.

Although it is possible for roles to be established by chance, appointment, and by the withholding of information (withholding of important information may make the group dependent upon the individual), these means are not generally supported by research findings. Of more importance is an ability to perceive the kinds of roles that are needed within the group. Group leaders, for example, often plan how they can assume their roles. In doing so, they tend to send certain kinds of messages to other members of the group. One kind proposes that they be leader. Putting it mildly, this is not often greeted with great enthusiasm. Another approach is to make a specific proposal about a course of action the group should take. If the group agrees, the door is open for more suggestions, whereupon the group gradually comes to accept the individual as their leader. And a final method is to make a general, abstract proposal about group action. Positive group responses to such proposals clear the path for assumption of leadership.

Several factors affect the learning of roles within the group. One is the clarity with which positions are perceived by occupants, aspirants, and counterposition occupants. In addition, agreement about expectations among members and within the minds of each individual are important considerations.

A good deal of research on role formation—especially that of leader—has been done by Bormann (1969) and his students at the University of Minnesota. Bormann worked with groups that were given various tasks but had no assigned leader. After several hours of discussion, members began to specialize in particular roles. Some gained status and esteem. Discussants did not automatically assume roles, but rather each worked out his role jointly with the others. The process by which a given person came to specialize was a dynamic set of trial-and-error episodes in which a given individual tried out various role functions and was encouraged or discouraged to continue by the responses of the group.

Bormann and Bormann (1972) lucidly illustrate the development of roles in a leaderless group discussion:

> Each of the men in our model group could do every task that is required to have the group succeed. Each, however, can do some of the things the group needs to have done better than others. Joe, for example, has been trained in technical matters. He is talented in planning and building machines. Bill is more adept at making plans for group action. He likes to divide a job into its component parts and find people to do the various tasks. Harry is good at testing ideas. The group has many different specific tasks that must be done, and to do them, they have to depend upon the resources and skills of the five members.
>
> Remember that the work group is a social event. In addition to getting

the job done, the group needs to take care of certain housekeeping chores of a social sort. Again all five could do all of the social things, but each is more skilled at some than at others.

We will begin the process of group structuring with a social concern. The members feel the typical primary tension common to the first group meeting. Don and Wilbur have been tension releasers in other groups and both have some talent in this human relations skill. They both enjoy the rewards that come from releasing social tension—the laughter, the social approval, being well liked. Generally, the person who assumes the tension release function becomes the most popular member. Don and Wilbur are both alert to any signs of primary tension, and they find a stiff social atmosphere uncomfortable. They both must try to "break the ice." Don has his characteristic way of being funny. He begins by making small talk about anything that comes into his head. When he sees someone respond in a friendly way, he makes a mildly insulting comment and laughs to indicate it is all in fun. In addition, he has memorized a vast store of "stories" which he tells at the slightest provocation.

Wilbur also has his own style of humor. He is something of a clown and pantomimist. He is clever at doing impersonations and has an expressive face. Don begins to break the ice by making small talk and then insulting Harry. He waits for the response. He does not get a big laugh. The others may smile a bit, but their response is tentative. Don cannot tell whether they like his sally or not. Wilbur is encouraged to give it a try, and he does a little pantomime routine. He watches to see how the others liked his little act. Again the response is half-hearted. Don tries again; Wilbur takes another turn. The others watch the two demonstrate their wares, and gradually they make up their minds as to whether Don or Wilbur should specialize in releasing tension or whether they might share the function. In the latter case, they would be affectionately referred to as a "couple of clowns."

The selection process is accomplished subconsciously. The group members are generally not aware of what is going on. They notice only that, say, Don is tactless and something of a smart aleck and that Wilbur is really pretty funny. When Harry comes to this conclusion, he begins to laugh at Wilbur and to ignore Don's attempts at humor. Then Bill and Joe may begin to see Wilbur's humor and begin to laugh at him. If Don continues to insult people or tell his "old" stories, the others may begin to groan and in other ways let him know that he ought to "knock it off." After a time, Wilbur will do more and more of the tension releasing and Don will stop and move on to other functions. At this point, the struggle for the high status function of being well liked and releasing social tensions will be over. Wilbur will be a specialist. He will expect to be funny, and the group will expect him to step in when things get tense and inject a little humor to relax the atmosphere. If Wilbur fails to play his role—if he appears at a group meeting one day with a long face and is quiet and glum, the group will resent his change. Wilbur, they'll say, is not himself today. They'll ask him if he's sick.

Should Wilbur try to get serious and make an important decision for the group, they will probably laugh at him.

Once the social tensions are broken, the group will go to work. Now they need someone with a "take charge" skill to step in and get them rolling. Bill and Harry have done this task for other groups, and they enjoy the rewards of being the take charge person. As soon as Harry feels that the primary tension has been released, he grows restless and wants to get down to business. He says, "All right. Let's get going. I suggest we begin by . . . ." He does not get immediate obedience. The other members do not say, "That's a good idea. Let's go." They seldom even nod approval. They say little one way or another. Now Bill is encouraged to try his hand. He says, "I don't quite understand what you mean. Would you run through that again?" Harry patiently explains his plan of action, thinking to himself that Bill is not very bright. Bill now sees what Harry is driving at but says, "I'm not sure that we have to do it that way. How about this? Wouldn't this be better?" Bill now makes a suggestion of his own as to how the group might go about its work. Gradually the group begins to follow Bill's directions and orders more often than they follow Harry's. At that point, Bill will have emerged as the group's *leader*. (pp. 15–17)

In the same way, other roles within a group typically are mutually arrived at by each member and the group.

Types of roles in small groups

Two basic classes of roles tend to emerge: those roles associated with task dimensions and those roles associated with social or group maintenance dimensions of the group. Many theorists and researchers have described what they perceived to be critical roles within a group. The points of view of some representative theorists will be presented in the forthcoming subsections.

Task roles. Although theorists agree on certain roles—such as those of initiator and evaluator—they differ in the scope and specificity of roles they propose as being necessary for accomplishing group tasks. Bormann (1969) notes the roles of initiating action, doing routine chores, testing soundness of information, dividing up group work and assigning jobs, gathering information, following orders carefully and doing the job assigned, giving suggestions as to possible ways to go about doing a job, drawing inferences, and evaluating inferences and plans of action.

Benne and Sheats (1948) describe the roles of the initiator-contributor, the information seeker, the opinion seeker, the information giver, the elaborator, the coordinator, the orienter, the evaluator-critic, the energizer, the procedural technician, and the recorder.

Guetzkow (in Cartwright and Zander, 1968) refers to the keyman role, which involves receiving information, formulating

solutions, and sending answers. Another role is that of endman, who merely sends information the others do not have and later receives answers from others. Some participants within the group are merely relayers, who pass on missing information from others and relay any answers received.

Cartwright and Zander (1960) put forward these task roles: initiating action, keeping member attention on the goal, clarifying the issue, developing a procedural plan, evaluating the quality of work done, and making expert information available.

Social roles. Bormann (1969) notes the roles of being funny and releasing tension. Benne and Sheats (1948) discuss the roles of encourager, harmonizer, compromiser, gatekeeper and expediter, standard setter, group observer and commentator, and follower. Cartwright and Zander (1960) propose these social or group maintenance roles: keeping interpersonal relations pleasant, arbitrating disputes, providing encouragement, giving the minority a chance to be heard, stimulating self-direction, and increasing the interdependence of group members.

The quest for an objectively defined or commonly accepted list of roles has not been very successful. And development of such a list is not probable. Roles tend to be recategorized by researchers concerned with different dimensions of group behavior.

Task roles and social or group-maintenance roles are the two basic types of roles in groups

exercise 1

Observe a problem-solving group discussion. Classify the role behaviors that seem to be exhibited. What task roles seem to be demonstrated? How do they affect the work of the group? What social roles seem to be operating? How do they influence the atmosphere of the group? Do any task roles affect the social-emotional aspects of the group? What effects do they have? Do any social roles help or hinder the group's task fulfillment? Were any roles absent that should have been performed? How do you feel about the relative importance of task versus social roles in problem-solving groups?

Role conflict

Many reasons account for role conflict or strain. For one thing, *interpersonal conflict* may create problems. Members of a small group, for example, may disagree on what kinds of behaviors are included in a given role. They may disagree about the "rights" permitted the leader. Some may feel the leader has the right to make decisions for the group, while others may feel the leader may suggest courses of action, but the decision can only be made by the group. They may also disagree on the situations to which the role applies or whether the role behavior is required or simply preferred.

In addition, strain may occur due to *intrapersonal conflict*. Parents may find it very difficult to be both friends and disciplinarians to their children. There may be conflicting differences in successive roles a member must play, or the member may be required to occupy two or more different roles simultaneously. Graduate teaching assistants often feel in limbo; they occupy both teacher and student roles. Many of them find that playing both roles causes them to go through a somewhat painful identity crisis. Role strain may also develop because the rights associated with a position may not be sufficiently rewarding to motivate group members to carry out the obligations of that position. Many professors refuse to be appointed department chairmen. For them, the rights associated with the position do not compensate for the headaches and tons of busywork associated with the position. Finally, we might note that role conflict may develop because conformity to the expectations of one role may interfere with goal achievement by the role partner. The group leader, for instance, in negatively evaluating a proposal by a group member may interfere with the member's desire to make a substantive contribution to the group.

So the question arises, Given the occurrence of role conflict, how is it resolved? We'll look at approaches taken by the group and by the individual to resolve role conflict. The group or organization may use indoctrination manuals and training programs, and rituals and ceremonies to reaffirm the rights and duties of members to the group. The individual, too, uses certain methods to resolve role strain. He may establish his own ranking of values. In his role as a teacher, he may decide that it's more important to play the part of disciplinarian than the role of encourager of individuality. He may use rationalization, or he may leave the group. Typically, when role conflict occurs, the person resolves conflict in the direction of greatest attraction: he chooses to play the role required by the group having the greatest significance to him.

exercise 2

Recall a group that had tensions, arguments, and poor task accomplishment. Identify the role conflict which may have triggered the original tensions. Were these role conflicts of an interpersonal or intrapersonal nature? What were some of the social-emotional and task difficulties encountered because of this role conflict? How were these difficulties resolved? Would other methods of resolution have been preferable?

Roles and small-group behavior

As in our consideration of norms and small-group behavior, we'll use the component dimensions of our model to discuss specific relationships between roles and behavior in small groups.

Communicator. The first relationship we'll examine is that between roles and the communicator. We must realize that roles create a social structure. Some people cannot tolerate an unclear social situation, and for them specifically defined roles are necessary. Most of us feel the need for structure or psychological "closure." Most people, as we've seen, cannot tolerate leaderless groups, especially when the group has problem solving as its purpose. We must keep in mind, however, that others cannot operate in an overly defined (and to them restricted) social structure. In a small group, then, the trick is to have roles that are adequate to provide some structure, but not so rigid that members feel there is no room for individuality or creativity.

A large series of studies have demonstrated (Miller and Burgoon, 1973) that when performing counterattitudinal roles there is a tendency to change attitudes and values to become consistent with the role. Choosing a new role or having a new one forced upon oneself generates strong psychological pressures toward changes in attitudes and behavior to conform to expectations of the role. An executive in a small office may go on vacation and ask one of the staff members to take over for a couple of weeks. Sometimes this worker may fill the boss's role *too well*.

Much research on roles has focused on the leader. There seems to be a relationship between those who achieve the leadership role in a group and intellectual ability. Intelligence, however, seems to be an important though not sufficient (by itself) quality. The personality tendency of ascendance, by contrast, appears necessary to achieve the leadership role. That is, a group member must have not only the smarts but also a strong drive to reach the top to attain the leader's role.

The leader or task specialist initially may be liked because he satisfies the desire of the members for fulfilling their task. But he also arouses envy because of his prestige. He also creates resentment because he talks a good deal of the time, and because he makes other members keep "on the ball." The more he talks, the more uncertain other members become toward him. Eventually they transfer some liking from him to another person who is less active and who expresses their negative feelings. This social-emotional specialist is the best liked member of the group. He symbolizes the values and attitudes that have been upset, curbed, or threatened by the necessity of fulfilling the task.

Apparently it is almost impossible to be both task and social-emotional leader of a group. Group resentment prevents fulfillment of both roles. In addition, personalities attracted to and able to perform these roles tend to be dissimilar. The social or group maintenance specialist must like and be liked if he is to meet these needs in the group. In contrast, the task specialist must be emotionally aloof. If he is to guide the group in achieving its aims, he cannot become so emotionally attached to other members that he cannot use his power over them.

There are a good number of rewards that come with achieving the leadership role. These include satisfactions gained from successful achievement of group goals and satisfactions inherent in the leadership activity itself. Further, the leader's role has a high degree of status, which is the importance given a position in a group. On the other hand, his costs include effort spent, worry over failure, criticism and blame aimed at him, and the emotional distance he is required to maintain.

Life as a follower is not all that bad. One can latch on to the skirt or coattail of the leader and share the sense of achievement. One can also satisfy the need to depend on someone, to identify with a strong leader, and to be free of the costs of assuming a leadership role. The follower, however, also has his pound of flesh to sacrifice. He must live with a lower status, have less control over the group's functions, and forget about the spoils of leadership.

Message. Important implications for group behavior can be gained from research on the relation of roles to message perception. "Variations in a message (praise or blame), the institutional setting (family, school, work, military), and the authority relationship of the communicators (superordinate, peer, subordinate) were used to measure the effect of context upon the same series of messages. The findings give strong support to the conclusion that messages depend for their meaning on the authority relationship of source and receiver, the setting in which the messages are exchanged, and the evaluative content of the message." (Barnlund, 1968, pp. 165–66) As communicators playing different roles in diverse groups, we should be aware of the relation between roles and varying levels of message interpretation. As we've observed earlier, evaluations made by a superior to a subordinate are interpreted most favorably, evaluations by a peer next most favorably, and evaluations by a subordinate least favorably.

There exists an interesting tendency for group members to interpret messages that are "out of role" as disclosing more of the senders' true selves than those giving "in role" answers. (Jones, Davis, and Gergen, 1961) The use of roles apparently inhibits personalized interaction. Communicating with another group member as a *person* appears to be unnecessary and unlikely within clearly defined role structures.

As group members we perform transmitter or receiver roles. (Zajonc, 1960) In these roles we tend to handle message content quite differently. In sender roles we are inclined to use more detail, have greater complexity, and organize material more tightly than when in receiver roles. As speakers we tend to get all wrapped up in our own ideas. As receivers, on the other hand, we tend to leave out details, simplify complexity, and lose sight of the organization of a message. Apparently when listening we don't work as hard at getting the other person's messages as we do in creating our own messages. The point to recall here, though, is that both sending and receiving of messages within a group are subject to the influence of role assignments.

Interaction. Role structure strongly influences the flow of messages within a group. Members tend to direct more talk to people they consider playing important roles, such as leader. People in more important roles tend to talk more to the whole group. These findings tend to support the conclusion that persons occupying important roles receive the most consideration by other members of the group.

A very important finding on the relation of roles to group task accomplishment is that groups tend to be more successful when role differentiation is clear and well defined. For example, a group without an accepted leader will experience role conflict which decreases the productivity of the group. It is only after role conflict within the group has been resolved relative to selecting a leader, that the group can begin to function effectively and harmoniously. It's understandable how members become more productive after they have established a system for working together. Differing roles help members understand what communication is appropriate and when. For example, the member who is accepted as fulfilling the tension-release role knows he should step in whenever conflicts tend to get out of hand, and thus allow the group to get back on a productive track. The more effective the communication, the more likely the group's task needs will be fulfilled.

What happens when group members do not fulfill their expected roles? A member may be excused for deviant behavior if he has proven himself in some fashion. If he makes helpful contributions to the group he may store up what are called *idiosyncrasy credits*. (Hollander, 1958) These allow him to depart from the prescribed role behaviors to some extent. For instance, a member who has earned his right to group leadership through his previous contributions to the group will be allowed to transgress against a standard as long as his behavior is not harmful to the group. He may be forgiven if he loses his cool every so often, because the group members realize the strain he's under in bearing the role of leader. If, however, his actions hurt the group, members react with greater hostility than when a lower-status person does the same thing. Indeed, when role behavior departs too much from the expected role, the occupant of the role, not surprisingly, is often evicted.

There exists a general tendency for role conformity to increase with increases in cohesiveness of the group. Cohesiveness, as we mentioned earlier, is a consequence of the various sources of attraction to the group held by each individual. "With few exceptions, the group's cohesiveness increases rather dramatically when roles are stabilized." (Bormann, 1968, p. 192) Stabilization of roles allows group members to know what to expect and what others expect of them. There are fewer conflicting and jolting communicative exchanges. Members can relax and concentrate on the job without having to worry about how people are going to act.

---

communication diary

1. *What general class of small-group roles do you most enjoy playing—task or social-emotional? Why?*

2. *What specific role behaviors do you play fairly well? Fairly poorly?*

6. Norms and roles

3. *Indicate the roles you play in at least three small groups to which you belong.*
   Analyze the reasons for similarities or differences in your role performance in these groups.

---

exercise 3

In the left column below list the five major roles you have played in previous class discussions. In the right column place a check mark alongside those roles you believe others recognized you as having played. Next, fill out the Role Participation Feedback Sheet to provide information to other group participants on roles you perceive they have played in previous discussions. When the instructor has collected the feedback sheets, he will read them aloud. Tally the perceptions that other class members have of major roles you played in previous discussions. How do they compare? What implications do these findings have for role behavior in small groups?

MY PERCEPTION OF ROLES I'VE PLAYED	PERCEIVED BY OTHERS
1.	(Place check mark according to instructions)
NOTE: Leave enough space for student to list five roles.	
2.	
3.	
4.	
5.	

ROLE PARTICIPATION FEEDBACK SHEET

For each participant, including yourself, write in the two major roles played in class discussions. These will be read aloud by the instructor.

NAME	ROLE 1	ROLE 2

1.
   NOTE: Leave enough space to list all class members.
2.

etc.

Social structure plays a crucial part in affecting communication within the small group. Group *norms*, those "rules" governing behavior within the group, have much to do with successful accomplishment of group tasks. Norms also bear directly upon the attainment of harmonious relationships between group members. Most *communicators* within small groups conform to the group's norms, although we sometimes allow certain valued members to depart somewhat from the norms. Norms play crucial roles in influencing members to accept *messages* reflecting the group's point of view, in affecting negative and positive interpretations given to messages, and in shaping the nature and number of messages we send to members who deviate from the group's norms. Adherence to norms has a positive relationship to group cohesiveness—one of the most important aspects of the *interaction* dimension. Norms also aid in group problem solving—through helping to create value and attitudinal similarity and by acting as substitutes for personal power and thus producing simpler, more efficient patterns of communicative behavior.

While some norms within a group apply to all members, others pertain only to certain persons or subgroups of persons within the group. These subclasses identify *roles* existing within a group. Roles refer to positions people play in small groups and, as with norms, have a variety of behaviors tied to them. In small groups, two prominent roles that tend to emerge are task roles and social roles. Roles affect *communicators* in small groups in many ways. Some group members cannot tolerate a group situation in which role requirements are not clearly specified, while others cannot operate effectively in an overly defined role structure. Most communicators within groups tend to focus on either task or social activities of the group—this is especially true of group leaders. Evaluative *messages* presented by leaders are responded to more favorably than are evaluative messages offered by group followers or members. A strong role structure lessens the need to personalize messages within the group. As transmitters we are more detailed, complex, and organized in our messages, while as receivers we leave out details, simplify, and lose sight of message organization. In terms of *interaction*, roles affect the flow of messages within the group—members tend to direct messages to the leader, while the leader speaks to the entire group. Clearly defined roles aid problem solving by establishing a system for working together. Finally, roles improve cohesiveness by allowing members to concentrate on the group's activities without having to worry about how other group members are going to act.

ADDITIONAL READINGS

Barnlund, Dean. "Social Context of Communication," in *Interpersonal Communication* (Boston: Houghton Mifflin, 1968). This section is an in-depth review of concepts and findings on the relation of norms and roles to interpersonal communication. The section also contains a superior collection of bibliographic sources.

Bormann, Ernest. *Discussion and Group Methods* (New York: Harper & Row, 1969). Chapters 9 and 10 present in clear detail the theory and patterns of role emergence within small groups.

Cartwright, Dorwin, and Zander, Alvin. *Group Dynamics* (New York: Harper & Row, 1968). Parts 3 and 7 provide a detailed examination of norms and roles. A classic small-groups text.

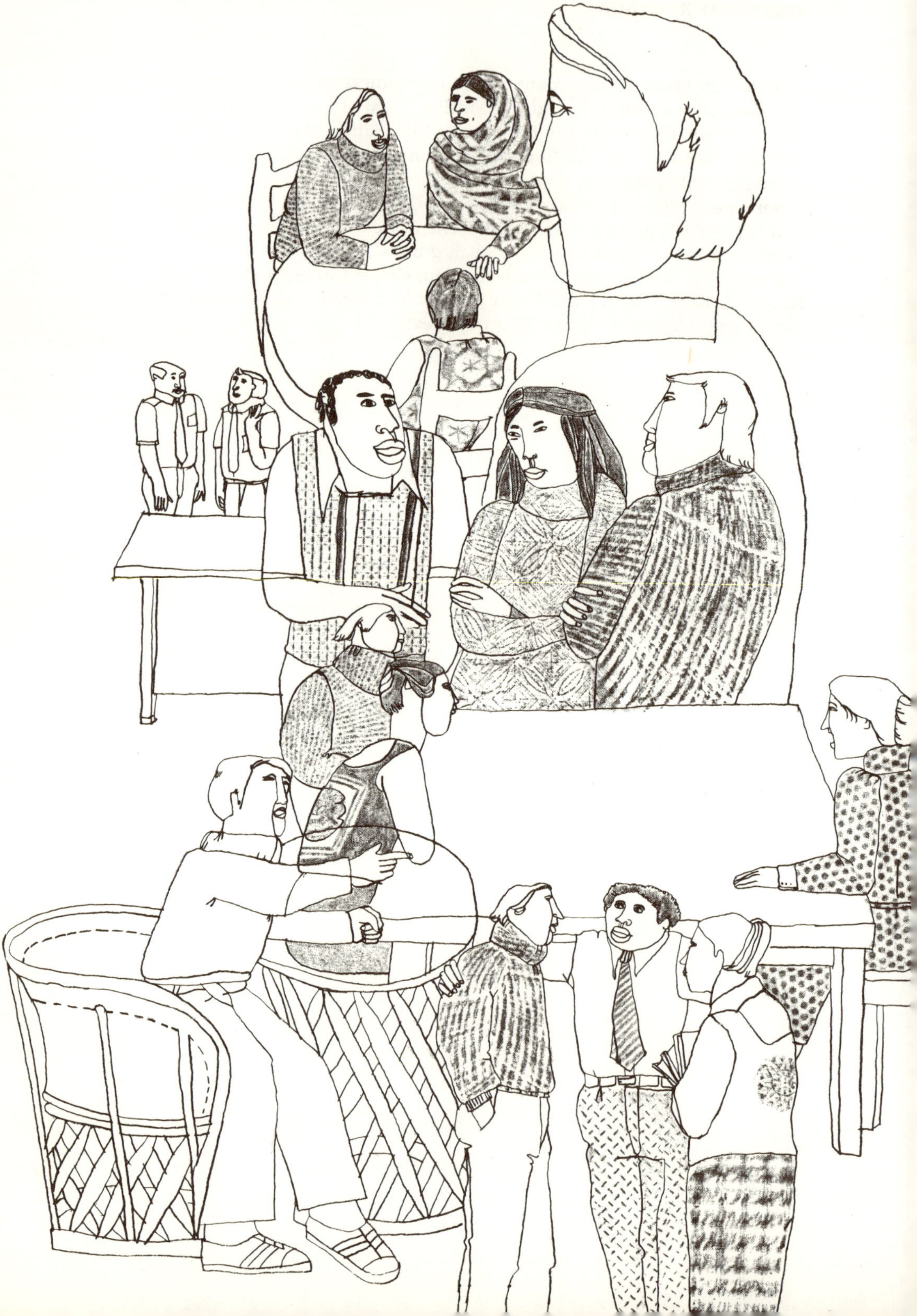

7. Cohesiveness

PREVIEW

What is cohesiveness?
　Cohesiveness is a process by which group members are attracted to each other, motivated to remain together, and share a common *perspective* of the group's activity.

How does attraction operate in the group?
　Attraction operates on two levels:
　Interpersonal: amount of attraction that individuals feel for other group *members*.
　Group: amount of attraction individuals feel for the group's *function*.

Upon what is group satisfaction dependent?
　Satisfaction depends on membership per se, effective group performance, and material rewards for membership.

What is group productivity?
　Productivity is group outcome in terms of expected results.

So far, our discussion of the interaction system has been concerned with approaches to problem solving and the complexities of conflict behavior. We think that these aspects of interaction are important because they are useful in describing group *behavior* given certain tasks or responsibilities. But, more often than not, knowledge of a group's particular method of solving a problem does not reveal the extent of commitment or desire to produce a good solution. Likewise, specifically identifying parties to a conflict or describing their conflict issues may not explain why they tolerated the disagreement in the first place.

What we're getting at here is that group membership depends not just on the behaviors that individuals perform within the particular group. In addition, the *atmosphere* under which the group works is indeed an important factor in maintenance of membership. Specifically, we want to spend the next several pages analyzing the interaction factor of *cohesiveness* as it is related to group behavior. In a way, we are oversimplifying when we refer to cohesiveness as an atmosphere. But, for most of us, that feeling about a group which can be synonymous with loyalty, one-ness, or togetherness is often best described as cohesiveness.

Recall that in chapter 6, we said that cohesiveness could be defined as the "total field of forces which act on members to remain in the group" (Festinger, Schachter, and Bach, 1950). Stated another way, we could speak of that "total field of forces" as "things or people" that keep us functioning as members of the group.

Regardless of the many ways in which we achieve cohesiveness, we are pleased when we recognize that it is present. What is cohesiveness? What are some of the causes of cohesiveness? What are some of the normal outcomes that we can expect from a cohesive group? In this chapter we want to address ourselves to those questions in an attempt to see if we can arm ourselves with criteria that will allow us to analyze more effectively the groups that we belong to.

Before proceeding to a discussion of the causes and effects of group cohesiveness, let us briefly put this particular group process in perspective. For a moment recall our Group Process Model. Our basic contention all along has been that variables and processes are constantly interacting and affecting change. Thus variables are both causes and effects of other model variables. We restate this point here because there is a general notion that cohesiveness is some "state" that groups achieve, and that once having achieved it, they relax knowing that they are finally "together," or cohesive. Not so. Group cohesiveness functions in the same manner as the other group variables that we've been discussing. The cohesiveness state is constantly in flux—it constantly changes.

What we want to do now is to arbitrarily choose variables that relate to group cohesiveness. First, we'll spend some time defining group cohesiveness as we see it; then we'll cover some variables that are generally identified as determinants (causes) of cohesiveness. We'll talk about some immediate and ultimate outcomes (effects) of group cohesiveness. Finally, we'll come back to the group process model and suggest some additional ways in which one can view group cohesiveness as a small-group communication process.

Cohesiveness defined

For the most part, we all attach some meaning to the term *cohesiveness*. To some of us it represents some Utopian state in which we are happy as group members—probably a state always to be somewhere over the horizon for many of us. For others of us it is best defined by referring to one of our groups. For example, it may be the fraternity, a class, a family, a debate squad, and the list goes on. The point is simply that we may have some trouble pinning down a word definition of cohesiveness, but usually we can think of some group that exemplifies it. And yet for many of us, the concept of cohesiveness may call to mind very traumatic experiences. How so? Recall that in chapter 6 we suggested that cohesiveness may be directly related to group conflict? Well, for many of us our memories of our most cohesive group may call to mind many instances of very dramatic group conflict.

Regardless of which group we may find ourselves in, the fact remains that we have some notion of what cohesiveness is and we will generally link it with positive impressions of a group experience. We have defined cohesiveness earlier in this chapter as well as in chapter 6. But, to be perfectly candid, that definition is a bit stuffy and pedantic for most of us to relate to. Let us say that *cohesiveness is a process in which group members are attracted to each other, motivated to remain together, and share a common perspective of the group's activity*.

---

exercise 1

Construct a list comprised of groups to which you belong. Rank order them using degree of cohesiveness as the prime criterion. For example, the group you perceive to be the most *cohesive would be 1, the next most cohesive would be 2, and so on. Now answer the following questions.*

1. Is your "most cohesive" group one in which you have held membership longer than in the others?
2. Does your ranking have anything to do with the amount of influence (or lack of influence) that you have in the various groups?
3. Do any of the groups you listed relatively low in cohesiveness contain highly cohesive subgroups?
4. Is the degree of cohesiveness related to the standards of behavior (norms) that operate in the groups?
5. Would these rankings have been the same several weeks ago?

Such a definition allows us to think of group cohesiveness as both cause and effect of group behavior. Additionally, it gives us three interrelated aspects of the process to examine: (1) the individual's attraction to the group and other group members; (2) group properties that encourage members to stay in the group; and (3) dimensions of the group's task (purpose) that provide members with reasons for sticking together.

Attraction

Actually, we can think of attraction, or attractiveness, as operating on two levels. First, there is the *interpersonal attraction* that individuals feel for other group members. And, second, there is the attractiveness that a group holds for potential membership. In the first case, we feel close to a group because we recognize that the other members of the group are much like us, or like we want to be. In the other case, we are drawn to a group because we like and admire the group for what it does and is.

Cartwright (1968) reasons that attraction to a group for a particular member is based on the member's "assessment of the desirable and undesirable consequences attendant upon membership in the group." (p. 95) Of course this makes sense and we have probably experienced such a motivation in joining groups. The fraternity or sorority "rush" operates first and foremost on the notion that individuals will "like" each other. Sure, it is important that individual houses have captured the most scholarship awards, intramural athletic trophies, and sponsor the better parties. But when we strip away all these trappings, prospective members as well as regular members are concerned with the basic quality of liking and compatibility that the "rushers" and "rushees" have for each other. How then does Cartwright's criterion apply in such an instance?

The prospective pledge looks at the house, the past reputation, and other material characteristics. But in the final analysis, he probably makes his choice on the basis of the group members —the "actives." On the other hand, the house members are primarily concerned with the interpersonal relationships that exist between themselves and the prospective pledges. Do the pledges look as though they would "fit in" with the actives?

Our example here may be trivial but we think that it demonstrates that a major determinant of group cohesiveness is the extent to which individuals—in this case actives and rushees—are interpersonally attracted to each other. It is silly to think that later cohesiveness can grow out of a circumstance in which individuals are *not* attracted to one another. Of course, once membership is attained, the attractiveness becomes a self-fulfilling prophecy. That is, once members are accepted by the group and once this acceptance is reciprocated, all participants must do what they can to justify that decision. Thus one sees few members leaving such an organization once membership has been approved.

It is true that this notion can be boiled down to a "what's in it for me" question being asked by both prospective and established members. But, after all, can we deny that we usually join groups for such reasons? Thus attraction has elements of justification (what will I get out of it?) and volition (how free am I to make this choice?). This is not to deny that interpersonal attraction is jeopardized when belonging is not voluntary. We are simply acknowledging that, given a choice in belonging, the element of interpersonal attraction has a great deal of significance in the development of group cohesiveness.

On another level, individuals are attracted to groups on the basis of what the group stands for, its operating norms, and its potential for energizing the individual's personal motives or goals. A special Greek-letter organization may cause some students to join because of such motivations. Imagine the first-term freshman at a large university who wants to make friends and establish some kind of social life. Such a circumstance would encourage rushing a fraternity or sorority. The interpersonal attraction that we spoke of earlier is naturally important, but the individual's prime concern is to find a "place" in the "system." To the extent that the organization allows him to do this, it is natural for him to be interested in it.

But there are groups that draw members primarily because of the task-oriented dimensions that they possess. For example, Young Democrats, the American Civil Liberties Union, the John Birch Society, and similar organizations would provide some type of *group attraction* for people primarily interested in the group's function and not in its level of interpersonal attractiveness. As we discuss the differences, keep in mind that these two levels of attraction—interpersonal and group—are *interrelated*. What we are saying here is that there are priorities in terms of attraction that individuals employ in seeking group membership.

Group attraction may derive from the individual's drive for security, altruistic goals, or a number of material factors. But regardless of his motivation for being attracted to a group, the fact remains that the group must afford him the opportunity to identify with it just as interpersonal attraction must give him the opportunity to establish meaningful personal relationships with group members.

We agree with Cartwright (1968) when he offers the following analysis of variables that determine an individual's attraction to a particular group:

1. His *motive base for attraction*, consisting of his needs for affiliation, recognition, security, money, or other values that can be mediated by groups.
2. The *incentive properties of the group*, consisting of its goals, programs, characteristics of its members, style of operation, prestige, or other properties of significance for his motive base.
3. His *expectancy*, the subjective probability that membership will actually have beneficial or detrimental consequences for him.
4. His *comparison level*—his conception of the level of outcomes that group membership should provide.

As one examines these variables, it is easy to see the interrelation between interpersonal and group attraction that exists. The motive base exists primarily as a group attraction class of variables. An individual has drives for recognition and wealth and he chooses the group that seems to serve that need. For example, the job applicant may have a desire to sign on with a major corporation with an extensive training program so that he can soon rise to the top of the corporate ladder. Or an individual may choose an academic major (a group) in economics because it seems to offer him more material satisfaction than, for example, a major in political science or speech communication. But regardless of the group that he chooses, his motivation remains basically the same—he is determined to achieve his personal goals with the chosen group to serve as the mediator of those goals. Once in that group (in this case, the major), he may acknowledge that he likes the others who share the group and thus become attracted on an interpersonal level. The fact remains that his drive for certain personal goals has led him to membership in the group which he perceives can satisfy those drives.

To reinforce that choice, it is necessary for the group to provide *incentives*. The individual is promoted regularly, he receives salary increases, use of the executive conference room, or tenure. The individual's attraction to the group is predicated on both the needs that he has *and* the ability of the group to systematically reward his choice of that particular group. In addition, there is the underlying expectation that the individual has concerning the goodness or badness of the group as it relates to his own life. Will he be ostracized by his family if he marries into a certain religion (group)? Will he alienate his friends by joining a certain political group? The individual is constantly faced with choices and decision points; when this occurs he must evaluate the favorable and unfavorable consequences that may grow out of his choice of group membership and then make his decision. The point is that he is then faced with an evaluation of the strength of his attraction to the group members (interpersonal) or to the group's purpose and function (group attraction). Finally, the individual must be concerned with the relative merits of being attracted to certain groups and individuals. On the basis of his past experience, his information as to the group's purpose, his knowledge of individuals in the group, and his personal needs, he must evaluate the wisdom of joining the group.

Thus we can look at attraction to individual members of the group as well as to the group itself as being comprised of characteristics (variables) that allow the individual to pursue the realization of individual goals. Additionally, it ought to provide the ongoing reinforcement of his choice. Whether or not an individual is initially drawn to the group because of other group members or because he wants affiliation with the group, we must treat attraction as a prime determinant of group cohesiveness. Stated another way, an attraction relationship suggests that there is a

In order to have a cohesive group, the members must be attracted to each other

certain degree of compatibility among group members and that this factor is directly related to how well the group sticks together.

Thus far we have been discussing attraction as a potential *cause* of a cohesive group process. It might be wise here to spend some time on the nature of attraction as a legitimate outcome or effect of cohesive group activity. What we are getting at here is the incentive properties of the group that are provided to reinforce the attraction relationship. We should not of course operate on the assumption that, once some level of compatibility or attraction is achieved, the cohesive group is "home free." On the contrary, the group has the task of continually reinforcing that attraction so that members will remain in the group. We will be talking about maintaining membership in a little while. For now, we want to suggest that unless the group membership recognizes that attraction varies, the group faces the very real danger that the relationship will be destroyed. We do not want to prescribe here. What we do want to do is to call your attention to the fact that the reason most individuals withdraw from a group to which they were initially attracted is that the attractiveness was not constantly updated, reinforced, or made meaningful. Have you ever taken an elective course that started out with a bang, proceeded into a dull class midway through the term, and finally ended with a whimper at the end of the term? Or have you had your expectations raised regarding a certain movie only to find that after the first twenty minutes the only exciting thing happening in the theater concerned the couple ahead of you? Or, perhaps more often, have you been attracted to another person and excited about the possibility of establishing a meaningful relationship only to find after several dates that your expectations were violated? These examples simply suggest that an initially high level of attractiveness that some group may hold for you can be destroyed in the absence of ongoing reinforcers.

By the same token you have probably experienced many circumstances in which a high initial level of attractiveness that some group held for you proved to be a good thing because the group "delivered." That is, as the group became more cohesive and more loyalty developed, the liking relationship (attraction) became stronger. It may be the case with a course that you have taken. It may have happened with some political group that you joined. It may have occurred with a romantic relationship that you are currently enjoying. Regardless of the nature of the group, we can conclude that attraction can be affected by a cohesive group atmosphere.

exercise 2

Using the groups you listed in exercise 1 as references, answer the following questions:

1. In which groups was *interpersonal* attraction the primary motivation for membership? Explain.
2. In which groups was *group* attraction the primary motivation for membership? Explain.
3. Can you draw any conclusions regarding the degree of cohesiveness in certain groups and the type of attraction that led you to those groups?

In summary, then, we can see that the first component of our cohesiveness definition—attraction—can be viewed as operating on two levels. It exists when an individual is drawn to group members initially and enjoys the interpersonal relationship that follows from such an attraction. Or it can exist when an individual is attracted to a group because it appears to be capable of meeting his needs and will serve as the vehicle for his objective. Moreover, we can see that attraction can be a prime determinar in the establishment of group cohesiveness because it allows th group to grow from a basis of compatibility. Finally we can make a case for the existence of attraction as a result or effect of group cohesion. As the group is allowed to operate in a highly compatible atmosphere, the level of attraction grows. In the absence of mutual reinforcement and justification for remaining in the group, individuals will lose their feeling of attraction for the group, and loyalty or commitment to the group will decrease.

We turn now to a consideration of group properties or characteristics that encourage individuals to remain as members of the group. Here we will be talking of the variables of satisfaction and productivity.

Satisfaction

We experience satisfaction in a number of ways as we go about our business as group members. We may derive satisfaction simply from belonging to the group. Certain prestigious groups rely heavily on the selectivity criteria that their group employs in choosing new members. Thus merely to be a member is grounds for pride or a sense of well-being. In addition we may be satisfied as a result of an effective group performance. If, for example, our group was concerned with raising money for a disadvantaged family as a Christmas gift and we did just that, there are certainly reasons for having a good feeling about ourselves and our group. And, finally, we reach a high level of satisfaction when the material rewards for performing our group tasks are in line with the effort it took to complete the task. It is true that many of us are overworked, underpaid, and unappreciated, but, generally, we keep doing our job regardless of the group, because the material benefits are adequate.

In essence, we can think of member satisfaction as being composed of the elements that we discussed above. Specifically, we can say that degree of satisfaction depends upon membership per se, effective group performance, and material rewards for membership. How do these relate to cohesion? Is satisfaction necessary for a cohesive group atmosphere? What are some ultimate effects of member satisfaction?

Our earlier discussion of cohesiveness was concerned with the notion that as group members experience a higher level of attrac-

Group members must be motivated to remain together

tion with each other or the group task, they generally experience a higher level of group cohesiveness. This is particularly relevant here as we discuss member satisfaction and the role it occupies in an analysis of group cohesiveness. In a sense, we can think of satisfaction as an outcome or effect that usually comes to members of cohesive groups. Really, it makes sense that the more cohesive a group is, the more satisfied it is. On the other hand, we can see that the converse is also true: the higher the degree of satisfaction, the more cohesive the group. In light of all our cautions of the *process* nature of group activity it seems silly now to repeat the point. Nevertheless, let us do it again: group characteristics—for example, satisfaction—can exist as the cause and effect of other group characteristics. In this case, satisfaction can generally be perceived as an effect or outcome of a cohesive group atmosphere, but can be thought of as a cause of it as well.

It may be helpful here to return to our analysis of cohesiveness as we defined it earlier: a process in which group members are attracted to each other, are motivated to remain together, and share a common perspective of the group's activity. How does satisfaction fit in? Well, if we think of satisfaction as being related to membership per se, effective group performance, and material rewards, we have to conclude that neither satisfaction nor cohesiveness can exist without the other.

But perhaps the relationship among elements of cohesiveness and satisfaction is more complex than that simple statement suggests. Let's take a brief look at the cohesiveness components (attractiveness, motivation to remain, and common perspective) as they might relate to those elements that are included when we discuss satisfaction (membership, performance, material rewards). Now we are not so silly as to try to isolate any one cohesiveness component and tie it up with some satisfaction condition. As we have noted on several pages of this book, factors of the group process are dynamic, always changing, impossible to isolate. What we want to do instead is to look at the development of member satisfaction as it might relate to the cohesiveness process. We begin by examining the attraction dimension of cohesiveness.

It would be foolish to say that the higher level of attraction that one has with other group members or with the group, the higher will be his level of satisfaction. While it may be true for many of us in the course of our group experiences, we can think of many instances in which we continue with some activity that seems attractive to us but is certainly far from satisfying. A similar thing happens when we "can't get enough of that pie." Thus we gorge ourselves in a state of near-gluttony. Likewise, we may continually become attracted to an individual who may provide no satisfaction for us at all. Perhaps an example may serve to make our point here.

Most colleges and universities regardless of their size have special programs of study. For some, it may be Honors College, for others it may be a semester abroad, while still other schools may have an intern teaching program. Regardless of what they may be called, the conditions are usually the same: limited enrollment, attractiveness in terms of flexible requirements, and prestige for the student.

Let us say that you are attracted to one of these programs because of the people you know who participate in it as well as the fact that the program itself is a good one. Thus you see that the group meets our criterion of attractiveness for later cohesiveness—its members look good and so do the group purpose and ambition. You are invited to join the group, you do so, and you now become a participating group member. In terms of the cohesiveness criterion of motivation, what do you experience? Well, first of all, you are a select member of your student body. Certain basic course requirements are waived, you are given a flexibility that you have been seeking since you enrolled in college as a freshman. These factors, in addition to weekly field trips, close relationships with faculty, and independence of thought, all combine to provide you with reasons for remaining in the special program. Finally, you find that you have much in common with other group members. You all share the love for learning in an independent atmosphere, you all like being on your own, and there is a similarity of personality characteristics that make this experience rewarding from both task and social perspectives. So according to everything that we've said about cohesiveness, your group has it. You feel that this is a collection of very close people. Are you satisfied? On all counts, the answer seems to be an emphatic YES. You are a member of this group (membership criterion), the group does what it is supposed to (performance), and you are getting credit for your work in the program (rewards). Everything is coming up roses. But let us vary one of the factors and take a look at the mix.

We'll still assume that the group meets all the criteria for cohesiveness. What we see, however, is something going on that affects your satisfaction with the group life. For one thing, you find that membership per se is not a prestigious thing. How has this perception changed? Well, you note that not all members of the group have met the minimum requirement of grade-point; that, instead, some people are in the group because of pull, or *who* they know instead of *what* they know. (Sound familiar?) Another thing you notice is that a few people are doing all the work. Thus the *group performance* is really the performance of a *few members*. Finally, you become disgusted with the number of credit hours that you are being given for the number of contact hours that you must put in. Are you satisfied? Hardly. How much longer will the group be cohesive? Not much longer. What does this prove? We think that it supports a couple of notions.

First, it is reasonable to assume that cohesiveness and member satisfaction are interrelated to the extent that it is difficult to speak of one without the other.

Second, it suggests that satisfaction, like cohesiveness, must be reinforced at various points of the group experience. Stated another way, the level of satisfaction varies and must be attended to continually.

Our discussion of cohesiveness and satisfaction indicates that several conclusions can be drawn. First, satisfaction is a matter of individual perception, that all the pressure in the world that members of a group exert on another member will not make one bit of difference as long as he is dissatisfied. Second, satisfaction can result from and can cause group cohesiveness. Third, the degree of member satisfaction with a particular group depends on the requirements of membership in the group, the group's performance, and the material rewards for membership in the group.

exercise 3

Again, thinking of the groups you belong to, rank these groups in terms of your overall satisfaction level.

1. Are the rankings similar to those of exercise 1?
    a. How can you account for these similarities or differences?
2. In which groups are you satisfied primarily because of incentive or reinforcement?
    a. What is the nature of the reinforcement?
    b. Are you consistently reinforced?

We are aware of research literature that suggests findings relating to member satisfaction. Those findings are equivocal at best. What is important to us as prospective group members is the extent to which we are content with membership in a particular group. We may be quite satisfied in a low cohesive group because we are allowed to do our own thing. On the other hand, we may constantly strive for a high level of cohesiveness and when we reach it we may say that we are satisfied. It is a matter for individual judgment. But one thing we can agree on: the group process is composed of our feelings of satisfaction and cohesiveness. To the extent that we can work in a group that meets those needs we will be more effective group members.

Productivity

It may seem absurd to discuss productivity at this stage in our analysis of group cohesiveness. In fact, we have discussed it at numerous points along the way. When we spoke of performance, we were talking about productivity. When we spoke of rewards, we were indirectly discussing productivity. Indeed, it is impossible to speak of any other group characteristic or member behavior without implying some notions regarding the group's productivity. What do we mean by productivity? How is it measured? How does it relate to cohesiveness?

In a very simple sense we can say that it is impossible to know a group without identifying its "product." Whether that group is a family, a football team, or a Senate subcommitte, we would find it hard not to know what the group is supposed to do simply by hearing the title. For example, what is the task of a curriculum committee? a group discussion class? a sensitivity group? The particular way in which a group goes about its task of problem solving may vary any number of ways, but we tend to know and evaluate a group on the basis of what it is designed to do.

We will define productivity as *group outcome in terms of expected results*. In a way, we can think of productivity as a ratio of completed to intended tasks. You know from experience that groups do not always get everything done that they set out to do. In fact, it's probably a safe bet that many group members don't expect to finish many jobs. And how many times have you worked on a class project with other students only to remark at the conclusion of the project that the job would have been "right" if more time had been available? Assignments are often put off until the last minute because students feel that they work better under pressure. It doesn't really make any difference if the group were to be given an extra week or the student an extra month, the end product would probably be the same. Thus, if the work is scheduled about the same, what are the factors relating to productivity that would make a group more or less cohesive?

We probably have stored somewhere in our "catalog of sayings" the assertion that the group with the best product is the most cohesive. Makes sense, doesn't it? The group that achieved the most was the group that was the closest in terms of working relationships, had more meaningful perspectives of the task, and so on. And along with that saying would go one which argues that the productive group is the satisfied group. Maybe we should stop right here, for there is little sense to arguing with such statements. And in fact it may be true that the group that produces the best (or the most) outcomes is the most cohesive and satisfied. Yet we have some nagging suspicions based on working with groups which suggest that often group members, having completed a task, look for reasons for the success. In retrospect, the members can argue that the group's success is dependent on the closeness and the perceived satisfaction.

What we have said in the two previous sections pertaining to cohesiveness and satisfaction is certainly appropriate when we

*To form a cohesive group, members must have a
common perspective of the group's activity*

discuss group productivity. A number of factors contribute to the perception of group accomplishment. Sometimes in the euphoria of a job completed, group members may rely on the tactic of handing out praise for the team effort that went into the task. We still keep coming back to the point of the dynamic changes that occur as a group works on its task. And on many occasions following a class group's happy statements of the values of cohesiveness in the successful achievement of a task, we find individual members having second thoughts regarding the reasons for success.

Recall we noted that attraction, motivation, and common perspective are necessary conditions for cohesiveness within the group. What our experiences seem to suggest is that attraction may be forced (assignment into groups by the instructor), motivation is a matter of assignment (do it or flunk), and that the only real condition leading to group accomplishment may be a sharing of a common perspective of the group's activity. How cohesive is a group that relies on threat for success? Is that the common circumstance for groups to which you belong?

What are we getting at? Simply this: viewing group productivity as effect only (the end product) severely limits the group's ability to develop cohesiveness. What we ought to be looking for in terms of productivity is a motivation for continuing on to other tasks. If the group activity is in fact a process, then we must observe that each outcome is the cause of future outcomes. If we look at productivity as the *result* of group activity instead of the *reason* for group activity, we restrict the effectiveness of future group behavior.

While it may not be true for the authors of this text or for the students reading it, you would be surprised to know that for many individuals enrolled in (or teaching) a particular class, the end of the term *is* the successful product of the term. In other words, members of the group simply try to get through the group's term of existence.

What can we say about the relation between group productivity and cohesiveness? We can say that, in fact, a group *can* be productive without attaining a high level of cohesiveness. We realize that this may be interpreted as saying that cohesiveness is unnecessary to productivity, but let us admit what we can perceive operating in many organizations (perhaps in this class). The company that pays its employees "by the piece" certainly seems to have something besides a "feeling of we-ness" operating as its profits skyrocket.

Secondly, we should examine group productivity as related to cohesiveness in terms of how the group's attained goals matched up with its intended objectives.

Finally, we should remember what we noted earlier with regard to the maintenance of member satisfaction when we are looking at the worth of group productivity. If members are given motivation to remain within the group, the quality of productivity should be affected. Yet, just as the motivation is perceived as ongoing, the group's product should not be viewed as some terminal behavior—to end when the group has its last meeting. If we are concerned with one dimension in the analysis of small-group communicative behavior, it is the fact that groups are expected to *produce* without regard to variables such as attractiveness, motivation, and satisfaction. But the relation between *cohesiveness* and group productivity is directly dependent upon the nature of such variables.

For the most part, we have been speaking of cohesiveness and group characteristics of satisfaction and productivity. We have argued, perhaps redundantly, that cohesiveness is not a state to be reached, then forgotten. It is, like other process variables, constantly changing as both cause and effect. We then moved on to discuss the interaction of cohesiveness and variables of satisfaction and productivity. Our conclusions, while not earthshaking, bear repeating. Productivity, when viewed as the end-all for the group, is dysfunctional and will gradually erode the members' satisfaction with the group. There must be some dynamic motivation continually reinforcing member satisfaction with the group. Finally, these variables—cohesiveness, satisfaction, productivity—depend on the nature and extent of attraction with the group members and with the group function per se.

In essence, what we have been concerned with is the model component of *interaction* and with the interrelation of variables within that component. What we need to do now is to speak briefly about the relationships that occur with regard to the other components of our model—communicator, message, and situational context. For this analysis we will ignore the variables of satisfaction and productivity. You ought to keep in mind, however, that the types of relationships which may exist between cohesiveness and elements of the other model components reflect similar relationships between satisfaction, productivity, and the other variables.

Communicator

As you know, the communicator component of our group process model contains those elements (variables, factors) which classify the individual's attitudes, motives, values, personality characteristics, and similar dimensions of the group member. How do communicator factors interrelate with interaction factors such as cohesiveness?

What sort of statements can you make about the extent of cohesiveness you would expect to find in a group made up of both highly and lowly involved individuals? Would we expect the highly involved people to reinforce the lowly involved? Hardly. On the other hand, those that are highly involved would support each other. For example, student membership on university boards of trustees has been an issue of importance to many institutions of higher education. Assume a board of trustees composed of eight businessmen, the university president, two faculty representatives, and one student. Can you see any hope for cohesiveness? Sure, there will exist some degree for those issues on which the members are equally involved. But to be perfectly honest, the student is at an initial disadvantage, because he is *perceived* to be low in involvement on all issues of university administration and governance. Note that it does not make any difference how involved the student perceives himself to be; the trustees' past experience (after all, all students are malcontents) militates against much member attraction. To be sure, our example may be dated, farfetched, or irrelevant. The point is that to discuss cohesiveness and cohesive group activity independently of the people involved is to look at just one facet of the diamond.

More importantly, we must keep in mind the dynamic activity of these variables. While the attitudes may *cause* the circumstances to be against cohesiveness, it may well be that member attraction may lead to a change in member attitude. Our same old concern: that variables be seen to *affect* and *be affected by* other variables in the system.

Thus when we consider the "people" component of our model and examine it in light of cohesive behavior we are led to conclude: interaction and communicator variables interrelate; cohesiveness can result from and lead to causes in communicators; and the changes are ongoing—they do not end with an effect or begin with a cause.

Situational context

The development of cohesiveness within the group depends quite heavily on factors of the situation. We can see this simply by examining our usual impressions of classroom assignments in a group discussion course. How realistic is it to discuss issues in front of other class members? Are important discussions asking for value judgments confined within fifty-minute time periods? Do people in the "real world" sit and evaluate a conference or discussion for the purpose of grading it?

Are the questions silly? Outdated? Irrelevant? The answers may be, but the questions appear to be contemporary with many group courses. We think that such things as grading, assignments, performance may be perfectly valid. What we question is the validity of placing the situation in a classroom. We think that it is expecting a little too much for a group to achieve cohesiveness when the situational variables—structure, physical characteristics, and so on—work against member attraction and satisfaction. Moreover, we think that the notion of productivity is distorted. Can one really expect students to "solve" some problem of international significance in the course of a fifty-minute classroom discussion? How do the students perceive this task? What are their attitudes? What is their mode of problem solving?

You noted, of course, that in the above paragraph we called in other major components of the group process model, which ought to suggest that group communication is not an independent activity. For our purposes here, we are concerned with the variable of cohesiveness and how it affects or is affected by the situational context of the group activity.

Is cohesiveness a function of group norms or does it lead to the establishment of new group norms? Is leadership identified clearly within a highly cohesive group? Do roles stabilize as the group gains cohesiveness?

We think that much is to be gained from asking these questions. But we believe much more is gained by realizing that it is absurd to think that the group can be identified as cohesive without regard to the nature of the situational context variables that are operating.

Message

And what of the verbal and nonverbal cues that go into our picture of cohesiveness? What of the content of messages? Can a group become cohesive without regard to *what* is being said and *how* it is being said?

As members seek to establish liking and attraction relationships with each other, the message elements assume an increasing importance. People seek to set up nonverbal messages letting others know of their attraction for them. We tend to think of such things as belonging to a romantic relationship in which people "flirt." Yet similar behavior leads to cohesiveness within a group as a result of message variables. As the group becomes closer, each member stakes out territory that is his and is recognized as such. Certain members sit in certain chairs, certain members speak after others, and the list goes on. The group has established norms for operating which dictate the level of cohesiveness. These norms serve as the motivators for people to remain in the group.

These variables also change as a result of certain levels of group cohesiveness. As members of the group become closer, more impact is given nonverbal messages. Thus cohesiveness and message cues work in an *interrelated* manner. The changes occur without regard to cause and effect—things just happen.

Our point here is that as variables of the message component of the group process model change to affect the extent of group cohesiveness, these variables are changed by the consequent cohesive behavior. Confusing? Not really. You've probably experienced many of these message changes without regarding them as changes.

For example, in this class you have probably developed a meaningful and cohesive relationship with someone. Your level of productivity has been affected as a result, and the more you produce the more the changes in the messages that you exchange. All the while, you are becoming more cohesive, and attraction is increasing. As problems come up, you handle them and go on to new ones. It is not a vicious circle for you, because you have found some motivating force that keeps you in this group. This is cohesiveness.

It is no doubt clear to you by now that, in many respects, cohesiveness shares important characteristics with the communication process. In fact, you will recall that we defined cohesiveness as a "process" suggesting a highly dynamic force constantly changing as the group develops. There is a tendency to forget this as we move through our consideration of cohesiveness and its relation to each of the components of the group model. We may want to think of cohesiveness as one of the defining characteristics of the communication process. Certainly its role in our group experiences cannot be overemphasized. In addition, as our definition notes, a crucial factor of cohesive groups is that people remain together. Of course we can see this to be an aid in strengthening the overall communication pattern of the group.

Essentially, we can think of the processes of cohesiveness and communication to be inextricably tied up in small-group settings. For the impact of communicative behavior in the group can only be as strong as the extent of member cohesiveness. When the time comes that we begin to think of group cohesiveness as a "given," we will surely note serious impairment in the communication effectiveness of group deliberations.

Our travels through the cohesiveness variable have been filled with a lot of side trips. We began by saying that cohesiveness can be viewed as a process in which group members are attracted to each other, motivated to remain together, and share a common perspective of the group's activity. Our analysis of this process revealed the attraction to be of both an interpersonal and a group nature. Then we began to speak of member satisfaction and group productivity. We know that these variables are also of the interaction class and serve to complement the cohesive behavior that members experience.

Finally, we took a brief look—with many questions—at the interrelationships that exist among variables of all components of our group process model. And, again, as we have done so often, we reemphasized the point that there is a tremendous activity that exists among *all* these variables.

Cohesiveness is indeed complex. It is a norm for many of us—for many of us it has never existed. In the groups that you perceive to be cohesive, what are the forces that keep people together?

ADDITIONAL READINGS

Berscheid, E., and Walster, E. *Interpersonal Attraction* (Menlo Park, Calif.: Addison-Wesley, 1969). The authors' discussion of attraction as it is related to liking, anxiety, and proximity, among other variables, is easy to read and invaluable in understanding the complexities of attraction. The use of examples and illustrations that can be easily understood by the student enhance the readability of this book.

Cartwright, D. "The Nature of Group Cohesiveness," in Cartwright and Zander, *Group Dynamics: Research and Theory* (New York: McGraw-Hill, 1968). Even though this chapter may be somewhat difficult to read the first time through, it is well worth rereading for valuable insights into the causes and consequences of group cohesiveness. Of special importance is the model (p. 92) outlining the determinants and consequences of group cohesiveness.

Davis, J. *Group Performance* (Menlo Park, Calif.: Addison-Wesley, 1969). Davis's discussion of cohesiveness as a variable affecting group performance is a "must" to understand the interrelation between cohesiveness and the effects of group performance. His treatment of cooperation and competition as factors related to cohesiveness deserves special attention.

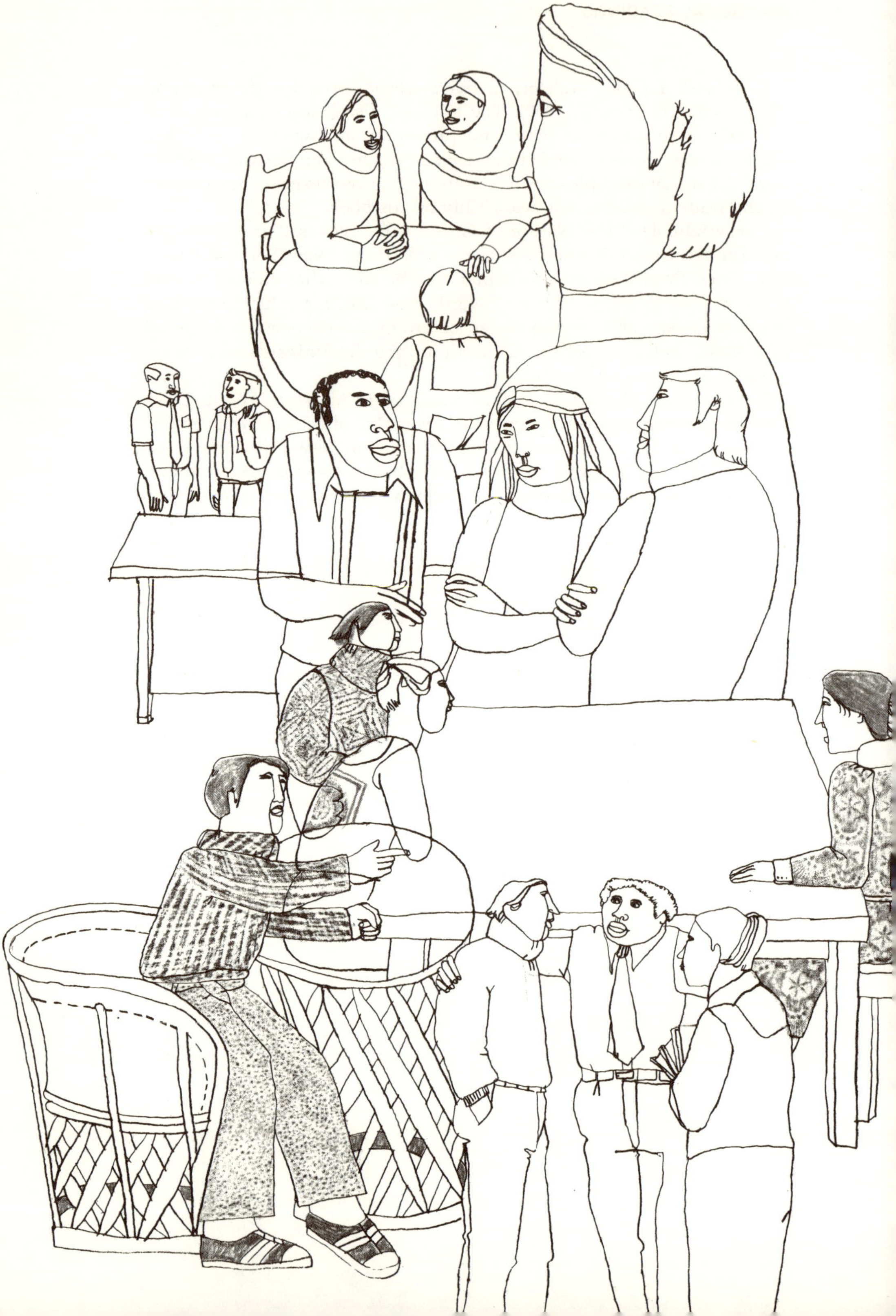

8. Conflict

PREVIEW

What is conflict?
    Intrapersonal conflict: the internal struggle an individual experiences when placed in a decision-making situation in which he must choose between equally attractive and mutually exclusive alternatives.
    Interpersonal conflict: an open difference over equally attractive and mutually exclusive alternatives by individuals who perceive themselves to be in disagreement.

What are two basic perspectives in the study of conflict?
    Productive/nonproductive dimensions of conflict.
    Individual orientations of competition or cooperation.

What are primary communicator *factors related to conflict?*
    Attitude
    Dogmatism
    Power

What are primary message *factors related to conflict?*
    Verbal characteristics
    Nonverbal cues

What are primary interaction *factors related to conflict?*
    Cohesiveness
    Member satisfaction

What are primary situational context *factors related to conflict?*
    Physical setting
    Spatial arrangements
    Group purpose

It would be very difficult to review one of our average days without admitting that much of our communication during that period involved some sort of conflict. Whether the conflict happened over the breakfast table within the family, over coffee at the Union with our friends, or during a class discussion, the fact remains that our usual group activity is an arena for conflict behavior.

But we know, thanks to the mass media, that our groups are not unusual. We are informed every day of the existence of a wide variety of social conflicts. Our morning newspaper headlines details of a current international conflict. On the way to class or work, we are informed by a radio commentator of increasing tensions in the black-white conflict. And the evening television newscaster tells us of a political party conflict. In the event that none of these sources gives us all the detail that we want, we are able to pick up a weekly newsmagazine that amplifies the details of conflicts that seem important at the time.

In this chapter we want to deal with many factors of conflict that describe this kind of behavior as it occurs in typical day-to-day groups.

Recall our discussion in chapter 1 of the basic postulate that group communication operates as a system of behavior. We noted that no one dimension, or variable, operates in isolation, and that a change in any one dimension leads from or to a change in all other variables of the system.

Similarly, we can say that conflict within a group can be viewed as a *subsystem* of the interaction dimension of our communication model. If we view interaction as the *dynamic of the group communication*—those processes resulting from the give-and-take of the group membership—then conflict can be viewed as a possible result of that interaction. How do we define this conflict system? What are its major dimensions? When is conflict productive, and when is it nonproductive? How do competition and cooperation relate to conflict? How do changes in the conflict system affect changes in the communication system? How do changes in the communication system affect changes in the conflict system?

An overview of conflict

Types of conflict

We are all decision makers of one kind or another. Whether we are buying a car, choosing an apartment, selecting a mate, or picking a class time, we often find ourselves faced with a decision-making situation in which we must choose between two similar objects or events. More often than not, these alternatives are equally attractive and mutually exclusive so that choosing one means rejecting the other. The conflict, or internal struggle, that we experience prior to such a decision is usually referred to as *intrapersonal* conflict and many psychologists (e.g., Festinger, 1957) argue that this type of conflict precedes nearly every decision that we make. In other words, intrapersonal conflict resides *within* the individual and is generally thought to be resolved when the person makes his decision as to which alternative he wants. Of course, once this decision is made then the individual goes about the job of justifying his choice.

While the bulk of our discussion in this chapter is concerned with the various types of disagreements that exist among individuals and groups, we should remember that the dimensions of intrapersonal conflict are often reflected in an individual's communication with his fellow group members. For instance, an individual member of the group may experience some state of intrapersonal conflict concerning the group's handling of a specific task. It is a pretty good bet that he will clash openly with other group members before that decision is reached (Coser, 1956). We simply cannot overemphasize the importance of intrapersonal conflict as it might relate to satisfaction with other group members and group tasks.

Actually, intrapersonal conflict usually contains most of the elements that we will see in other major types of conflict. What are some of these elements? Well, for one thing intrapersonal conflict deals with the existence of two equally attractive and mutually exclusive alternatives, along with the drive or motivation for decision making as a method of resolving the conflict. The notions of equal attractiveness and mutual exclusivity are crucial to our discussion of conflict as it operates in the individual *and* the group. In very simple terms, we are recognizing the fact that if one option or choice is perceived to be more attractive, there is really no basis for conflict. Of course this equally attractive factor implies that both options are available to the individual. The point here is simply that minimal conditions for any conflict circumstance are equal attractiveness and mutual exclusivity of alternatives. *Intrapersonal conflict occurs when an individual experiences internal struggle when placed in a decision-making situation in which he must choose between equally attractive and mutually exclusive alternatives.*

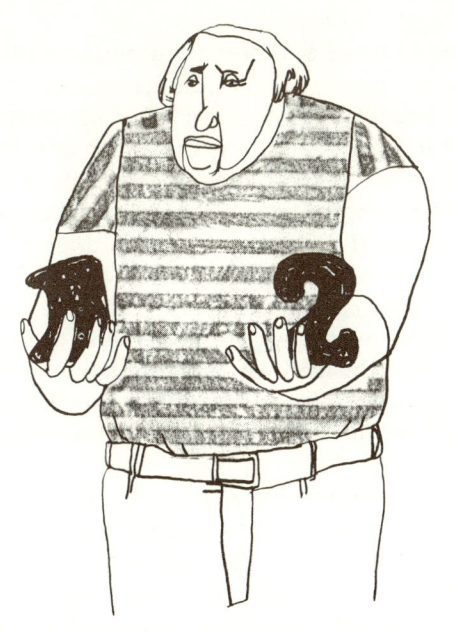

With these standards and necessary conditions in mind, let us modify our situation. Instead of just one person involved in the decision-making process, let us add another so that there are now two—that is, a small group. The options remain relatively the same, except that now we have two persons communicating with each other about which option to exercise. Moreover, they are in open disagreement over which one to choose. For one person, the only reasonable course of action is to attend the movie. After all, it is *Love Story*. The book was a best-seller, the cast is excellent, all conditions are favorable. Besides, baseball is such a slow game. Oddly enough, the other party to the disagreement does not see things so clearly. After all, the movie is one of those soap operas, the Dodgers are in first place, they have a winning streak going, and the weather is beautiful. Unfortunately, such topics of conflict are not always so harmless or innocuous to us. But to the people involved, the issues are critical and the situation is very important.

What we want to emphasize here is the introduction of two additional factors to our earlier intrapersonal conception of conflict: (1) we have added *another communicator* to the decision-making situation; and (2) we have added the notion that the two communicators *perceive themselves to be in disagreement*. Therefore, we now speak of conflict as operating on an *interpersonal* level. *Interpersonal conflict occurs when there is an open difference over equally attractive and mutually exclusive alternatives by individuals who perceive themselves to be in disagreement.*

It is this type of conflict that we are most familiar with in our day-to-day group activity. Therefore, let us more closely examine the terms of our definition. *An open difference* requires us to look at the behavioral dimension of the disagreement. Often, we think of the conflict between group members as operating on a very subtle level. This concept of conflict makes it extremely difficult for us to resolve the disagreement or to channel it into productive group activity. It is necessary that we view conflict as always taking place in *interaction* between two or more group members (Coser, 1956). In so doing, we are better able to describe in some systematic manner the core of the problem. So if we think of conflict as a *behavior* that grows out of hostile or antagonistic attitudes we are on our way to more effective conflict resolution or management.

We noted earlier that the alternatives must be equally attractive. This does not mean that both alternatives are desired or regarded positively. It is often the case that we are required to make some decision involving two distasteful alternatives. For example, our task might be to determine how we can add needed revenue to our organization's treasury. Let's assume that everyone has agreed that the money is needed. The primary task now is to decide upon the manner in which to raise the amount. Or, assume for the moment that you belong to a religious group that is preparing a lecture series. The series is being designed to inform your audience of various perspectives on an issue that your church condemns. The choice of a speaker who would reinforce the church's position is a relatively easy decision to make; the selection of an opposition speaker from a list of several people qualified to present the "other side" might be more difficult. It is, of course, unnecessary to belabor the point with numerous examples. What is important is that we realize that the "attractiveness" of the alternatives refer to the relative equality of their positive and negative characteristics.

The *exclusive* characteristic of the alternatives under examination by the opposing parties refers to their *opposite nature*. We can understand this characteristic of conflict by realizing that if one party to the conflict attains his goal or objective, the other party cannot. Thus the two alternatives, or the issue of the disagreement, must be mutually incompatible. Deutsch (1969) has suggested that we can define conflict as simply the existence of "incompatible activities." As we concentrate more on the defining characteristics of conflict and its modes of reduction, we will be able to better understand the many ways in which group options can be perceived as incompatible.

Perhaps the key defining characteristic of our definition of conflict is the requirement that individuals *perceive themselves to be in disagreement*. Conflict is often, but not always, brought about by individuals who perceive a situation in very different ways. Now it is of course true that no two individuals see the same thing in the same way; we have often heard the saying that, "One man's meat is another man's poison." Yet to understand the disagreement under question, parties to the conflict must have some similarity of understanding of the conflict issue. Unless the parties to the conflict actually see themselves in disagreement *with each other*, the issue will not be amenable to resolution. We see such examples of this operating when individuals react to each other as representatives of other groups rather than as opponents for the particular conflict under discussion. For example, is the "conservative" member of the discussion group reacting to the "liberal" member's argument, or is he reacting to the many stereotypes and experiences that he has stored in his mind? At times like this, when the conflict is more symbolic than real, the parties do not accurately perceive themselves to be in disagreement over the same issue and the constructive management of that conflict is virtually hopeless.

As we noted in our earlier discussion of the system approach to the study of group communication, it is extremely important to keep in mind the constant interrelationships that exist among the many factors (elements) of the system. As we look back over our discussion of conflict as a system, we can certainly see the increasing complexity as relevant factors increase in number. We can see now that there are several major dimensions of our conflict system: parties, issues, attractiveness of alternatives, exclusivity of alternatives, and perceived disagreement. Moreover, we can see that engagement in *interpersonal* conflict usually flows from some degree of *intrapersonal* conflict.

communication diary

Think for a moment about the nature and occasions of your experience with conflict in your small groups.

1. *In which of your small groups do you experience the most* intrapersonal *conflict?*
2. *In which of your small groups is conflict productive? nonproductive?*
3. *Are power relationships clearly defined in your various small groups?*
4. *Does your individual orientation differ depending on the group in which you are participating?*

Basic perspectives of conflict

For most of us, the existence of conflict—regardless of how much we know about it—still connotes a negative group activity. We think it appropriate to deal with this common impression right now. There are two dimensions—perspectives—of conflict behavior that we think important to discuss before moving on to our treatment of conflict and the communication system. One of these perspectives refers to how useful (productive) conflict may be in our group communication activities. The second perspective has to do with the state of mind (orientation) that the individual brings to his group. An understanding of these basic perspectives of conflict will help you to better understand such behavior as it relates to the various components of our communication system.

Productive and nonproductive conflict

Our analysis of conflict thus far has acknowledged that conflict is generally thought to be a negative group activity but that it can be reflective of a productive group. Can these two seemingly contradictory assumptions be thought of as compatible? For the time being, let us state the following principle regarding group conflict: *Interpersonal conflict within a group will be productive or nonproductive depending upon the group task*. What we are trying to stress is that one should not have the attitude that conflict is always to be avoided in group decision making.

We usually describe conflict that is productive as *functional* conflict, because it often serves to aid the group in the accomplishment of its specified task. Recall that conflict is often the result of preexisting hostile or antagonistic attitudes. The continued suppression of such attitudes could do more to restrict the group than to further its goals. Thus the overt display of these attitudes—that is, conflict behavior—would help the group to rid itself of such underlying hostilities. It has been argued that the most functional dimension of conflict in group activity is that it clearly defines the issues under discussion. For example, as we will see later, conflict can serve to generate cohesiveness in the group, since it tends to unite some individuals who would normally refrain from such associations (Coser, 1956).

We can also think of conflict behavior as functional because it often demonstrates that the members of the group trust each other and are very comfortable taking certain risks. Think of the group most fulfilling to you. Is conflict useful? Does it lead you to trust other group members more? Does it aid you in your decision making? Are your group relationships more reliable and stable because you are not afraid to engage in conflict behavior? The chances are good that you answered yes to these questions and the reasons are quite clear. For we have all experienced at one time or another within our groups that conflict has served the positive function of aiding us in group decision making. What are other conditions under which we can say that group conflict is productive or functional?

Group conflict can be a *useful vehicle for the proposal of different solutions to the group problem*. If group members can openly disagree with each other without fear, the opportunity to pose unique and creative solutions to problems facing the group is maximized. How many times have you felt as though you could pose a workable solution but the ground rules under which the group operated caused you to suppress it?

Conflict can clearly define the power relationships that exist within the group. Power (French and Raven, 1959) is usually defined in terms of perceived influence that exists within individuals or groups. Often, the powerholders within a group engage in a struggle for group leadership. Conflict allows these members to argue their case openly. At the same time it gives all group members an opportunity to participate in the group's decision to bestow power on one or more individuals. If conflict is an acceptable group behavior, member satisfaction is increased because of the right to participate in the bestowing of power. Additionally, it allows the group members the opportunity to keep all struggles "within the family." By doing this, the group becomes a stronger collection of individuals and is more prepared to create for itself a cohesive atmosphere.

Finally, recognition of interpersonal conflict within the group can *reinforce the individuality of group members*. Here we refer to the basic need of the individual to be "his own man" within the confines of group membership. Admittedly, group membership per se involves a certain amount of giving up individuality in favor of group action. Conflict can be useful within the group because it allows the individual member to present his position regardless of how far that position differs from the group norm. In a sense, this principle of productive conflict underlies all other useful purposes of interpersonal disagreement. Member satisfaction, feeling of participation in the group's activity, the notion that each position is respected—all of these somewhat intangible characteristics are reinforced. These benefits occur when conflict is acknowledged as a functional dimension of group activity.

In general, we can say that conflict has been productive when members are satisfied and that they have gained—both as individuals and as group members—from the conflict (Deutsch, 1969).

Usually we think of group conflict as being dysfunctional (harmful) when group members feel some measure of dissatisfaction or loss as a result of the conflict. It is certainly true that some groups simply have no mechanism for tolerating conflict. As a case in point, the amount of functional conflict that can be tolerated in a group composed of university administration *and* undergraduates is limited. Likewise, the tolerance of conflict in an authoritarian system such as the military is nearly nonexistent. In very simple terms, *if the group's task is imposed on it by outside authority the useful dimensions of intragroup conflict are dramatically restricted.* In a sense, we can see that conflict behavior on the part of group members is usually nonproductive toward the group's goals when the system within which the group operates is incapable of handling the conflict. Keltner (1970) offers a good example of such a case when he discusses the problems surrounding the 1968 Democratic convention in Chicago:

> The rigid police system was unable to tolerate the minor disturbances of the students' crusade or the comparable rigidity of the militant leaders who were spearheading the demonstrations. Such mutual rigidities prevent the development of an equilibrium and riots result. Almost the same type of *polarized rigidity* may be found on every campus where troubles have erupted in recent years. (p. 230)

While Keltner may be speaking of *intergroup conflict*—the struggle *between* existing groups—we can see the generalizability to intragroup conflict. In a sense, people demonstrate a type of polarized rigidity when they assume an "all or nothing" attitude toward the problem under discussion. How often have you been involved in group communication with people who refused to see any value in sharing or compromising a position?

Finally, *conflict behavior within a group tends to serve a nonproductive function when group goals are subverted in favor of individual objectives.* Here we are speaking of those who join groups for purely individual gain and who engage in open disagreement with other group members for purposes of furthering their own objective. People of this type are never reluctant to engage in conflictual behavior, and their strategy is generally the "showdown." The problem with such behavior is that it inhibits the group process and may cause the group to escalate the disagreement to the point where resolution is impossible. We will speak more on this subject when we discuss the relation between communicators and group conflict.

Generally, we should think of interpersonal conflict within the group to be serving nonproductive or task-frustrating functions when the conflict goes beyond its initiating causes and appears to continue long after these causes have been forgotten or become irrelevant (Deutsch, 1969).

Individual orientation

It should be clear by now that the productive or nonproductive characteristics of conflict within the group depend on a number of variables. These factors include the group's task, the individual objectives, the initiating issues, and the location of power within the group. Underlying all these factors, however, is one that determines the individual member's perception of the struggle. That factor is the perspective that the individual brings into the group. In a way, we can refer to this as his *orientation* for operating. Generally, we can speak of one of two orientations that individuals bring to the group circumstance: competitive and cooperative. These orientations should be conceived of as lying on opposite points on a continuum that ranges from individual orientation of pure competition to a position in which the individual is purely cooperative. In order to better understand these orientations, let us speak of them as they relate to successful resolution or management of the group's conflict.

No doubt you have noted that we have referred to the handling of a conflict with such interchangeable terms as *reduction*, *resolution*, and *management*. We do so because in its simplest sense, the removal of a conflict can usually be termed the removal of a particular group problem. Therefore, whether we partially reduce the disagreement (reduction), eliminate it to the parties' satisfaction (resolution), or channel the conflict into an ongoing productive group function (management), we have solved a group problem. Thus we do not consistently make distinctions between the terms—our only concern is that the conflict be dealt with. In general, then, our primary criterion for discussing the productive/nonproductive functions that conflict may play hinges directly on the capability of the group to handle the conflict. Similarly, when we speak of individual orientations of competition and cooperation toward group activity, a determining characteristic of the value of that orientation is its relation to the treatment of group conflict. With that in mind, let us examine these individual orientations and discuss them in terms of how they contribute to the reduction, resolution, or management of interpersonal conflict within the group.

It is not unusual to hear the terms *conflict* and *competition* used synonymously. More accurately, we should view competition as a *form* of conflict among individuals and groups (Beck, 1971). We can think of competition as a precondition to conflict, but conflict does not necessarily have to be of a competitive nature. Perhaps a more precise definition of competition might be helpful as we discuss an individual's competitive orientation toward group activity. An individual who possesses a competitive goal orientation perceives his relationship in clear win-lose terms. The first example that comes to mind for most of us refers to sports activities. Individuals are aware of the rules of the particular game specifying that the one with the most points, better record, fastest time, and so on will be the winner—all others will be losers. Of course, there are degrees—1st, 2d, 3d—and there are qualitative differences in the rewards—gold medals, silver medals, and so on. But the basic requirement of those participating in the contest —let us call it a conflict—is that as one approaches a particular goal, the other is faced with some form of defeat.

On the other hand, the individual with the cooperative orientation believes that the "reward" of the conflict can be shared. This particular individual orientation does not preclude conflict; rather, it acknowledges that the most efficient means of handling a group struggle is through some cooperative process. Perhaps Deutsch (1967) best summarized the differences between the cooperative and competitive orientations:

> If the people have a pre-existing cooperative orientation toward one another, they are likely to resolve a conflict of interest by a cooperative process, if they have a prior competitive orientation they are likely to resolve it by a competitive process. (p. 46)

In other words, the manner in which we deal with conflict depends on the orientation we bring to the group. For example, we can hardly expect five individuals who compete at every turn in small-group deliberations to resolve their differences through cooperative strategies. What is *your* individual orientation as you participate in your various small groups? What is the orientation of your fellow group members? Is your group's predominant method of conflict resolution cooperative or competitive?

We should keep in mind that conflict can exist with either a competitive or a cooperative orientation. Our orientation is the prime factor determining whether conflict reduction, resolution, or management will be employed. For a moment let us look at an example of a group circumstance that involves conflict within each of these contexts.

Our classroom discussions are group activities that generally take place within a cooperative environment. The group members are on display and attempt to work together to accomplish some group objective that will show all the participants to be "good" group members. Conflicts that occur within the period of the discussion are generally handled according to the many decision-making procedures that we have discussed in chapters 1 and 5. The cooperative orientation does not preclude the existence of violent disagreements, but they are resolved using some agreed-upon rules of operation. The goals are often consensus and member satisfaction.

Now, however, let us assume that we have some members who know that the grading of a particular group assignment will be made on the basis of *individual* contributions. The discussion behavior is not difficult to understand. Members vie with each other to outshine one another. It is extremely difficult for one individual to agree with another, even within the confines of an acceptable problem-solving procedure. The result is a conflict that is nearly impossible to resolve. Why? A very simple answer can be found. For the group members there could only be a win-lose situation. While the ostensible purpose of the group was to discuss for the group's good, the reward system was structured for the emergence of "winners" and "losers." Again, these questions seem relevant. Does your normal group activity exist within a competitive or cooperative orientation? Do *you* bring a competitive or cooperative perspective to your group activity? Remember, the orientation that the individual brings to the group must be consistent with the group orientation. Conflict reduction, resolution, or management is a difficult process at best. An inconsistency between individual and group orientation makes the treatment of conflict virtually impossible. We will speak more to this point when we explore personality variables in operation within the group.

So far our discussion has been designed to explore conflict behavior as a complex *subsystem* operating within the larger communication system that we presented in chapter 1. We know that conflict has as its determining characteristics the open disagreement over equally attractive and mutually exclusive alternatives. We have discussed the interrelation that exists between *intrapersonal* and *interpersonal* conflict, noting that the dynamics of the conflict behavior may play one type of conflict against another. Interpersonal conflict that occurs within the group (intragroup conflict) can be viewed as both productive and nonproductive depending on the group task. Finally, we examined the two basic orientations that the individual brings to the group and discussed these in terms of the resolution of a conflict. From this point on, when we discuss conflict "resolution" we will be referring to the process of solving a group conflict—whether that process refers to the complete elimination of the conflict, the reduction of it to the members' satisfaction, or the management of it for subsequent group activity. We turn now to a discussion of the relationship of conflict and communication within the group setting.

---

exercise 1

MESSAGE ANALYSIS
1. Members of the class should be paired off into dyads. Dyads should position themselves in different parts of the room or in different rooms.

2. One member of the dyad is identified as A, the other as B, for the duration of the activity and the members of the dyad proceed through the following activity:

Description: Member A describes to B what he (A) observes about B. A is to comment on nonverbal cues only—clothes, face, etc. All statements are to be descriptive, nonevaluative statements. When A has finished, B performs the same activity concerning A. Neither member of the dyad is to react to comments made by the other at this time.

Hypothesis: During this second round, A states his hypotheses about B—without any comments from B—relevant to B's attitudes, values, beliefs, behaviors, and so on. The point here is to generate as many evaluative statements as possible about the individual. When A has finished, B performs the same activity by making evaluative statements about A. The following statement might be the kind that would be generated: "You would probably vote Democratic."

Verification: During this third round, both parties react to the hypotheses generated during the second round. B begins by reacting to the hypotheses—evaluative statements—that A made about him during the second round. A does the same in terms of the statements made during the second round about him by B. Each member of the dyad should also comment at this time about any statements made during the first round.

QUESTIONS

1. Did you find it difficult to offer nonevaluative statements in the first phase of the exercise? Why or why not?

2. How accurate were the hypotheses about your attitudes, values, etc.?

3. Was it difficult to predict your partner's attitudes, etc.? Why or why not?

Conflict and group communication

As we noted earlier, conflict is the result of the group dynamic or interaction. Up to this point we have been exploring the dynamics of conflict per se—how it is defined, how it is resolved, and what its general characteristics are in intrapersonal and interpersonal settings. We turn now to the examination of conflict in its context—the communication system of the group. Our procedure will be simple. We will return to our basic components of the communication system that we defined in chapter 1—communicator, message, interaction, and situational context. We will look at conflict behavior as both cause and effect of certain conditions within each of the communication factors. We do this to remind you of our basic postulate: *communication is a system*. Conflict behavior arising within the group causes changes within the total system. Conversely, changes in components (factors) within the communication system affect changes that result in group conflict.

It is of course impossible to note all the variables that operate within the communication system. Our selection of components represents our best guess as to the basic factors of a group communication system. Likewise, our selection of factors that we choose to examine here represent a best guess as to important conflict-related variables. It may well be that certain factors that you think most relevant to conflict as it might exist within your group(s) are not discussed here. We hope that the principles of interrelation that we demonstrate—that conflict can be simultaneously cause and effect—will be generalized to your own situation.

Communicator

The communicator component of our model refers to those individuals who send and receive the messages within the group setting. We will stress three communicator variables or characteristics that relate to interpersonal conflict behavior in the small group: attitudes, dogmatism, and power. It is true that additional variables of self-esteem, source credibility—to name only two—certainly affect and are affected by interpersonal conflict within the group context. Yet, as noted earlier, we will discuss those that we think representative to help focus our thinking on the systematic relationships that exist in the small-group communication system.

Attitude. For the most part, we can see that conflict occurs as a result of earlier hostile feelings or attitudes (Coser, 1956). Recall from our discussion in chapter 1 that attitudes can be thought of as these favorable or unfavorable evaluations we have toward people, objects, ideas, or behaviors. These evaluations are thought to be among the most important factors influencing communicative outcomes (e.g., Cohen, 1964; Zimbardo and Ebbeson, 1971). The role of the communicator's attitude in the development of conflict cannot be overemphasized, for it involves not only the individual's evaluation of the issue under question but also his evaluation of the context and the other parties to the conflict. How does an attitude lead to conflict? Let us look at an example that will serve to indicate the potential of this communicator characteristic in the development of a conflict situation.

Let us assume that individuals are participating in a problem-solving discussion for the purpose of arriving at a position identifying the role of the undergraduate student in curriculum development. The group is composed of faculty and students, and the external constraints placed on the group are minimal. Thus, this group has the freedom to develop a position that will probably be implemented by the university administration. Therefore, the *intrapersonal* conflict should be at a minimum: the students feel that the role ought to be a strong one, the faculty—assume here a traditional faculty—feels that the status quo is sufficient. At this time there exist hostile attitudes, but no overt conflict or disagreement. Will overt antagonism result? The evolution of conflict from these hostile attitudes depends on a variety of factors.

First, how involved are the students? How flexible are the parties to the discussion? If, for example, the students are seniors in their last semester of college, the question may not be as important as the upcoming job interview, the current course load the student is taking, or any number of other extraneous factors. The point here is that the mere existence of hostile or antagonistic attitudes is not a necessary condition for ensuing conflict. What is crucial is the level of involvement that the students have on the issue. We know that an individual who is highly involved in an issue is not likely to be persuaded to change his position. (Sereno, 1968)

A second factor relates to the parties' attitudes toward each other. Here we refer to our earlier discussion regarding the orientation of the individual group members. Are the faculty members entering the group session with a win-lose attitude? Do the students see this as an opportunity to "get" the establishment?

What we can say at this point is that while conflict is likely to grow out of the existence of prior opposing attitudes, such attitudes are not in and of themselves sufficient conditions to *cause* conflict behavior. Moreover, the existence of other attitude-related variables that we have suggested above may mediate the effect that the contrary attitudes might produce.

In general, then, attitudes can be treated as the root of conflict, but they do not necessarily lead to conflict. Rokeach (1960) argues that to understand the attitude variable we must look not only at the object of the attitude—in this case the conflict issue—but also at the various characteristics of the situation. Such factors would necessitate that we keep in mind the relative position of the parties' attitudes with regard to status, how the issue is defined, the form of leadership, and many other such factors. All of these and more would give us some indication of whether or not the mere existence of competing attitudes would lead the communicators into a conflict situation.

Now let us assume that, all things being equal, the parties do engage in conflict—that is, the attitudes have caused conflict. What is the dynamic of the group now in operation? In other words, where does the group go from here? It is reasonable to assume that conflict behavior can have an effect on the competing parties and in turn cause a change in their attitudes. We now can see conflict as a *cause*, the communicator attitudes as an *effect*, of that conflict behavior. This change in attitude would constitute conflict resolution of some degree and would therefore result in a solution to the problem. The change in attitude need not be a complete reversal—this rarely happens in such cases; it may be a modification of the parties' positions, a reinforcement of existing attitudes, or the parties' agreeing on some third position.

The point here is not so much what happened to our particular group; rather, it is that the communicator variable of attitude leads to conflict behavior (open antagonism), and conflict behavior in turn leads to a change in the communicator attitudes. This, in its simplest form, is the system in action: one factor affects another, which affects another. In this case, conflict is both effect and cause of some other variable in our group-communication process.

Dogmatism. The orientation that an individual brings to the group setting is directly related to the type of personality characteristics that he possesses. Past experiences with familiar individuals enable us to make fairly accurate guesses about how he will behave in a group setting. We see some people as "authoritarian," others as "cocky," others as "timid," and still others as "weak sisters." On the basis of seeing a particular individual in operation, we are able to predict his prominent personality attributes. Rokeach (1960) has identified the individual who demonstrates blind loyalty to a system as one who is highly *dogmatic*. The highly dogmatic individual is defined as a closed-minded individual who generally remains loyal to directions and instructions given by authorities outside the particular system in which the dogmatic person operates.

In a sense, the variables of attitude and dogmatism are inextricably bound together, for it is difficult to envision an individual with a strong personality characteristic such as dogmatism without seeing him also as holding very involved attitudes on a variety of issues. However, our discussion now will be limited to the role of this personality factor of dogmatism as it affects and is affected by conflict behavior within the group.

Research (Druckman, 1967) indicates that the highly dogmatic individual will solidify his position during negotiations with an opponent. Stated simply, the dogmatic personality probably does not perceive himself to be in conflict according to our earlier definition, for he does not see any alternative to be workable except his own. The highly dogmatic individual is also much more resistant to compromise than is the lowly dogmatic individual. Therefore, if conflict does occur with the dogmatic individual, he is firm in his position and rarely compromises to resolve the conflict. Assuming that this factor can lead to conflict, we could then ask the question "Does conflict result in inducing dogmatism?" If our principle relevant to the system model of group communication is valid, we must answer in the affirmative. In fact, we have all probably witnessed such an effect of conflict behavior.

For example, look to your own experiences as a member of a particular group: this class. You began this class without a particular position on the course materials, and were probably pretty low on the dogmatic scale. After several weeks you have internalized a certain amount of information. During that period of time you have probably had your share of conflicts with the instructor or fellow students. You have modified your attitudes somewhat. More importantly, you have probably evolved to the point at which you are somewhat rigid with regard to certain positions or arguments. Similarly, you have experienced the solidifying of your personality in a number of groups primarily through your conflict experiences with those groups.

In general, the personality variable of dogmatism leads the communicator into various conflict circumstances in a group setting. Since he is highly dogmatic, he will probably resist the group's influence and will resist more conventional forms of conflict resolution such as compromise. It is very possible that because of the conflict he will become more convinced of his position. At any rate, the conflict system in operation has served as both an antecedent (cause) and consequence (effect) of his dogmatic character. The next time you engage in a group communicative activity, identify for yourself those members that you perceive to be high or low in dogmatism (including yourself), then observe their behavior once the group engages in conflict. It should be a very interesting and illuminating experience for you.

Power. As we indicated earlier, power as a communicator variable refers to the potential of an individual's influence in the group. To most of us, this factor in the group communication system is usually descriptive when we think of conflict within a group. For example, the terms *power struggle, vying for power,* and *power play* have come to represent conflict behaviors of one type or another that we think of as existing in a variety of group situations. Generally, such descriptions connote a negative impression of group conflict. Examined with some objectivity, however, we can see that this communicator variable has much to offer us in terms of describing group conflict.

Let us begin our discussion of power by acknowledging that it can be manifested in a variety of ways. For example, we can perceive of people possessing several different characteristics of power. In fact, French and Raven (1959) identify five bases of power. These "bases" refer to the relationship between the parties and specifies the source of the power. It is well to note here that power is not an absolute factor inherent in the communicator; rather, it is a relative characteristic that *compares* the participants with one another.

Reward power is defined as one individual's ability to present rewards to or for another. In a sense, this refers to one individual being in a position to give another some additional incentive for a positive activity or behavior. *Coercive power* is the ability of one individual to affect the behavior of another because he is in a position to punish him unless the behavior is performed. *Legitimate* power specifies that an individual has the assigned right—because of the organizational structure, for example—to expect another individual to conform to his wishes. *Referent* power gives one individual power over the other because the latter wishes to identify with the former—the feeling that "I want to be like you, so I'll do what you want me to." Finally, *expert* power means that one individual has more influence than the others because he is perceived to be knowledgeable—an expert—regarding a specific problem or field. In one way or another, virtually every characteristic that we can think of relating to the amount of and source of a person's capability to influence others can be categorized into one or more of these five categories. How does power as a communicator variable affect group conflict? How is power mediated or affected by the conflict system? What kind of power, if any, do you see operating in your various groups?

It is not difficult to see how conflict grows out of perceptions of power relationships. Most of us have at one time or another—probably in this classroom—engaged in an open disagreement with an individual over some issue that calls expert power characteristics into question. The notion, for example, that an instructor's statement is "true" because he said it, that some statement in this book is accurate because the authors are experts can lead to conflict behavior very easily. The power struggle—the conflict

—is confounded by previously held attitudes or highly dogmatic predispositions. The point here is simply that we all strive for some type of power position. The saying that "information is power" suggests that the more knowledge one has in a certain area, the higher position in the organizational structure he should occupy. Quite often in a classroom discussion the positions of power are occupied by those individuals who read the assigned chapter simply because they have more information than those who did not complete the reading. Through these examples, the principle remains the same: individuals are placed in power positions because they have something that the other members of the group do not have. With these general ideas in mind, let us examine conflict as it might evolve from each of the types of power.

Engagement in conflict with an individual who has reward power is risky business. One faces the possibility of losing the future rewards as well as the conflict confrontation itself. This of course assumes that the individual who possesses the reward power operates within the group from a competitive orientation. If the reward is perceived to be a win or a loss, the ultimate resolution of the conflict can be harmful (dysfunctional) to the group's goal. On the other hand, if reward power is invested in group members who operate from a cooperative orientation, the results can be mutually satisfying for all group members. In the case, for example, of a faculty-student conflict over a particular grade that has been assigned, the reward power position is constant. The best that can be hoped for is a compromise, not a shifting of the responsibility to the student. On the other hand, the situation may involve a prospective donor and an organization representative who is soliciting a sizable amount for his institution. The disagreement may result in any number of possible resolutions, one of which may be to increase the donation dramatically. In this case, the parties have mediated the power position so that *both* parties have been instrumental in the resolution of the disagreement.

Coercive power conflicts are not probable, but if they do occur, the resolution is usually one without beneficial ends. An individual holds a coercive position in an invariant manner—that is, it does not change—and anything short of a coup will not yield the conflicting parties beneficial results.

Legitimate, referent, and expert power positions are similar in that they all imply the holding of some intangible credibility factor in addition to the obvious material position. Conflict growing out of a difference with individuals holding any of these positions can be beneficial to all concerned. It is unlikely that conflict growing out of a difference with or between individuals holding referent power will frustrate group goals or objectives, since there is a strong drive on the part of the individuals to identify with each other. These are cases in which parties to the conflict will generally hold a cooperative orientation toward resolution of any disagreement, and the resolution should provide high member satisfaction.

In simple terms, conflict grows out of differences in perception of the power relations, and the quality of the resolution to the conflict depends almost entirely on the individual orientation to the situation. If it is competitive, then competitive (win-lose) criteria will be employed and the member satisfaction and group productivity will be minimal. If the orientation is cooperative, conflict may still occur, but the processes employed to resolve it will lead to high member satisfaction and, presumably, greater group cohesiveness.

In a general sense, conflict is most productive when it leads to a clear definition of power relationships. As Coser (1956) has noted, conflict is most functional (productive) when it aids in the establishment and maintenance of a group balance of power.

The number of communicator variables in operation within the group communication system is infinite. However, knowing the roles that attitude, dogmatism, and power occupy will go a long way in helping us to deal with conflict as it arises. Moreover, the impact of conflict in the stabilization of power relationships, the discovery of new power positions, and the maintenance of a group balance of power should allow the individual to better identify emerging power-based conflicts. As we continue our discussion of the components of the group communication process and the role that conflict occupies as a subsystem within that process, we should continue to think of conflict behavior as both cause and effect of other factors.

---

exercise 2

CONSENSUS/CONFLICT

1. Generate a list of topic areas that are very important on your campus. (A list of ten to twelve should do it.)

2. As individuals, rank-order these campus-related topics on a most-important-to-least-important basis. (Do not combine any topics.)

3. Break down the class into five-member groups at random.

4. Now, as groups, rank-order these topics on a most-important-to-least-important basis. (Do not combine any topics.) Do not average or vote as a means of arriving at the group consensus.

QUESTIONS

1. How close to *your* initial ranking was the final group order?

2. Which members of your group were most powerful? Why?

3. Describe the outstanding differences (conflicts), if any, in your group.

The message

In chapters 3 and 4 we indicated that the message element of the group-communication system is examined from *verbal* and *nonverbal* perspectives. Our treatment of conflict behavior in the group setting will treat these dimensions. Here, however, we want to examine conflict behavior as it grows out of message transmission and of the effects on postconflict message transmission that such open disagreements may have. As we indicated in chapter 1, there is evidence that both the *word* (verbal) and physical/vocal (nonverbal) behavior can lead to conflict within the group setting. How does conflict result from the communicative message?

In a sense, we can say that nearly all conflict is manifested by verbal behavior. Recall that we confined our definition of conflict to *overt antagonism*, thus ruling out the mere holding of hostile attitudes to indicate conflict. We come to know that individuals are in conflict when they indicate *verbally* that they are in opposition. Whether it is name-calling or open and rational disagreement, the conflict that surfaces is first identified by the language used by the competing parties. However, the conflict can also be attributed to the many nonverbal messages that are given by one member to another. The facial smirk, drumming one's fingers on a table while another is talking, the furrowed brow—all of these and many more similar messages are all recognized by the receiver. Therefore, while we can say that the conflict is represented in verbal form, we must keep in mind that the words used may simply reflect dissatisfaction with nonverbal communicative behavior.

From a different point of view, we can see that conflict behavior can dramatically affect the postconflict verbal and nonverbal messages that are transmitted. Having once engaged in conflict that has been characterized by loaded language, facial contortions, and highly intense gesturing, we may note that group members change their future communicative behavior by modifying their language and nonverbal cues. In one sense, we can view negative feedback as a form of conflict behavior, for an individual may be telling us—through word, facial expression, or tone of voice—that he is opposed to our position. Do we modify our presentation of the message to take future reactions like this into account?

In the course of an hour's discussion on a particular topic in which group members are highly involved, we may see conflict arise, be resolved, and lead to more conflict several times. It is well to keep in mind that the message in the group communication context acts as a vehicle for conflict and its resolution.

Recall for a moment our earlier discussion of competitive and cooperative orientations. The individual orientation that is brought to the group situation is conveyed through the messages that the communicators transmit. It is made clear to us very early in the group's deliberations which orientation the members possess. The elements of the message indicate the amount of trust that individuals have in us, the extent to which they will openly give their views, and the manner in which they will resolve any conflict that occurs. The message element of the group communication system tells us each individual's opinion (presumably, the statement of his attitude), his personality characteristics, and how powerful he perceives himself to be. The message allows us to resolve a conflict by removing a person from our group or by adopting his divergent point of view; it allows us a mechanism that we can use to be openly honest with our words or to reveal nonverbally that we are dissatisfied with the group's activity.

Simultaneously, conflict behavior within the group affects the message and is in turn affected by it. It affects the message by leading to a modification of the manner in which individuals communicate their positions to the group membership. It is affected by the message in that it gives parties to the disagreement a common medium through which to communicate. Without the message there can surely be no conflict; but without the message there can be no group.

The next time you participate in a group activity—this class, for example—attempt to model the message-conflict relationships that occur. Observe which message elements by specific members seem to generate interpersonal conflict within the group. Additionally, observe any changes in the communicative messages that may result from the conflict.

Interaction

As we move through our discussion of conflict behavior within the group communication system it should be clear that it is extremely difficult to isolate any one component of that system and speak of it in relation to conflict circumstances. Obviously you are noting that the components we have discussed thus far—communicator and message—are interrelated. The component that we are about to discuss—interaction—is no different. In fact, one can conceive of the interaction of the communicative process as the overall dynamic of the group. When earlier conflict theorists (Simmel, 1955; Coser, 1956) discussed conflict, they emphasized the factor of interaction. Mack and Snyder (1957) referred to conflict as a "social-interaction process." It is the interaction element of the communication system that makes the system a *group* process. The problem-solving characteristic of the group, the various group factors such as cohesiveness, conformity, task-orientation, goal-motivation—all these are group properties that cannot be discussed without recognizing the *interactive* nature of the group members. We will discuss two variables within the interaction dimension of our group communication system that we believe to have a great deal of importance when discussing interaction and intragroup conflict. These two variables are cohesiveness and member satisfaction.

Cohesiveness. For the most of us, the most desirable term we can think of in describing our "best" group is to call it cohesive. Group cohesiveness is a concept that generally refers to the high degree of closeness that members feel about their group. It has been defined more precisely by Festinger, Schachter, and Bach (1950) as the "total field of forces which act on members to remain in the group." We can think of it not only as a good and loyal feeling that we may have about our group, but also as a kind of drive that keeps us active members of that group. What role could conflict play in developing cohesiveness? In what way do cohesive groups perform conflict behaviors? Which of your groups are cohesive? Why?

Again, we want you to think for a moment of your favorite group; it can be your primary social group, task group, or any other for that matter. Assuming that you perceive this group to be cohesive, how did it get to that stage? Chances are that there were many situations in which members were openly hostile or antagonistic toward each other. Issues were brought up, conflict ensued, resolution may or may not have occurred. It has been found, for example, that in cohesive groups there is more of an attempt by members to influence each other and, in turn, to be influenced by each other (Cartwright and Lippitt, 1961). As we indicated earlier, the notion of influence is critical to an understanding of conflict behavior. It seems reasonable for us to assume that in groups in which we engage in some form of behavi[?] for purposes of influencing each other that there will be a cert[?] amount of conflict. Individual members with either competing or cooperating orientations would work toward group goals and, in the process, develop warmer, more cohesive attitudes.

During the conflict, individuals react more openly and presumably become more trustful of each other. Of course there is always the possibility that individuals will reject each other. However, even this kind of behavior can lead to cohesiveness within the group. Related to conflict as it develops, cohesiveness is perceived trust and risk-taking. All these behaviors tend to give the group member the feeling that his opinions and positions are worthwhile. Thus, even if his position is rejected, he becomes an even stronger group member simply because he was recognized and his position respected. Of course much of this is inferential. Does it square with your experiences? Have you found that group conflict can lead to a more cohesive group? What are some other related factors?

It is certainly not difficult to understand the existence of conflict as an *effect* of a cohesive group. As group members trust each other more, as they begin to solidify into a unified group, and as they understand each other as individuals, they feel freer to take risks that they would not have taken with a less closely knit group. As individuals become more cohesive they tend to feel less threat from each other and place more trust in each other's judgment. They also probably react more openly without the fear of rejection or isolation. Several common measurements of cohesiveness have included perceived friendliness and acceptance of members' ideas (Duetsch and Krauss, 1965). Therefore, the conflict that arises in a cohesive group would appear to be very amenable to resolution. For the most part, we can probably say that conflict is more productive in a cohesive group than in an uncohesive group.

Member satisfaction. Directly related to the cohesiveness of a group is its member satisfaction with the group activity. Member satisfaction is used here to refer not only to the ongoing perceptions of the group's activity, but also to the product of the group deliberations. *Conflict is probably the toughest test of member satisfaction.* The extent to which individual group members expend their energies in resolving some disagreement obviously takes away from the available energy to implement the group solution. Yet we can see that in a situation in which member satisfaction is high, minimal conflict could occur. Exceptions to this would occur if the members were competitive-oriented and based their satisfaction on the "win" that they could secure. However, in groups with a cooperative orientation, conflict behavior would occupy very little of the group's attention. What are some factors related to group member satisfaction that would lead to virtually no conflict? Such factors as perceived similarity of interests, similarity of personalities, and a high level of group cohesiveness could provide for high member satisfaction with the group's activity along with minimum conflict.

The relationship between conflict and cohesiveness is certainly interactive. Cohesive group members engage in conflict and are able to resolve the difficulty with normal cooperative processes. For those members who have a high degree of satisfaction with the group goals and activity, minimal conflict occurs. When it does, the normal mode of conflict resolution is through cooperative processes. Conflict acts as a cause of member satisfaction in much the same manner as it does with cohesive groups. It is demonstrative of trusting and loyal relationships and it reinforces the group membership in terms of condoning risk-taking behaviors.

Situational context

Just as the interaction element of the communication system reflects the dynamic of the group, the situational context reflects those factors of the physical and social setting in which the group acts. In this section we will briefly discuss the relation of conflict behavior and various dimensions of the group context.

We have already referred to the most powerful determinant of the context: the individual orientations that members bring to the group. The orientation must be examined in light of the *group norms* in order to evaluate the productive or nonproductive quality of the conflict. As we noted earlier, if a discrepancy exists between individual and group orientations, then conflict will be common and the mode of resolving it will be difficult to ascertain.

The *physical characteristics* of the group setting can affect and be affected markedly by conflict behavior. In a sense, architectural features, spatial arrangements, and physical locations for the group communication can be treated as nonverbal dimensions of the communicative message. We have already discussed the impact of such nonverbal dimensions on conflict behavior.

The *group purpose or task* is another major determinant of the existence of conflict. Conflict behavior can lead to a modification of group task; conversely, conflict can be an integral component of a group's purpose. For example, a group established for purposes of self-maintenance can exist as an encounter group in which conflict is a necessary ingredient. A group that has as its primary purpose the sharing of information needs a mechanism to deal with the conflict that may occur when information presented by one group member is in opposition to that presented by another member.

The situational context factor of group structure is directly tied to potential conflict. Whether that conflict occurs in response to perceived role differentiation or simply when an individual performs some behavior that is in opposition to the group norms, some understanding of conflict behavior is necessary.

Conflict can either occur as a result of situational context factors that are fixed by the group membership, or conflict can cause changes in the context. It is important to note here that no matter how rigid the group structure, it is still composed of individual perceptions of the group members. It is important to understand whether the conflict is related to the structure per se or to the individuals who are supporting that structure. Our earlier remarks concerning the nature of individual-institutional conflict are particularly appropriate here.

We have tried to demonstrate the complex interrelationships that occur between conflict behavior as a subsystem and various components of the group communication system. It is important to remember that we have not exhausted the list; in fact we have barely scratched the surface. Your experiences as a group member may have led you to consider many more variables in operation than we have discussed. But the principles that we have suggested should have some generalizability to your own experiences. Whether conflict is productive or nonproductive, it is still both cause and effect of changes in the group communication system. And we have not tried here to indicate that those changes occur only within the specific component that we were discussing. Thus, for example, conflict may cause some change in the communicator component of the group communication system, while at the same time changes may occur in the message, interaction, and situational context components. The shape of our system is constantly changing and the potential for conflict to occur at any time within the system requires that we constantly be in a position to propose methods of resolving that conflict. In a very general sense, the recognition of conflict behavior is a method of resolution.

Characteristics of the conflict subsystem

We are now in a position to offer some general principles about the operation of conflict within the larger group communication system:

Conflict is an ever present phenomenon that occurs across all levels of group activity.

Conflict behavior is a subsystem of the group communication system.

Conflict is basically of two types: intrapersonal and interpersonal.

Conflict is productive or nonproductive depending upon the group task.

Individual orientations of a competitive or cooperative nature determine the method and ease of conflict resolution.

Conflict serves simultaneously as cause and effect of changes in the communicator, message, interaction, and situational context components of the group communication system.

ADDITIONAL READINGS

Keltner, John W. *Interpersonal Speech-Communication: Elements and Structures* (Belmont, Calif.: Wadsworth, 1970). A comprehensive and easy-to-read treatment of conflict and its relationship to communication behavior. The presentation of the dimensions and systems of controversy-conflict (p. 231) is particularly useful for the small-group member.

Jacobson, Wally D. *Power and Interpersonal Relations* (Belmont, Calif.: Wadsworth, 1972). This is a very sophisticated and scholarly treatment of the power variable and its operation in a variety of circumstances. This work contains virtually all relevant research in the area. It may be somewhat difficult to read for the student, but worth it if the time can be taken.

Coser, Lewis A. *The Functions of Social Conflict* (New York: Free Press, 1956). This is probably the single most influential treatment of social conflict to be written. It is not an easy book to read and understand; it deals with a "number of basic propositions which have been distilled from theories of social conflict."

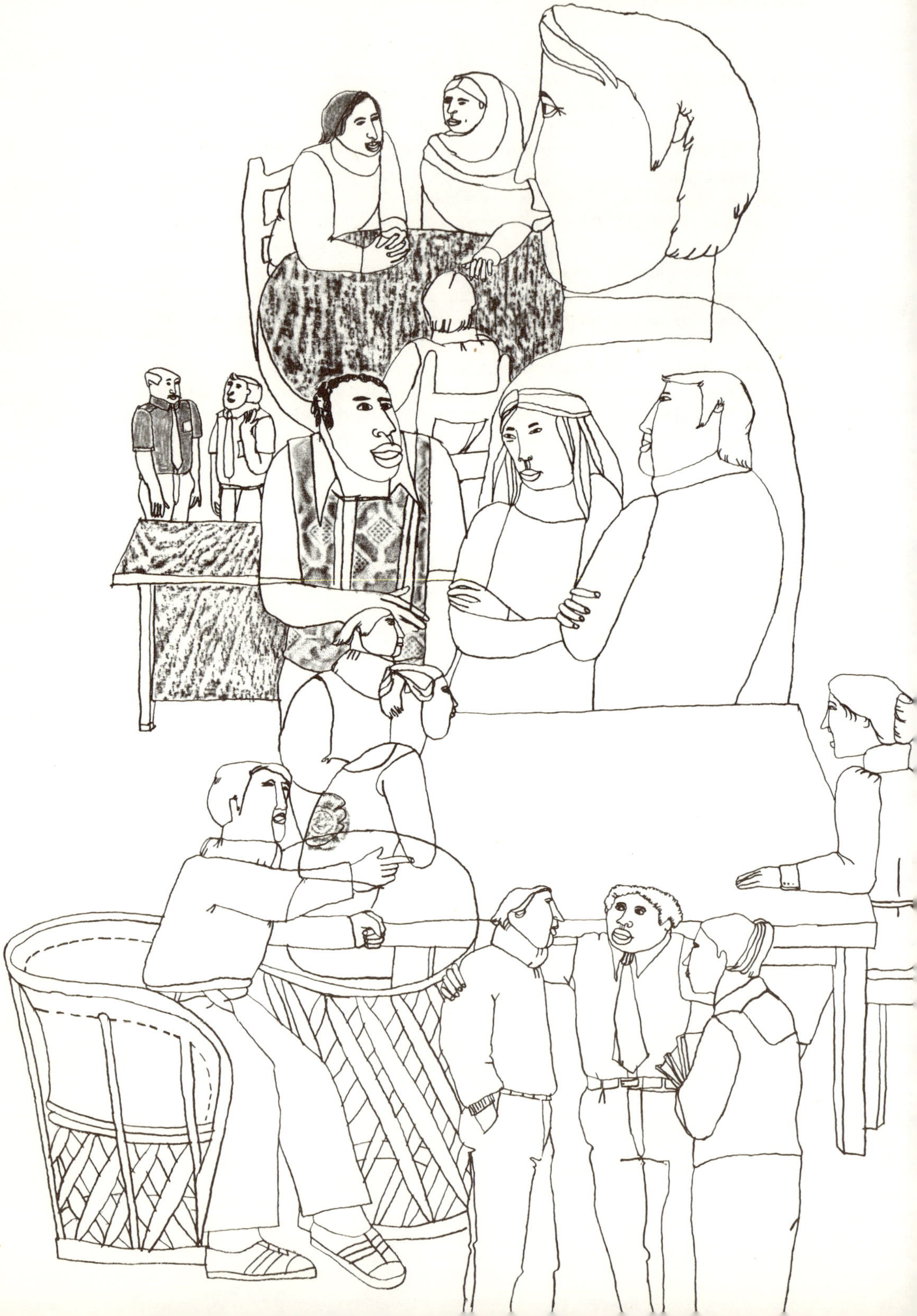

9. Leadership in small groups

PREVIEW

Leadership defined
    The term "leadership" has three major meanings:
        The attribute of a position.
        The characteristics of a person.
        A category of behavior.

Frameworks utilized in studying leadership
    Leadership may be studied under the terms of four basic approaches:
        The trait approach.
        The situational approach.
        The functional approach.
        The stylistic approach.
    Each approach is discussed; some basic operational procedures utilized in each approach are cited; and several findings are reported.

Leadership roles
    Different leaders may be suited for different roles. Roles may change as we move from one group to another or from one task to another. The various roles discussed are:
        Task-environment roles.
        Group-maintenance or social-emotional roles.
        Consideration roles.
        Structure roles.
    The effect of these roles during interaction with group members is discussed.

Leadership styles
    Style focuses on what leaders *do* rather than on their personal characteristics. Different styles tend to influence different kinds of interaction between members. We discuss the three frequently mentioned styles of leadership:
        Autocratic or authoritarian style.
        Democratic style.
        Laissez-faire or free-reign style.

During the early stages of our lives, many adults, especially parents, took the initiative in influencing our behavior, and served as models for our becoming what we are. Later, in our relationship with peers, we took the initiative in leading in some instances, and allowed ourselves to be led in other instances. The extent to which we led, or were led, depended, perhaps, on our own personality, the nature of our peer group, the group task, or the setting or situation in which we found ourselves.

Leadership not only involves the overt display of certain kinds of action in the group, but is also related to the perceptions and expectations of the members of the group. Certain kinds of behavior are perceived and characterized as leadership behavior; and a leader is expected to behave in a particular manner. We usually think of leadership in terms of one particular individual in a group; however, leadership may be shared by a number of individuals. The specific type of leadership may be determined by the demands of the task, the membership, or the purpose and activities of the group. As group membership, task, purpose, or activities change, the method of leadership used by a given individual may also change.

In exploring the question of leadership, we will use our group communication model from chapter 1. We will look at leadership in terms of the leader as communicator, the messages which he sends, his interaction with group members, and the context in which he communicates. We will discuss leadership within this framework so that you may gain a few conceptual tools to aid you in your study.

Here are some of the questions to be considered: What is leadership? What makes an effective leader? What is the best style of leadership? What influences leaders to behave as they do? What communication patterns commonly prevail between the leaders and followers? What the various roles that leaders occupy in groups? What are the prospects for training effective leaders? Our answers will be far from complete, but we hope they will take us further along our path to discovery.

exercise 1

The ideas in this chapter may be more meaningful if we performed this brief assignment.

1. Make a list of several instances in which you occupied a leadership position.

_____

_____

_____

  a) Specify those instances in which you were effective.

_____

_____

_____

  b) Specify those instances in which you were ineffective.

_____

_____

_____

2. Make a list of several instances in which you perceived yourself following the directives of a leader.

_____

_____

_____

  a) Specify those instances in which you were quite content to be led by a particular individual.

_____

_____

_____

b) Specify those instances in which you were *not* content to be led by a particular individual.

_____

_____

_____

3. Jot down some reasons which may give support to your feelings in the four specific situations you have just reviewed.

a) Why were you effective?

_____

_____

_____

b) Why were you ineffective?

_____

_____

_____

c) Why were you content to be led?

_____

_____

_____

d) Why were you *not* content to be led?

_____

_____

_____

As we have examined our own experience, we hope that some patterns will have emerged to aid us in defining the conditions for effective leadership.

Since this book focuses on the dynamics of small groups in various situations of discussion, problem solving, decision making, task accomplishment, industrial operations, policymaking, and so on, we will begin by focusing on several definitions which may spell out leadership in terms of our model of group communication process.

The group leader as communicator

A convenient way of defining a leader could be to say that a leader is a person who performs leadership behaviors, that is, behaviors that have been labeled "leadership behaviors." What constitutes leadership behaviors depends on the perception of the person categorizing the behaviors. We may say, then, that a leader "communicates" leadership through the demonstration of behaviors that group members *expect* of leaders.

Katz and Kahn (1966) maintain that the term *leadership* has three major meanings: the attribute of a position, the characteristics of a person, and a category of behavior. In most discussions, the three meanings are employed simultaneously; that is, they are used to refer to a person who possesses certain qualities, who occupies a certain position, and who behaves in certain ways. The three meanings are not mutually exclusive; they are ways of recognizing that the influence potential of leaders may be related to different characteristics. A captain will be obeyed by his soldiers if he gives a certain order, regardless of whether he is the kind of person to whom they would ordinarily look for leadership or whether the kind of behavior he displays is very leaderlike according to their usual norms of expectations. In this case, his position alone makes him a leader.

In terms of the position taken by Katz and Kahn (1966) we may say that the group leader is the person so designated by members of the group. This designation may be a result of (1) some type of sociometric choice, or (2) the result of an appointment made by some external authority, or (3) the emergence of one particular individual who becomes outstanding in the group. Let us discuss these three attributions in some detail.

Attribution through sociometric choice

The sociometric approach to the study of leadership represents an attempt to construct a visual diagram of the patterns of liking and disliking within a group. This approach is based on the assumption that groups which consist of individuals who like one another will work more effectively than groups in which individuals dislike one another. Specifically, in terms of a choice of leader, a sociometric index is used to single out the individual who is best liked by the other group members. Sociometry makes use of a direct questionnaire which asks members to indicate whom they enjoy working with, whom they respect, whom they would prefer to avoid working with, who is their choice for leader, and so on. The responses are then placed in a matrix for analysis, and a profile or chart is obtained. Let us look at an example of a question asked and the sociogram that was plotted on the basis of the responses. (See figure 1.)

Question: You and nine other students in your residence hall are being called upon to plan a series of social activities for the Dormitory Council. Whom would you choose as leader?

Result:

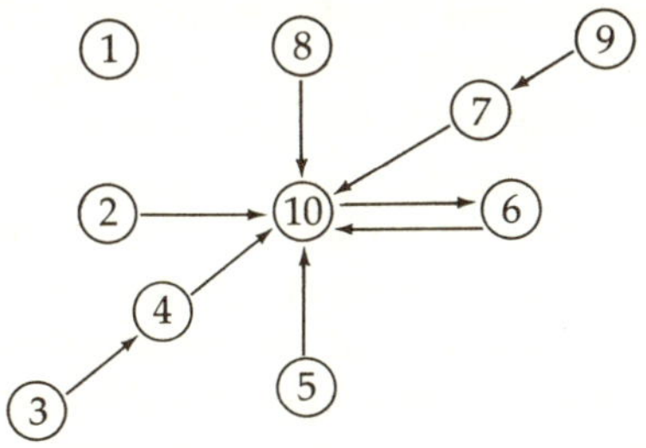

Interpretation: The clustering of arrows around no. 10 strongly suggests that the group wants him as their leader. No. 4 was chosen by no. 3, no. 7 was chosen by no. 9, and no. 10 chose no. 6. However it is interesting to note that all three of the students (other than no. 10) who were chosen opted in favor of no. 10. Note also that no. 1 made no choice and no one chose him. We would say that this example represents the sociogram of a group where the choice for a leader is clearly indicated.

Figure 1. Use of a sociometric method in a small group.

Leadership by sociometric choice represents one type of appointment. Its essential characteristic is that this type of appointment comes from within the group itself. Two relevant questions to be answered are: What accounts for a certain individual being chosen by many others? What accounts for certain individuals being rejected by others? These questions will be answered later when we discuss the *traits* that are manifested by leaders. For the moment, we want to discuss another kind of leadership in terms of the leader as a communicator.

Leadership through emergence

Sometimes, a leader is not chosen by sociometric choice; instead it is common to find one person becoming prominent in the group as time goes by. This type of leader is called an *emergent* leader. He emerges to the forefront in the group because the members perceive certain relevant attributes or traits in him, or because he himself takes the initiative in aspiring toward that prominence. Crucial to our model is the idea that the leader must be able to communicate certain relevant traits or abilities or tendencies to his fellow group members. The individual who is most effective in such communication will be the one who will emerge as the leader.

According to the components of our model of the leader as a communicator, the emergent leader is an individual who, in his interaction with others, demonstrates (1) a positive attitude toward the members and the task, (2) motives that are not selfish, (3) values that are shared by the members, (4) a relatively high degree of involvement in the project, (5) open-mindedness or low dogmatism in dealing with the suggestions of the members of the group, (6) a sufficiently high degree of self-esteem to give him confidence in his abilities, (7) the ability to persuade or influence others without coercion, (8) an appreciable amount of information about the task and the personal needs of the group, and (9) a manifestation of intelligence sufficient to adjust to whatever changes or novel circumstances that may arise during group interaction.

The keen distinction to be made between sociometrically chosen leaders and emergent leaders is this:

Leadership by sociometric choice is basically centered in "liking" relations, or attraction. The weakness of this type of choice is that in some instances, it's possible to elevate someone to leader just because we happen to like him, only to find out shortly that he may be totally lacking in ability.

Leadership by emergence is largely "behavior-oriented." Group members observe the manifestation of certain behaviors in a particular individual. Those behaviors are perceived to be "useful" or "beneficial" in promoting group goals, and as a consequence that individual is "allowed" to move toward leadership.

In contrast with the appointed leader whom we will discuss shortly, there is an assumption that the emergent leader is often forced into handling his interactions or relationships in the group with caution. The reason seems to be that he is constantly mindful that he owes his position to the goodwill or allowances of his fellow members. Consequently, he feels that he owes favors, and behaves with more deference than the appointed leader who owes no such favors.

Leadership through appointment

Let us see how *appointed* leadership fits into our model. Here is a simple proposition: *Formal designation as a leader, supervisor, boss, manager, chief, etc., will be a source of power.* Notice the term *source of power*. Adapted to our model we could say that an appointed leader *communicates* a possession of power. To a certain extent, we are all prone to give way to the dictates of directives of those who are powerful in our environment.

When a leader occupies his position by appointment, certain formal privileges and duties are attributed to his position, and there are also certain expectations concerning his behavior. It is important to note, however, that while the titular or appointed position of leadership increases the probability that the appointed person will display leadership functions in the group, there may be conditions under which he may not be able to exert effective power or influence over the other members. You may be appointed as leader by an external authority, but if the members do not want you as their leader you may be rather ineffective in your attempt to control or guide the group toward goal achievement. We can see, then, that the matter of leadership and member reaction operates on a two-way street. In short, there must be a willingness to exchange roles and relationships in order to lead effectively.

Leadership traits

Whether we are dealing with the question of emergent leadership or appointed leadership, the qualities or traits that must be communicated are vitally important. Let us identify some of these traits. As we do this, we should bear in mind that no single trait or cluster of traits can be used to predict the successful leader.

Stogdill's (1948) review of leadership research demonstrated that leaders tend to excel nonleaders in the following:

1. Capacity (intelligence, alertness, verbal facility, originality, judgment)
2. Achievement (scholarship, knowledge, athletic accomplishments)
3. Responsibility (dependability, initiative, persistence, aggressiveness, self-confidence, desire to excel)
4. Participation (activity, sociability, cooperation, adaptability, humor)
5. Status (socioeconomic position, popularity) (See Gouran, 1970.)

The fact that Stogdill's review reflects findings that predate 1948 may force us to consider changes in perception of leadership that have developed within the past twenty-five years. How have we changed in our view of leaders?

Geier's study (1967) may have the greatest interest for students of group communication. He identified five *negative* communicable traits associated with failure to achieve effective leadership in small-group discussions: being uninformed, nonparticipation, extreme rigidity, authoritarian or dogmatic behavior, and offensive verbalization.

Such findings notwithstanding, research has pointed to so many traits in an attempt to describe and predict leadership that in effect nothing of appreciable usefulness has resulted. Jennings (1961) concluded that "fifty years of study have failed to produce one personality trait or set of traits that can be used to discriminate between leaders and nonleaders." We suggest that the difficulty in examining traits and successfully identifying them is due to the fact that many of the studies have dealt with the leader as a communicator in total isolation from the people being led (that is, those who receive the communication) and from the situations in which leaders exert influence. Thus our model in chapter 1 is vitally important in that it demonstrates the entire loop or cycle through which leadership influence should travel.

Fiedler (1960) used a novel approach to study the traits that are possessed and communicated by a leader. He disregarded those traits which may help a person to emerge into a leadership position, and chose to concentrate on *one* trait which may be associated with effective leadership once a leader already occupies his position. Fiedler asked leaders to estimate the similarities and dissimilarities between themselves and other group members. Through this estimation he derived a trait which he called *social distance*. He discovered that some leaders were narrow-distance leaders, and others were wide-distance leaders. Let us examine the difference between these two types of leaders.

The narrow-distance leader tends to see his co-workers as being quite similar to himself. He is tolerant of his co-workers, and tends to accept or reject them on bases other than their ability to work with him. He cultivates warm relations with group members, does not emphasize task accomplishment, and is not as effective in promoting productivity.

The wide-distance leader, on the other hand, sees his co-workers as being quite dissimilar from himself. He maintains a considerable aloofness and has a tendency to reject those with whom he cannot work. He emphasizes task accomplishment, and is very conscious of productivity.

Whether we favor the "single trait" or a "cluster of traits" approach, we should always be mindful of the situation in which leadership is exerted. Take Fiedler's single trait—social distance—for example. Could you suggest different situations in which a "wide social distance" leader and a "narrow social distance" leader would be effective?

---

exercise 2

Using the following scheme, try to make some predictions about types of activities and types of followers.

PREDICTION OF EFFECTIVE LEADERSHIP

Wide-Distance Leader

Types of Situations	Types of Followers
e.g., military campaign	e.g., low self-esteem

Narrow-Distance Leader

Types of Situations	Types of Followers
e.g., group discussion	e.g., intelligent peer group

Once we have performed this exercise we should begin to see how crucial both the situation and personality of the followers are when we consider leadership as influence. The same considerations should be applied as we review some of the other discoveries about communicable leadership traits.

Various researchers have found that leadership is related to physical size, physical appearance and dress, self-confidence and self-assurance, sociability and friendliness, will, determination, energy, intelligence, and sensitivity to the feelings, attitudes, and needs of other members of their group. As we review this assortment of traits, we may think of situations in which certain of these traits may not necessarily enhance the effectiveness of leadership.

We have been discovering that it is not easy to pinpoint traits of the leader as a communicator. We are dealing with a complex phenomenon. The best that we can do is to highlight a few traits that seem to stand out in several group situations. What are some "simple" (?) characteristics or traits of effective leaders? We suggest the following:

Intelligence. It may be a common-sense notion that persons appointed, elected, or otherwise perceived as leaders rate higher in intelligence than the rank and file members of the group. Kiessling and Kalish (1961) found a significant positive correlation between leadership ratings and scores made on standardized intelligence tests. Similar results were reported by Showell (1960) who investigated the relation between leadership ratings of army trainees and the scores on the Army General Classification Test.

Adjustment. Leadership roles are probably more demanding than nonleadership roles in the small group. If this is true, it is likely that any manifestations of "neurotic" tendencies may interfere with leader effectiveness. Our perception of an individual's ability to adjust or adapt to a situation may contribute to our willingness to perceive him or her as a leader. Fitzsimmons and Marcuse (1961) studied the relation between adjustment and leadership. They testify to some overlap between the leaders and nonleaders but they also contend that their results indicate that leaders had fewer "neurotic" traits than nonleaders. The researchers concluded that leadership tends to operate most effectively when negative personality traits are absent or minimal.

Deviancy. Leaders tend to deviate from the group norms more than do other members of the group. A number of studies suggest that leaders tend to be freer of group pressures than most people. One study of the behavior of members of cliques showed that the leaders and the members with the lowest status tended to conform the least, whereas middle-status members conformed the most (Harvey and Gonsalvi, 1960). Lindgren (1969) provides the following explanation: "Very probably, because leaders are less neurotic they are able to use their ability to think independently in the service of the group, whereas low-ranking members are not. High-ranking group members, furthermore, are evidently able to express deviant views in ways that are less likely to upset other group members, whereas lower-status members either have not learned this technique or are not interested in doing so."

Perhaps leadership is not so much a function of deviancy as it is a function of knowing *how much* and *when* to deviate. We should bear in mind that leaders tend to be more concerned about group solidarity than most people. Thus, quite possibly, there is a method in their deviating. In one study of small-group interaction, leaders agreed with others more and made more attempts to reduce tension than did other members of the groups (McClintock, 1963). It is possible that leaders are likely to be people who maintain a reasonable balance between maintaining group cohesiveness and expressing nonconforming ideas and behaviors.

Perhaps, the essential difference between the high-ranking member and the low-status member is the high-ranking member's interest in the solidarity of the group. Consequently, they are less likely to compromise that solidarity by participating in the free expression of ideas and feelings that deviate too conspicuously from those of most members of the group.

In summary, what may we say about leadership traits? We may suggest, on the basis of the evidence, that three general categories of personal attributes appear to be related to effective and successful emergent leadership in small groups: qualities of *sensitivity*, *flexibility*, and *responsibility*. An effective leader (1) must be sensitive to the needs and demands confronting his group and each of its members, (2) must be able to guide the group toward meeting demands and also be flexible enough to change his behavior as the needs or demands change from moment to moment, and finally (3) must be able to exert initiative in assuming responsibility for being among the first to display the behaviors necessary for the group's success. Note, however, that the specific traits, abilities, or personality attributes that meet such demands do vary from one group to another or from one type of activity to another.

This concludes our discussion concerning the first component of our model—*the leader as a communicator*. Let us summarize.

1. The basic ways in which a leader "comes into being" as far as the group is concerned: (a) leadership by sociometric choice, (b) leadership by emergence, and (c) leadership by appointment.
2. The traits manifested by leaders in certain circumstances (upon condensing a large but overlapping list of traits): intelligence, adjustment, deviancy, sensitivity, flexibility, and responsibility.

The study of traits or characteristics of individuals in leadership roles falls under a rubric of studies called the Trait Approach to Leadership. In the remainder of this chapter we will go on to discuss several other approaches to the study of leadership. We will begin shortly with the Situational Approach, following which we will talk about the Functional Approach and, finally, the Stylistic Approach. Each approach constitutes a different way of studying leadership. Researchers are in constant argument as to which approach is best. We will let you make your own decision.

Leadership and situational contexts

Some writers define leadership largely as a function of group goals. The leader is the person who takes the initiative and is successful in leading the group to its goals; however, goals differ from situation to situation. Our discussion, in this section, deals with what we may call a *situational approach* to the study of leadership. The discussion in the first section of this chapter involved a *trait approach*. As we study some of the situational determinants of leadership, you would discover that it takes into consideration such attributes as traits and style. We appreciate Bormann's definition of leadership; its underlying assumption is that *leadership is a function of the traits (personality attributes) of the members, the purpose of the group, the internal and external pressures on the group, and the interactions of the members.*

Let us review the factors in the situational component of our communication model in chapter 1. We would observe that when we think about the *situational context* we will have to consider such factors as

> physical characteristics (space, position, location, time, color, etc.)
> group function or task
> group social climate (cooperative versus competitive orientations)
> group structure (size, power, and work structure)
> group norms and roles

All of these factors, when operating, will have an influence on the leader's behavior. The leader should have the capabilities that are relevant to the situation prevailing at a given moment. A person who has a great ability for climbing mountains would stand a better chance of being chosen leader for an expedition up Mt. McKinley than would a person without such an ability. But what would you be willing to bet concerning his chance of being selected as leader of the Student Union Fund Raising Committee? It is safe to say that you would hedge your bet. Now that we understand the predicament, let us be armed with this useful axiom: *effectiveness is relative to abilities and situations.*

The most popular researcher of the so-called situational school is Fred Fiedler. He reports that successful leadership is the result of individuals in key positions using the particular style called for by the situation and the degree of psychological distance between them and other group members. Recall that we talked about "social distance" as a personality attribute earlier in the chapter.

Let us cite an example of the kinds of adaptability of styles in different situations.

First of all, in cases where the rules of the functioning group called for conformity in decision making, it was found that a highly dominant person was almost certain to emerge as leader. Second, where a more open, nonconforming procedure was followed in decision making, the high dominants were not nearly as likely to monopolize leadership roles.

Fiedler's approach—*the situational determinants of leadership* —attempts to specify those conditions under which one leadership style or another would be instrumental in increasing group productivity. The approach has also introduced the important concept of "situational favorableness"—that is, the extent to which the situation provides the leader with influence. Again, it becomes a concern for the leader to size up the situation in order to make a guess as to how much influence he would have in the particular situation. Fiedler also suggests that leadership style is determined by the needs that the individual seeks to satisfy in the leadership situation. This need fulfillment will become clearer when we discuss *social-emotional* and *task-facilitating* roles later in the chapter.

Also, whenever we talk about leadership as a response to situations, we should bear in mind the possibility that an element of threat may prevail in a given situation. When threat increases in a group, a less favorable leadership situation would tend to emerge. In such a circumstance, a knowledge of the threat should encourage a flexibility of style in the leader. "Good" or "effective" leaders are those who are able to cope with tense or critical situations.

In summary, we could say that leadership performance depends as much upon the situation as it does upon the leader's own attributes. Usually, it is not wise to speak of an effective leader or an ineffective leader; rather it is better to speak of a leader who is effective in one situation and may be ineffective in another. To the extent that we are concerned about leadership effectiveness, and to the extent that we may feel the need to educate or train ourselves or others for leadership roles, we should acquire the skills for creating "good" communication environments in which leaders can perform well.

When we talk of creating "good" communication environments, we bring into focus the needs of followers. The assumption is that followers have basic needs, and that they tend to follow those leaders who best help them to satisfy those needs. For example, the conspicuous "A" student in a group of students cramming for an exam may emerge as a group leader because he can be the most beneficial to the others in preparing for the test.

In the case of the conspicuous "A" student, we see a leader emerging on the basis of the function he can perform in the group. Many writers and researchers have studied the relation between group functions and group leadership. These studies have been gathered largely under the title of what is called the *functional approach to leadership*.

The functional approach to leadership deals with the identification of group functions that promote the fulfillment of the objectives, goals, or needs of the group. One theorist argues that any group member exerts leadership if the properties of the group are modified or changed by his presence. Leadership acts are those behaviors which perform these changes. We will examine some of the findings of the functional approach as we look at leadership in situational contexts.

The leader who is mindful of function is not free to determine the group's actions at will but is limited to a great extent by its needs and norms. He must be aware of those needs, norms, and behavior patterns of his group in order to structure the activities and interactions in such a way that the needs of the group are satisfied. As yet the literature on leadership has not been able to classify a set of functions that are specifically related to leadership. We know what some group functions are, but we do not know the extent to which we can correctly label those functions as being specifically tied to leadership functions.

Krech and Crutchfield (1948, pp. 417–22) proposed a list of fourteen functions that a leader may perform. These functions classify a leader as an executive, planner, policymaker, expert, external group representative, controller of internal relationships, purveyor of rewards and punishments, arbitrator, exemplar, group symbol, surrogate for individual responsibility, ideologist, father figure, or scapegoat.

This list is quite impressive, but it leaves a string of questions in its wake. What determines the emergence of any of these fourteen functions in the group? What determines which of the members will perform any of these fourteen functions? And what are the consequences stemming from the performance of these functions under different conditions in the group? Are there situations in which a "father figure" type of leader would fail miserably?

Answers to such questions are important! Perhaps we may be guided by what seems to be two important principles that sum up the information on leadership functions. The first is that any member of a group may be a leader in the sense that he may take actions that serve group functions. The second principle is that a given function may be served by many different behaviors. In short, the leadership function may be served by a variety of actions taken by a variety of people.

A moment ago, as we talked about functions, we seemed to be suggesting that leadership is some sort of "scatter-prone" phenomenon. You may be influential in a group at one time because of environmental demands or certain personal characteristics, or another person may be influential in the same group at another time because of different demands or personal characteristics. This suggests that we may be suited for different *roles*.

These roles may change as we move from one group to another or from one task to another. There is a rather economical system under which we may study roles as a factor in leadership.

Roles

Some leaders have a knack for controlling and dispelling interpersonal squabbles in small groups; others have a knack for forcing the group to accomplish its task. This difference in ability is crucial, and has led researchers such as Robert Bales to conclude that there may be two separate "specialists" among leaders of small groups—one, a task-environmental leader; the other, an interpersonal leader. Stated another way, we could say that one type of leader performs *task-related* functions, and another type performs *group-maintenance* functions. According to Bales, the interpersonal leader, or group-maintenance specialist, or social-specialist (they are all the same!) occupies a role that enables him to perform activities that contribute to the organization and harmony of the group. The task-environmental leader, or group-maintenance or task-specialist, performs activities that contribute more directly to the group's successful attainment of its collective aims and objectives.

We should realize, however, that several of the things that group members must do to achieve rewards from the task-environment tend to create frustration, and since the leader is delegated the responsibility for alloting rewards, punishment, praise, blame, etc., the task specialist will be blamed for the frictions, discontent, conflict, and misunderstandings that ensue. The social-emotional specialist concerns himself mainly with giving approval and improving member interaction, and he (more than does the task-specialist), tends to gain the liking of the other group members.

It would seem, then, that if a choice were available, then one should choose the role of social-emotional specialist. Let us be aware of the pitfalls. An excessive desire to be liked can become an interpersonal obstacle in itself. Remember the famous words of baseball's Leo Durocher: "Nice guys finish last." This desire to be liked by group members has been termed, in some instances, Individual Prominence and Achievement Behavior. This kind of behavior is directed toward the individual's own private goals; it does not help the group toward the common goal, and actually hinders group progress.

We should, perhaps, make the point clearer. We are in agreement that rewards must be given in promoting group activity, but the social-emotional specialist who obtains friendship purely on the basis of handing out rewards and candy-coated comments may unwittingly create a disintegration of the group around him.

Two roles somewhat similar to those just discussed have been identified in industrial settings. They are *consideration* roles and *structure-initiating* roles. Consideration roles include behavior indicating mutual trust, respect, and a certain warmth and rapport between the supervisor and his group. This does not mean that this dimension reflects a superficial pat-on-the-back, first-name-calling kind of human-relations behavior. This dimension appears to emphasize a deeper concern for group members' needs and includes such behavior as allowing subordinates more participation in decision making and encouraging more two-way communication. Structure roles include behavior in which the supervisor organizes and defines group activities and his relation to the group. Thus he defines the role he expects each member to assume, assigns tasks, plans ahead, establishes ways of getting things done and pushes for production. This dimension seems to emphasize overt attempts to achieve organizational goals.

Since the dimensions are independent, a supervisor may score high on both dimensions, low on both, or high on one and low on the other.... Production supervisors rated high on "proficiency" by plant management turned out to have leadership patterns high in Structure and low in Consideration....On the other hand, this same pattern of high Structure and low Consideration was found to be related to high labor turnover, union grievances, worker absences and accidents, and low worker satisfaction. (Bales, 1953)

A simple maxim emerges in response to the question of what kinds of roles we should utilize when confronted with group demands. There is wisdom in deciding in which area to concentrate our efforts, and that decision depends on the relative importance of good group relations versus a good group product.

As we study small-group communication today, leadership is viewed more in terms of the set of ideas that we have just developed—that is, it is viewed more as a particular kind of role than as a simple manifestation of personal qualities. However, there is some evidence that there are certain attributes of personality which propel certain individuals into assuming roles of leadership consistently in the many groups to which they belong. In other words, in spite of varying situations, certain people tend to emerge as leaders.

Aside from the consideration that a leader may *emerge* in a group on the basis of certain attributions of skills, is it possible that the mere physical or ecological features of the surroundings (seating arrangement, shape of table, etc.) may be an important factor in the emergency pattern? We think so.

Physical determinants of leadership emergence

One fundamental behavior seems to be that leaders tend to select the head position at a rectangular table, and that other people tend to arrange themselves so that they could see the leader. Strodtbeck and Hook (1961) recorded the seating arrangement in experimental jury sessions in Chicago. The jury room contained a rectangular table with one chair at the head and the foot and five chairs on either side. The jurors' first task was to select a foreman, and results showed that there was a recurring tendency for the person seated at one of the head positions to be elected foreman. But there was another remarkable finding! It was discovered that people do not choose seats randomly. People from higher socioeconomic classes selected head chairs more often than members of lower socioeconomic classes. Moreover, people occupying these head positions participated more in the discussions than people occupying the side positions.

Leavitt (1961) worked with other ecological formations in order to determine leadership emergence (see figure 2). Some networks consisted of wheels where messages went around the periphery, wheels where all the messages had to come to the center hub, as well as Y-shaped and incomplete circle arrangements. After

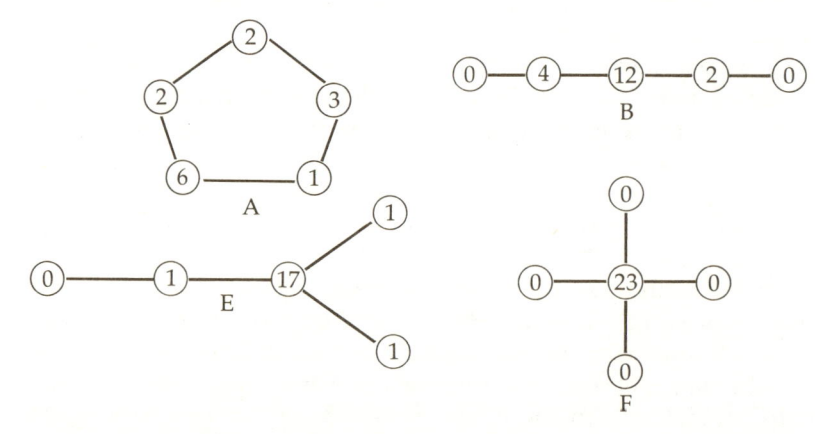

Figure 2. Emergence of recognized leaders in different communication patterns. The number at each position shows the total number of group members who recognized the individual in that position as the leader (Leavitt's data).

the sessions the experimenter asked each group whether one member had been a leader. Notice from figure 2 that about half of the group in the circular arrangements named someone as a leader, and that he was perceived among all positions in the circle. You will see, also, that 92 percent of the groups utilized in the study named leaders in the wheel arrangements, and this designated leader was invariably the person at the hub. Note also the centrally situated determinant of leadership designation in the Y and in the broken circle or line arrangements. We see, then, that leadership may be a function of maintaining a high degree of visibility or centrality in a group. This visibility or centrality places the leader in the forefront of communication with other members.

Leadership and message factors

In this section, we shall discuss effective leadership in terms of the messages that the leader transmits to the members of the group. Recall, from our communication model in chapter 1, that when we speak of "message" we refer to such factors as

verbal response (quantity, frequency, direction)
nonverbal response (physical, vocal)
content (argument, evidence, type of appeal)
method (organization, style)

Recall also the suggestion that perhaps 65 percent to 75 percent of the meanings conveyed in any message are conveyed through nonverbal means. This idea that most meaning is conveyed nonverbally rests on estimates by Birdwhistell (1970) and Mehrabian (1971). If this is true, it would follow that the influence of the leader may be derived more from what he does than from what he says.

Group members tend to respond favorably to those behaviors in a leader which demonstrate a "genuine" concern for the group, a willingness to make sacrifices in the interest of the members, and an ability to build cohesiveness in the group. Those behaviors are generally evident in his conduct and in his conversations with group members concerning the task and their relationship to the task. It may seem difficult to teach a person how to send nonverbal messages effectively. Yet an effort should be made. Since nonverbal messages may be strong indicators of inner feelings, the first task should be to develop in ourselves a feeling of goodwill toward group members. Nonverbal behaviors are dead giveaways; if we have a good attitude toward the task and members, the members may perceive that attitude through our behavior.

Let us talk, now, about verbal messages. Should we as leaders offer opinions, information, and evaluations to the group? Can power be retained if we, as leaders, refuse to participate more actively than others? Do we have to exercise persuasive abilities or good speaking skills? The answers to these questions are straightforward. A leader has a commitment to his group which demands that he occupy a decisive role if functions are to be fulfilled. The leader does initiate more frequent communication and is generally the most active member of the group.

A leader should offer conclusions, opinions, and regulate the affairs of the group. A leader who performs these activities creates greater satisfaction among members; they feel that their leader is an integral part of the group, and not just a regulator of group process. Moreover, if we, as leaders, do not fulfill these activities, such as "providing orientations toward, evaluations of, and suggestions about the situation when these are demanded by group members, other members will assume these tasks and remove our power" (Burke, 1966, p. 237).

Bormann (1969, p. 254) discusses some of these "messages" which leaders should or should not transmit. He says:

"People who became leaders had an interest in the group's work and understood it.... They did not suggest that the group's work was trivial or that its goals were unimportant. Nor did they suggest that they personally found the group's work dull and routine. When they spoke about matters of substance relating to the task, they demonstrated a firm understanding of the subject.... They raise the status of other group members whenever possible. They indicate by word and actions that the other person is important, likeable, and admirable. They give compliments and rewards."

We are stressing here that the leader must assume a distinctive role. This role will be manifested by his number of contributions, his ability to exhibit decisiveness and self-confidence, his ability to deviate from group norms without blatancy and consequently without retribution, and by his ability to resist power attempts from other members.

As far as the leader's speaking style or technique is concerned, we would suggest that such a skill is not as important as the quality of the information that he is able to deliver in the group situations. Of course, the leader may often have to resort to persuading members of his group, and styles of delivery may be crucial, but we feel that his persuasiveness and success in leading others will be derived more from his nonverbal behavior than from what he actually says in order to bring about compliance with his suggestions, demands, or directives. A rigid preoccupation with an agenda, or a particular style will deprive a leader of flexibility in responding to the various behavioral shifts in the group. In some instances, this inflexibility may tend to decrease the achievement of our group. The effect of messages notwithstanding, we should note that the behaviors that occur in a group may be a result of the *interaction* between the leader and the members. Interaction may hinder or facilitate the impact of messages. Let us study the nature of interaction in this next section.

Leadership and interaction with group members

Interaction, according to the communication model in chapter 1, deals with the dynamics of communication, the processes that result from the give-and-take between members of a group. The study of *interaction* in the small group deals with the processes that influence such factors as

> cohesiveness and conformity (identification with the group, attraction and liking, group pressure, similarity of opinion, satisfaction)
> conflict
> problem solving (networks, patterns of problem solving, etc.)

Let us examine, in this section, the manner in which leadership affects or is affected by interaction among members of the small group.

Bass (1960) points out that leadership is a kind of interaction between people. Any group member's attempt to change the behavior (including attitudes, values, and feelings) of one or more members of a group constitutes an attempt at leadership. But we should note that the mere attempt is not sufficient; the degree to which leadership has indeed taken place is indicated by the extent to which the intended change has taken place. Since, as we suggested in the preceding section, the major influence of a leader's behavior is derived from his nonverbal behavior, we should look at one particular feature which consists of nonverbal behavior and relatively less verbal behavior. The feature that involves such components is the *style of leadership*. Style is so vitally important to the interaction between leaders and members that many studies have been conducted in order to examine its various aspects. These studies constitute what is called a *stylistic approach to leadership*.

The study of the effects of style on the interaction between group members was given a boost by the classic works started by Lewin, Lippitt, and White (1939) and Lippitt and White (1943). These studies focused on what leaders *do* rather than on their personal characteristics. Even a casual observation of leaders at work reveals great differences in style. And if we were to observe more closely, we would notice that different styles tend to influence different kinds of interaction between members. Some leaders constantly give orders, demand obedience, and make all decisions without regard to the opinion of others. Some leaders, by contrast, are considerate, solicit the cooperation of others, and ask for opinion before making decisions. Three frequently mentioned leadership styles are

1. autocratic, authoritarian, or supervisory
2. democratic, consultive, or participatory
3. laissez-faire or free-reign

Briefly, the *autocratic* leader tends to gain obedience from his group by the use of formal authority, rewards, and punishment. He dictates policy and makes all decisions. The *democratic* leader draws ideas and suggestions from his followers and encourages them to participate in things that concern them. In some instances, he may let the group determine policy; in others, he may ask for their advice but makes the final decision himself. The *laissez-faire* or *free-reign* leader plays down his role in the group's activities and acts primarily to provide information, materials, and facilities for the group in accomplishing its objectives. He exercises a minimum of control. Figure 3 uses a graph to demonstrate how each of these three styles of leadership proceeds both verbally and nonverbally. As we look further into the work conducted by Lewin, Lippitt, and White (see White and Lippitt, 1960), we would observe how these styles affect the interaction.

Lewin, Lippitt, and White studied four matched groups of ten-year-old boys as they worked successively under autocratic, democratic, and laissez-faire styles of adult leadership. The groups engaged in activities such as making paper masks. The results, graphically portrayed in figures 4 and 5, demonstrate different patterns of interaction as a function of leadership style. Let us look at some of the more important results in these figures, which represent, respectively, the boys' behavior toward their leader and toward each other.

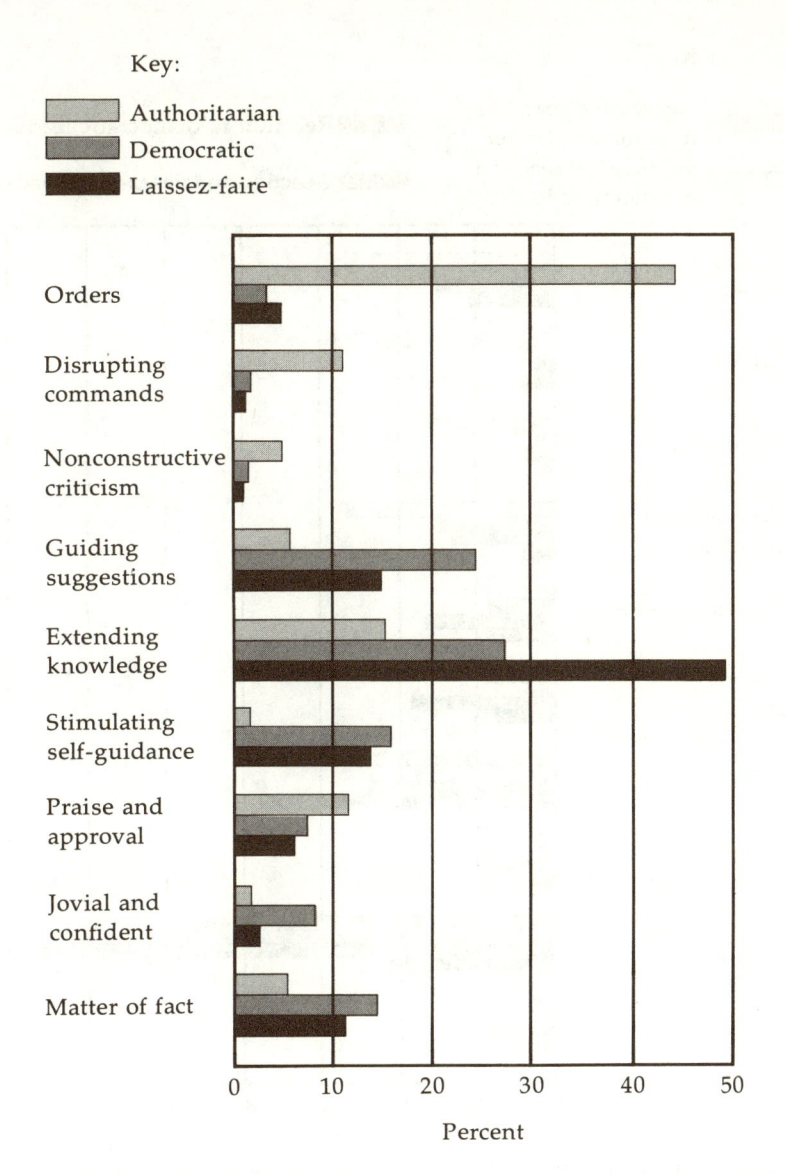

Figure 3. Comparison of behavior of average autocratic, democratic, and laissez-faire leaders. (From *Autocracy and Democracy: An Experimental Inquiry*, by Ralph K. White and Ronald Lippitt, p. 32. New York: Harper & Row, 1960.)

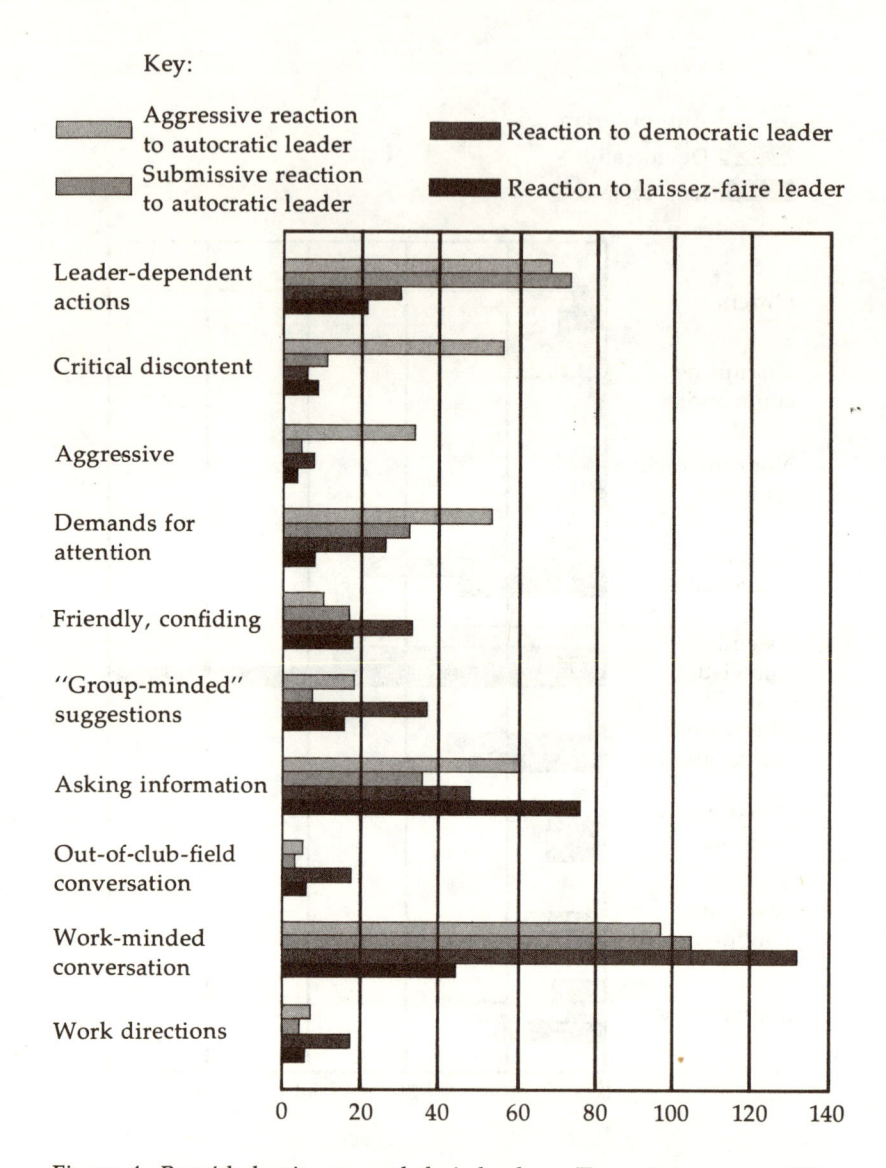

Figure 4. Boys' behavior toward their leaders. (From *Autocracy and Democracy: An Experimental Inquiry*, by Ralph K. White and Ronald Lippitt, p. 85. New York: Harper & Row, 1960.)

Key:

▬ Aggressive reaction to autocracy   ▬ Democratic

▬ Submissive reaction to autocracy   ▬ Laissez-faire

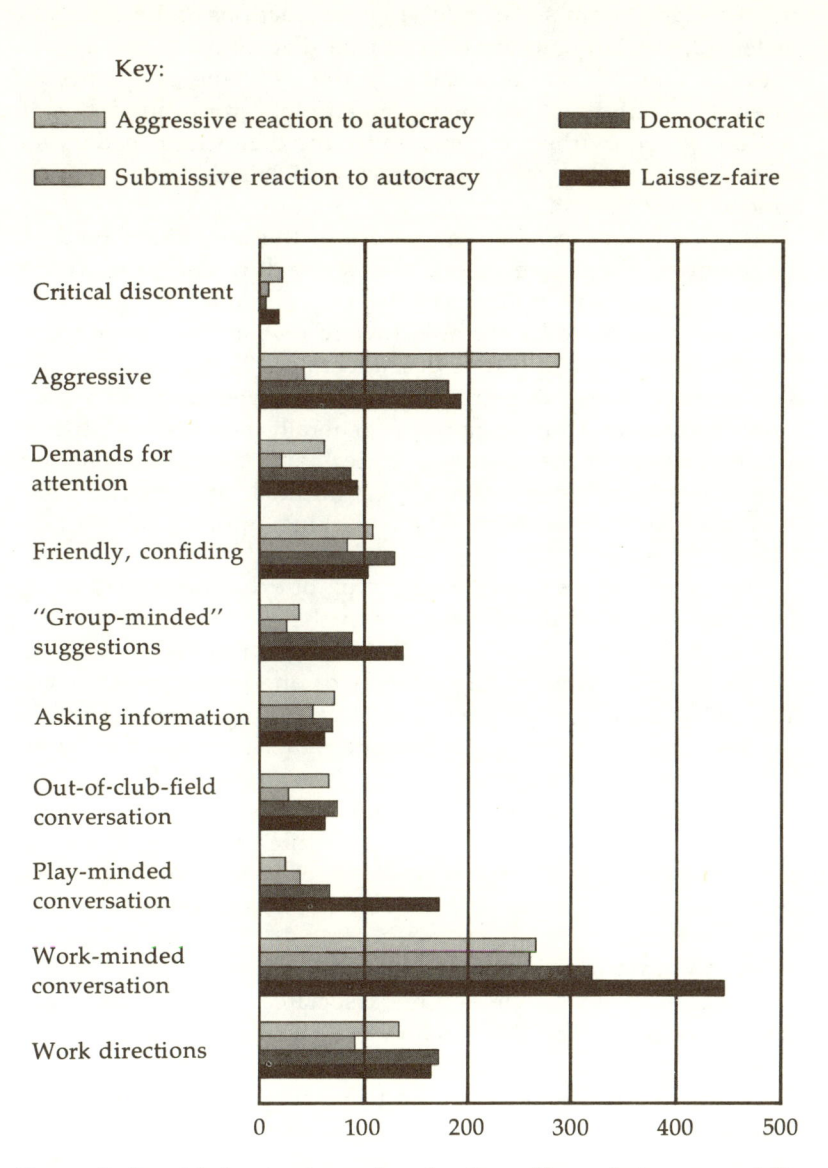

Figure 5. Boys' behavior toward each other. (From *Autocracy and Democracy: An Experimental Inquiry*, by Ralph K. White and Ronald Lippitt, p. 86. New York: Harper & Row, 1960.)

The chief differences to be noted in figure 4 are (1) the large number of leader-dependent actions in terms of both aggressive or defiant and submissive or "giving in" reactions to the autocratic leader; (2) the large amounts of critical discontent in the aggressive reaction to the autocratic leader; (3) the frequency of "friendly, confiding" conversation and of group-minded suggestions given by the members under the democratic leader; and (4) the contrast between democracy and laissez-faire in work-minded conversation.

In figure 5, you can see the nature of the interaction between the members themselves. Here, too, some differences are worthy of notice. You will notice: (1) the large amount of aggressive behavior manifested by the boys toward one another when working under an autocratic style of leadership; (2) the small amount of attention demands, group-minded suggestions, and play-minded remarks (this suggests a generally submissive attitude in the presence of the autocratic leader); and (3) the large amount of group-minded suggestions, play-minded conversation, and work-minded conversation when working under a laissez-faire style of leadership.

The reports of the observers pointed out that hostility and aggression were significantly greater in the autocratic than in the democratic groups. There was more scapegoating in the autocratic groups than in either of the other two; one group member was frequently made the target of hostility and aggression until he left the group, and shortly thereafter another boy would fall prey. Nineteen of twenty boys liked the democratic leader better than the autocratic leader, and seven of ten liked the laissez-faire leader better than the autocratic leader. And while there was no significant difference in the number of paper masks produced, the judges felt that those made by the democratic groups were qualitatively superior.

Several other researchers have discovered behaviors similar to those described by Lewin and his associates. Preston and Heintz (1949) used assigned leaders who were asked to play either a participatory or a supervisory role. (The role playing was crucial.) The participatory leader was told to be sure that each name was considered, to encourage participation in the discussion by all members, to discourage chance methods of deciding doubtful cases, and to complete the work in half an hour. The supervisory leaders were instructed not to participate in the discussion and to limit their responsibility to ensuring that the work was done in the stipulated amount of time.

Results showed that participatory leadership was more effective in changing attitudes than was supervisory leadership. It was also significant that participatory group members were better satisfied with the group's ranking, found the task more interesting and worthwhile, and rated their group discussions as more friendly and enjoyable than did members of supervisory groups.

Shaw (1955) also examined the effects of authoritarian and nonauthoritarian leadership in a laboratory setting. Groups of four college males were assembled and assigned instructed leaders who played either an authoritarian or a nonauthoritarian leadership role.

The authoritarian leader was asked to give orders, to accept no suggestions without criticizing them, and to make the group know that he was the boss of the group. The nonauthoritarian leader, on the other hand, was instructed to encourage suggestions, make requests instead of issuing orders, and to ensure that the group functioned as democratically as possible. Each group was given the task of solving three arithmetic problems by means of written communication.

The results demonstrated that the authoritarian groups made fewer errors, required fewer messages for problem solution, and required less time than did the nonauthoritarian groups. However, the ratings of satisfaction with the group were higher in the nonauthoritarian groups.

While studying these different effects, researchers stumbled upon one interesting bit of information. Apparently, it is much easier to be a good autocratic leader than a good democratic leader. The study by Shaw (1955) pointed up the fact that the best group and the worst group had democratic leaders; whereas autocratic groups remained steady or constant in interaction and productivity. Shaw submits the following advice: "It is easy to issue orders but difficult to utilize effectively the abilities of group members. If a leader doubts his ability to be an effective democratic leader, then he probably is well advised to play the autocratic role." (Shaw, 1971, p. 274)

Gouran (1970) reports that the democratic style proved to be superior to other styles in a number of respects, including the level of group cohesiveness developed, and the amount of independent behavior exhibited by the subjects. Berkowitz (1958) discovered that groups having more permissive leaders developed higher levels of cohesiveness than groups with less permissive leadership. Hare (1953) reported finding participatory leadership superior to supervisory leadership in producing opinion change. And Coch and French (1948) observed that employee participation in some decision-making activities in the Harwood Manufacturing Corporation tended to reduce resistance to change in working conditions.

Let us put all these observations into some kind of proper perspective. Is the democratic style basically superior to the autocratic style? Not necessarily. What we do know is that several factors may influence the style of leadership an individual chooses. His own personality and needs, as well as the particular circumstances under which he operates, may *force* him to adopt a particular style. The behavior of the other members of the group, or even the communication patterns or habits of the members, may influence the emergence of a particular style.

Here are some valuable pointers. We know that in communication networks that are highly centralized—that is, where information is channeled into one single position within the group, leadership tends to be more autocratic. Where the communication networks are more open and evenly distributed throughout the group, leadership tends to be more democratic.

Also, the style of leadership displayed tends to become more autocratic and authoritarian as the size of the group increases. Can you make some guesses as to why this change may occur? Additionally, a crisis may occur, the removal of which may depend on concerted group action, and the tension may produce a demand for a very quick adjustment in the functioning of the group. In such a circumstance, the autocratic or authoritarian style of leadership may be best suited.

The following exercise may be useful in summarizing your understanding of the effect of leadership on member interaction. Let us imagine the group situations listed. What style of leadership would be most effective in each situation in creating cohesiveness and increasing productivity or good results in each group. Remember that we are dealing with autocratic, democratic, and laissez-faire styles of leadership. Please indicate your choice in the blank space at the right.

---

exercise 3

PREDICTIONS OF EFFECTIVE STYLES OF LEADERSHIP
FOR DIFFERENT GROUP SITUATIONS

Group Situations	Type of Leadership Style
1. An evacuation crew at a tunnel disaster.	1. _____
2. A hearing committee concerned with disciplining a member of a group.	2. _____
3. A study group preparing for a final exam.	3. _____
4. A group of engineers, all of equal skill and rank, working on a project.	4. _____
5. A military commander and his crew at a fire base.	5. _____
6. An assigned discussion in your classroom among classmates.	6. _____
7. A new group to which you have been assigned as leader.	7. _____
8. A quarterback planning a play with second down and three to go.	8. _____

We are reasonably sure that you are prepared to justify the choices you have made in these eight situations. As you consider each situation, you would say, perhaps, that the most effective style depends on the leader himself, the followers, and the situation. It would also depend on the leader's own assumptions, feelings, and perceptions concerning the people around him. If he thinks of himself as being dominant, he may feel comfortable using an authoritarian style; if he thinks of himself as merely a facilitator, he may be more comfortable using a laissez-faire style.

But what about the nature of the task? What influence does this have on the type of leadership? Suppose you were the captain of a ship about to be zapped by a torpedo. It is highly unlikely that you would consult with your subordinates or "call a meeting" to decide on the course of action to be taken. On the other hand, if you were in charge of a group of creative scientists in some type of aerospace industry, chances are that you would use a laissez-faire approach regardless of how authoritarian you may tend to be. What we are really saying is that the good leader uses his head. He sizes up the situation, the task, and the personnel, and behaves in a manner that will enhance the accomplishment of the group's objective.

We have come to the end of our discussion on leadership as a factor within the framework of a group communication model. We have studied the leader in terms of his emergence through the demonstration of certain communicable traits; the leader as he is affected in varying situational contexts; the leader and the messages he transmits to group members; and the leader as an influence on the interaction among members in the group. The chapter finishes with a response to the question that is generally asked by students of small-group communication—particularly those who are interested in leadership. Can a person be *trained* to be a leader? Let us find out.

This chapter suggests that leadership may be best conceived as an interpersonal phenomenon of role relationships within a group, rather than as a trait in an individual. We also suggest that leadership may be defined as the frequency with which an individual in the group can be identified as one who influences or directs the behaviors of others within the group.

The manner in which leadership is performed tends to vary considerably. The leader's personal attributes, values, and motives, as well as the circumstance in which he operates, all go together to influence the actions he takes to modify the behavior of others.

There is some evidence to support the view that an effective leader is (a) sensitive to the needs and demands of the group and each of its members, (b) able and flexible in adapting his behavior to satisfy those needs, and (c) responsible enough to initiate new actions and suggestions when needed. While we do not wish the following suggestion to be exaggerated, it would appear that leadership may be strengthened and stabilized if the leader is able to maintain a certain amount of "social distance" between himself and his followers.

ADDITIONAL READINGS

Bormann, E. G. *Discussion and Group Methods: Theory and Practice* (New York: Harper & Row, 1969). Chapter 10 discusses some of the patterns of interaction that result in the emergence of a leader.

Cartwright, D., and Zander, A. *Group Dynamics: Research and Theory*. (New York: McGraw-Hill, 1968). Part 5 on "Leadership and Performance of Group Functions" presents seven studies involving the question of leadership (see pages 301–98). Studies 25 and 28 present excellent coverage of styles of leadership, and situational determinants of leadership, respectively.

Collins, B., and Guetzkow, H. *A Social Psychology of Group Processes for Decision-Making* (New York: Wiley, 1964). See Chapter 11 for an explanation of leadership traits and the differentiation of leadership roles.

Fiedler, F. *A Theory of Leadership Effectiveness* (New York: McGraw-Hill, 1967). Chapter 3 emphasizes methods for measuring leadership style. Chapter 15, particularly pages 247–55, discusses fundamental aspects of leadership training.

Shaw, M. *Group Dynamics: The Psychology of Small Group Behavior* (New York: McGraw-Hill, 1971). See pages 267–87 for a review of approaches to definitions of leadership, leadership styles, and a listing of twenty-four hypotheses concerning group structure and member status.

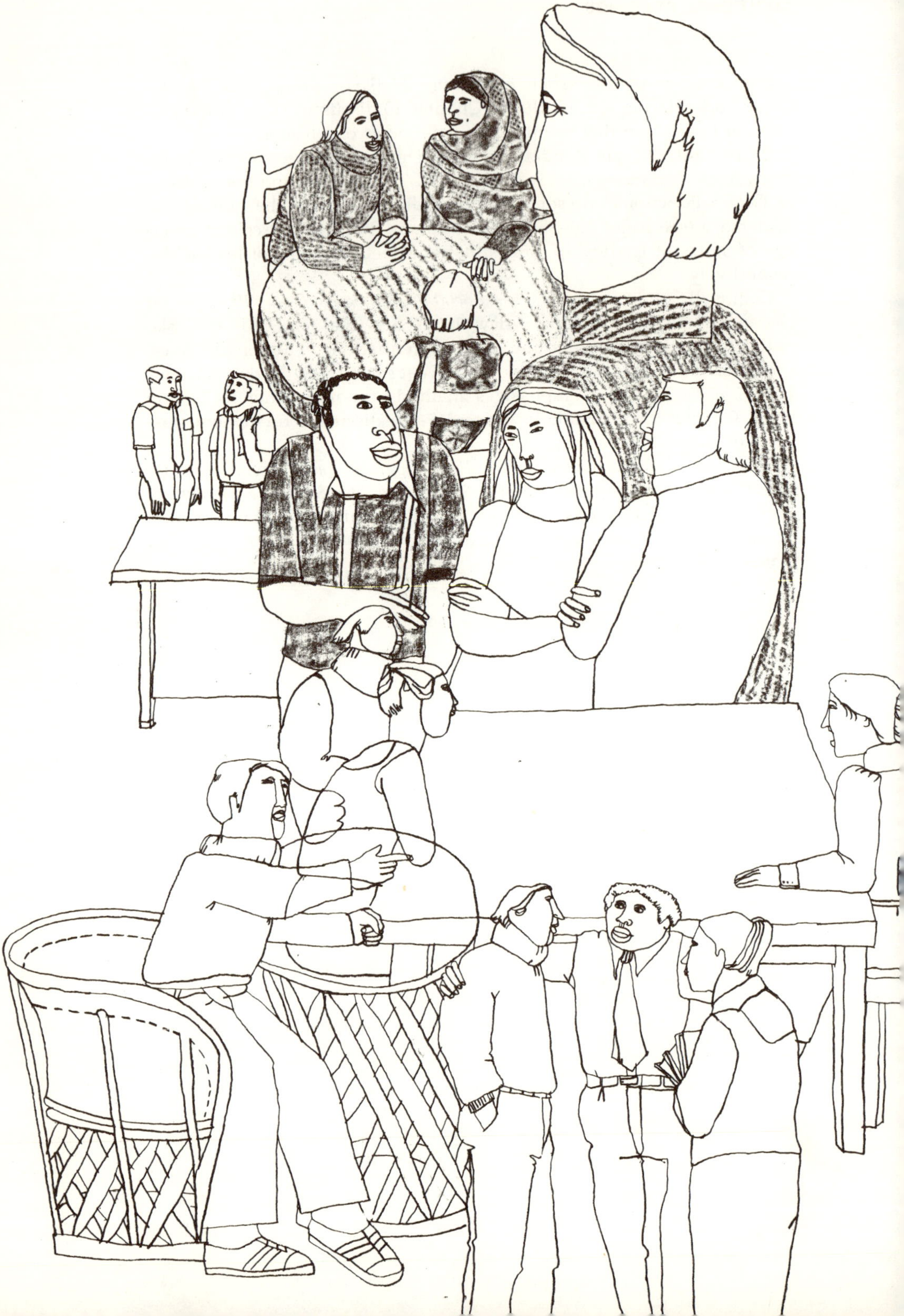

Controlling the Group-Communication Process

10. Methods of Discussion

PREVIEW

What is group discussion?
    Group discussion is a special form of group communication. It is defined as two or more individuals in face-to-face interaction for the purpose of information sharing, problem solving, and/or self-maintenance.

What are methods of discussion?
    A discussion method is a preselected procedure for conducting a group discussion.
    Six methods of discussion are examined:
        panel
        round table
        symposium-forum
        dialogue
        colloquy
        lecture-forum

We now realize that group communication is a complex process involving interrelations between communicators, messages, tasks, and situations. Earlier we attempted to describe communication occurring in small groups at one specific time and in groups meeting over a period of time. We noted then that communication in a group is specific to the group's membership, task, messages transmitted, and situation. Because of these complex interactions, it is difficult to predict the exact nature of the group process.

In the preceding chapters we have found that knowledge of how a group operates is important. Group members must understand the role of communicators, the type of interaction occurring in the group, and the demands of the situation. If we cannot predict how the group will operate, we cannot be certain that our group will accomplish its goal. To assure ourselves that our group will meet its goal, we must at times apply procedures that will control the operation of our group; that is, we should control how communicators will interact. This control will help us estimate what communicators will say, estimate how they will say it, and estimate or evaluate the situation in which the group operates.

In the next two chapters we shall deal with a number of methods and techniques for modifying, either directly or indirectly, the elements of our group process model. These methods or techniques, as we shall see, operate as constraints upon the communicator, his message, the situation, and group member interaction. Some procedures will influence one element of our model more than another; for example, brainstorming has its greatest effect upon the interaction between communicators. However, effecting a change in one component of our model will effect a change in all other elements to some extent. Using these controlling agents, we can modify or structure the group situation to conform to our group needs and thus, hopefully, facilitate a degree of group effectiveness.

Here in chapter 10 we will examine different methods or procedures for conducting a group discussion. We will first investigate the relation between group communication and group discussion. We will answer the question Are group discussion and group communication the same phenomenon? A second question we will answer is, What are the responsibilities of a group discussion participant? In the second section, we will investigate six discussion methods. Each method will be examined in respect to the following: its purpose; the format for group member communication; the situational context for using the method; the advantages and disadvantages of a particular method; and the basic procedures for implementing the method during a group discussion. Let us begin by discovering what is meant by the term *group discussion*.

---

communication diary

Return to your group communication diary.

1. *How many times do you ask others to solve your problems?*
2. *How many times do you ask others for information pertaining to:*

    school _____

    friends _____

    work _____

    family _____

3. *How many times do friends ask your assistance in solving a problem or in gathering information for some specific task?*
4. *Can you identify any consistent pattern of communication occurring when you talk with a group of friends?*

We can use the results of this exercise in the first section of this chapter.

What is group discussion?

Imagine the following situations:

SITUATION 1

The student senate proposes that students be given more representation on faculty committees. The president of the senate contacts the dean of students to inform him of the proposal. The dean of students asks for an informal meeting wth three student representatives. The four meet in the corner of the Student Union over a cup of coffee and discuss the problem of how to present the students' ideas at a meeting of the faculty committee on committees. One student suggests that each present a separate area of the proposal. The other students and the dean unanimously agree.

SITUATION 2

A meeting is held that afternoon by the faculty. Several faculty members are present when the students arrive. With faculty sitting in front and facing the students, a student takes the floor and explains the overall proposal. The other two students follow with separate reports on the desirability and implementation of the proposal. Following the presentation, the students are questioned by the faculty committee. The committee chairman takes the floor, summarizes the comments of students and faculty members, and appoints a subcommittee to study the students' proposal.

SITUATION 3

The following day the student senate reconvenes. The senate representatives at the faculty committee discuss the events of the previous day. Several senators pose questions and offer comments concerning the next step to be taken.

All three situations are examples of group discussion. Notice the similarities in each situation. First, all three situations had two or more individuals talking on a specific topic. Second, group members in each situation were involved in face-to-face interaction. Third, the primary modes of communication were verbal and nonverbal communication. And, fourth, each discussion situation had a specific purpose or goal.

We can define *group discussion* as a *process involving two or more individuals in face-to-face interaction for the purpose of information sharing, problem solving, or self-maintenance*. From this definition we can see that group discussion is a form of group communication.

Discussion involves face-to-face interaction. Each group member must see and hear the other. The members adapt and modify their behavior in response to each other's behavior. This is communicative interaction between group members. This interaction can be informal and conversational, as is common at parties when friends stand around talking, or it can be very formal and follow a specifically designed format, as in the case of the television program "Meet the Press." Ideally each member participates by making contributions which assist the group in reaching its goal. Thus cooperation between group members is crucial. We do not mean to suggest that conflict must be eliminated from a group discussion. The differences and disagreements that arise during a discussion are valuable assets in the group process. All members, however, must work toward producing a product that will meet the needs of the group.

In a discussion all members of the group communicate with each other directly. While it is possible to carry on a discussion through writing, the *major modes* of interaction are oral-verbal and nonverbal messages. We interact principally by talking with other group members, and our facial expressions, posture, gestures, and tone of voice all affect the discussion process. These nonverbal messages are *very* important.

Group discussion has a specific purpose or goal: information sharing, problem solving, or self-maintenance. Do not assume, however, that these goals are mutually exclusive. In fact, no problem-solving discussion can be carried on without the sharing of information by group members. A group discussion concerning itself with self-maintenance must be involved with gathering information concerning individual and group problems and solving problems created by personality differences in the group.

This purpose or goal must be apparent to all members. A committee may meet to solve a concrete problem, such as how to raise money for charity; a study group, which uses discussion for information sharing, may come together to prepare for a final exam. The crucial element in group discussion is that a common group goal or task is recognized by all group members.

In summary, group discussion has four characteristics: two or more people, interacting in face-to-face situations, verbal and nonverbal communication, and a commonly recognized group purpose or goal. We should recognize that these are also characteristics of group communication. Group communication and group discussion are synonymous. While the distinction is not significant, some teachers of speech communication have distinguished between the two concepts. They suggest that only serious and systematic talk about a clearly specified topic can be considered group discussion; the term connotes something more than a group merely conversing. However, only a relatively small percentage of group communication could not be termed group discussion—for example, people talking on the telephone. Group discussion is the most common form of group communication. The ideas and concepts presented earlier in this text have been concerned with *all* forms of group communication. Now that we have shown the relationship between group discussion and group communication, let us ask the question, What are the responsibilities of a group discussant or communicator?

---

communication diary

Return to your original diary entries and answer the following questions:

1. *Do all your group situations conform to our definition of group discussion?*

2. *What percentage of your communication in groups can be considered group discussion?*
   Compare your diary entries and percentage estimates with your fellow classmates'.

We're probably aware that some students are excellent communicators in a group discussion. They ask good questions, are excellent leaders, are able to analyze and synthesize information, make important contributions to the discussion, and develop solutions from the materials presented. Yet, when they deliver a classroom speech, they are not as effective: their presentation is poor, their speech is poorly organized, and their delivery is stilted or boring. We find that differences in successful performance can be attributed to the fact that each type of oral communication requires a different set of skills. The skill of organizing a large amount of information for a speech is not necessary for short give-and-take conversational remarks commonly found in most group discussions. In addition, persuasive strategies can be a detriment to the group process. Indeed, a forceful delivery, desirable in many public speaking situations, may be neither helpful nor acceptable within a group context. The appropriate and effective behavior of a communicator depends on his understanding of and adaptation to the specific communication situation.

Group discussion requires that each communicator have a specific responsibility for speaking and listening during the discussion. Sources and receivers of communication constantly change. Each group member is a listener, then a speaker, then a listener, and so on. However, when listening we are sending out important cues even though we're not speaking. We are simultaneously sending and receiving. The close proximity of group members makes group discussion members sensitive to the mannerisms of their fellow group members. The facial expressions, posture, and tonal responses will all affect the communicator.

The discussion participant is held immediately accountable for what he has said or heard. Dishonesty, faulty reasoning, and lack of evidence can lead to a challenge by another group member. The responsibility for validating another member's comments may rest with all members of the group, a group leader, or a recognized expert in the group. The group situation determines what individual or individuals are to assume this responsibility.

The purposes of group discussion are to share information, explore different ideas, develop solutions to mutual problems, and to learn how to function more effectively in the group. The object of communication in group discussion is to investigate, explore, and evaluate before arriving at a final conclusion. To achieve this end the discussant *ideally* evaluates each piece of evidence, or the solution, in terms of the group goal rather than his own personal goal. The discussant attempts to find the best evidence, the most reasonable solution.

---

exercise 1

A MEETING

Ten students at your college gather in your home to consider new rules for student discipline. Two students are from the student senate. The remaining students represent different campus organizations. During the first part of the meeting, the two senate members discuss the relationship between the senate and the administration. One student asks about the nature of the problem. The same two students discuss the problem for an hour. One student suggests that they all ask the administration for its recommendations regarding student discipline. The other group members do not respond. One student suggests they go out and have a pizza. The group disperses.

Answer the following questions:

1. Was this a group discussion situation?
2. What could have been done to encourage members to meet their responsibilities more fully?

3. Was any value derived from the entire group meeting?
4. How would you improve this group meeting?

Methods of discussion

The basic elements of communication remain unchanged in different group situations, but the communicative procedures used by group members during discussion vary with the group's purpose, the subject being discussed, and the people to whom the discussion is directed. In this section, we will examine six methods or procedures used by discussion groups. A discussion method is a preselected procedure for conducting a group discussion.

Group discussion can be placed upon two related continua from informal to formal and private to public. The two continua look like this:

Informal |――――――――――――――| Formal

Private |――――――――――――――| Public

The informal discussion is the most common form of group discussion. When we get together with friends at a party to gossip or "shoot the bull," we are participating in an "informal" discussion. We have an opportunity to exchange ideas, and conversations usually ramble from one topic to another. These informal discussions are also called private discussions. A private or informal discussion is carried on *only* for the benefit of those taking part in the discussion. For example, a conversation among friends at a party typically is not conducted for the benefit of everyone at the party. It is conducted only for those talking in the group. We find that the more informal a group discussion, the fewer the restrictions placed upon the method of interacting.

We might say, "My friends don't use any procedures or format when talking together at a party." There is some truth to this observation. While conversation with friends is an informal group discussion, it may or may not follow any specific format or set of procedures. Only when the group discussion is following a specific pattern, *preselected* by group members, can we label it a *method of discussion*.

Traditionally, discussion methods have been classified into six major categories: round table, dialogue, panel, symposium-forum, colloquy, and lecture-forum. The labels only serve to permit distinctions between different discussion strategies. We can place our six methods of discussion on our original discussion continua.

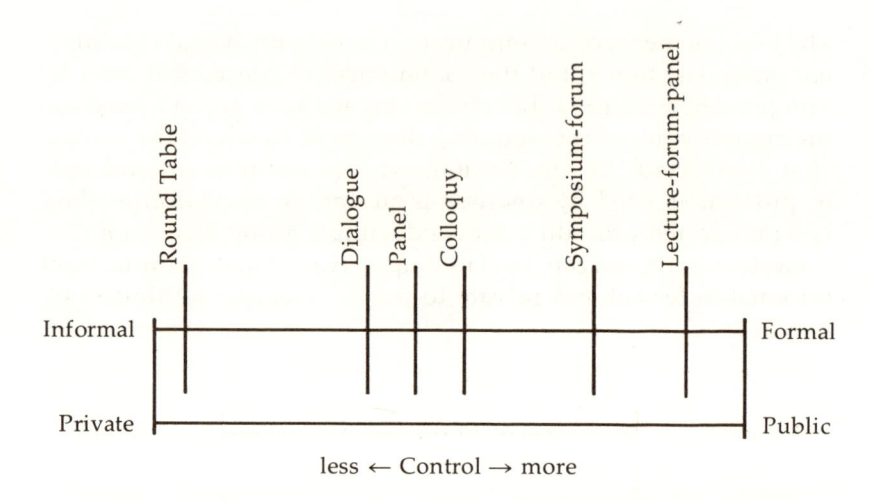

```
                  Round Table          Dialogue  Panel  Colloquy      Symposium-forum       Lecture-forum-panel
Informal            |                    |      |        |                 |                      |              Formal
                    |                    |      |        |                 |                      |
Private  |——————————————————————————————————————————————————————————————————————————————|  Public
                                    less ← Control → more
```

Note that we have added a new dimension to our continuum—control. We are suggesting that as the method of discussion becomes more formal it controls or restricts the presentation of the group discussion to a greater degree.

Only the round table can be considered solely an informal method of group discussion. The round table is the only method in which the communicator's messages are issued strictly for the benefit of the immediate group. This method places the fewest restrictions on the discussion process. The dialogue, on the other hand, can be either private or public. The remaining four methods always have an audience that is physically present during the discussion. A discussion for the benefit of an audience is called a *public* discussion. Classroom discussions are public, and nonparticipating classmates constitute the audience. A public discussion is more formal in its planning and execution than the private discussion.

All discussion methods, private or public, make use of a chairman. Do not confuse the terms *chairman* and *leader*. They are not necessarily synonymous. A group member may be made chairman in a group because he is recognized as the leader, or because he is appointed by some external authority, or because he may best fulfill the responsibilities necessary for the chairmanship of a particular discussion. The actual leader of a group might emerge during the discussion or remain a group participant because his expertise or ability to handle group members may best be served outside the position of discussion chairman. Having the recognized group leader as a group discussion participant, rather than as the group chairman, is not an uncommon practice in classroom discussions. This permits the leader to take a more active role in some cases without the restrictions of the chairmanship.

The discussion chairman has specific functions which facilitate the efficient operation of the group discussion. The exact functions will depend on the specific discussion method used by the group. A round-table chairman has the primary responsibility of promoting interaction between group members. The symposium chairman is concerned with introducing the discussion topic and the speakers, providing transitions between speakers, and summarizing the discussion. The importance of the chairman is determined both by the situation and by the discussion method. When the discussion method is informal—for example, a round-table discussion at home—the chairman's role could be minor. He might merely set the atmosphere for free interchange between group members and let group members proceed on their own. However, in a different situation, he might be continually forced to mediate internal conflicts that are inhibiting the exchange of ideas between discussion participants. Thus the chairman's role in the latter situation would be a major one. In public discussions the chairman's responsibilities are more formal, because he must control the format of the discussion method. There is, however, one overriding function that all chairmen have in common—assisting the group to reach its ultimate goal.

Let us begin our examination of discussion methods with the only method that is wholly private, the round-table discussion.

The round table

Remember the last time you got together with friends to study for an exam or the time you were appointed to a committee that met to decide how to raise money for a club of which you were a member? In each instance you were participating in a round-table discussion. A round-table discussion may be defined as a group discussion held without the presence of an audience, and with all group members entering into a free exchange of ideas. This method is used extensively in small decision-making groups and small learning groups. Notice that unlike the panel, the round-table method is held without the presence of an audience.

The group discussion in our last exercise was a round-table discussion.

The method is said to have originated with King Arthur and the Knights of the Round Table. (Whether this is fact or legend is not certain.) The king would present problems to his knights seated around his table, who would in turn discuss the problem in a climate of equality. During a round-table discussion, the group members may be seated around a table or merely sitting in a circle. The important feature of the seating arrangement is that all discussants can see and communicate with each other.

The round table consists of a chairman and at least two additional members. The chairman is seated in the circle with the other members. However, if a table is used, he may assume a central position by sitting at the head of the table. The chairman's primary function is to encourage participants to engage in a free interchange of opinions and ideas.

Ideally, the round table provides all group members with an opportunity to express their opinions and attitudes. This group interaction, it is hoped, will stimulate group members to refine their thinking, adjust their views of other members' ideas, and allow members to achieve some balance of opinions on an issue.

The round table rarely functions as we would like it to. Since the ideas are drawn from only a small number of participants, it is possible that the information needed is not possessed by the discussants. Imagine five white students trying to discover the effect of racial prejudice on an individual's self-esteem. Their lack of first hand knowledge about the topic could lead to an inadequate conclusion.

While the actual number of participants is flexible, too many participants make the group unwieldy and unmanageable. The larger the group, the less an individual may have an opportunity to participate and the greater the chance that one or two members will dominate the others. As the size of the group increases, all the members may not be able to maintain an intimate relationship with one another, and the individual's attraction to the group (cohesiveness) may decrease. If you want to experience these problems firsthand, attempt to carry on a round-table discussion in one of your college classrooms. Since college classes usually have more than twenty students, it is difficult to use this method as an integral part of the instructional process.

There is always the danger in a round table of group members rambling from topic to topic. The chairman must control the discussion and direct it toward its ultimate goal. The larger the group, however, the more difficult it will be for the chairman to exercise control.

> Procedure: *Round Table*
>
> 1. The chairman opens the meeting.
> 2. If necessary, the chairman introduces the members and introduces the question for discussion.
> 3. The chairman throws the topic open for discussion.
> 4. Members discuss the topic; the chairman summarizes throughout the discussion and provides transitional remarks when the discussion shifts from one phase of the problem to another.
> 5. At the completion of the discussion the chairman summarizes the discussion and closes the meeting.

We have discussed the only private form of group discussion. In the remainder of the chapter we will examine five methods of discussion that are categorized as public discussions. We will see that public discussions are more formal in their planning and execution. The discussion participants are more concerned with the audience and its responses to their behavior. The communication patterns are more restrictive, and the control over the type of group member interaction is greater.

The panel

If you asked your friends what discussion method they see most often, they would probably answer "the panel." The label *panel* has been used at times to describe the format in which a group of newspaper columnists interview a political candidate, a host converses with a number of guest celebrities on a television show, a committee of experts meet privately to develop organizational policy, and a specially appointed committee presents pertinent information to its club membership. Actually, only the committee reporting its findings to the larger group is truly following the panel method of discussion.

A panel can be defined as a discussion that is held before an audience, with all group members entering into a free interchange of ideas. Note that the discussion is carried on before an audience and not just for the benefit of group members. The panelist, as this group communicator is called, speaks for the benefit of the audience as well as to fellow discussion members. The function of the panel is to solve problems, arrive at consensus, or illuminate ideas for the advantage of the audience.

The panel members enter into a free interchange of ideas; that is, there is no preset order in which the panel members offer their contributions. To encourage this freedom of interaction, the group members must be seated so that communication between members can flow easily. Since a panel is presented before an audience, the semicircle seating arrangement is recommended to enable the audience to see and hear group members without difficulty.

A panel consists of a chairman and the group members. There is no set number of discussants, but it usually ranges from four to six. A television news program may use only three group members, thus giving each panelist more time to express his viewpoint. The more panelists in a discussion the more unwieldy and difficult to operate effectively.

Panel members do not bring prepared speeches to the discussion. This does not imply that they are not properly prepared. Careful preparation, anticipation of likely topics, need for facts, and so on, are vital in a discussion. Panelists are usually chosen because they can supply facts needed for well-informed discussion or because they represent views held by members of a larger group and can therefore act as their spokesmen.

The chairman, who is a panel member, does not have the same responsibilities as a regular panel member. He does not enter into the discussion as a participant. His primary responsibility is to allow the panel members to discuss freely and openly without interjecting his own ideas or biases. He presents the problem or topic to the group members for discussion but remains in the background. The audience has come to hear the discussion members; the chairman is an instrument for an effective presentation. He is concerned with the procedures of the meeting that help bring forth appropriate substantive content. He influences the substance of the discussion by his introduction of the group and its discussion topic, by any transitional statements that he makes between group members' comments, by bringing them back to the topic should they wander, and by the final summary. At the beginning of the panel, the chairman introduces the problem for discussion by giving a brief look at the background, the immediate cause for the discussion, and explanation of the way the panel will be conducted. He then introduces the panel members to the audience. He may make note of the group members' background and experience with the discussion topic. During the discussion, he may provide transitional statements between various group member statements. These comments are principally used for clarifying previous statements, summarizing the ideas covered, and for keeping the discussion focused on the main discussion topic. At the completion of the panel discussion, the chairman summarizes the results, briefly pointing out areas of agreement and conflict.

The panel is an excellent vehicle for group discussion. Its conversational informality generally makes it somewhat more interesting than other public methods of discussion. The informality creates a relaxed atmosphere, which in turn reduces the tensions and anxiety most communicators feel when speaking before an audience. Because all group members have a responsibility to the discussion, a feeling of teamwork and cooperation can be developed. Group member cooperation is a desirable end, but not necessarily a realisitic one. A panel composed of police officials and Black Panthers could not be expected to develop a harmonious relationship during discussion.

Using the panel method does present some potential problems. The informal conversational format can also hinder a group by making it difficult to follow specific organizational patterns. Many panel members become sidetracked and discuss tangential issues.

The group must be wary of communicators who tend to monopolize the conversation. Such individuals can prevent other group members from expressing their ideas and can in some cases cause group members to withdraw from the discussion. On the other hand, a group member may attempt to goof off and consequently not contribute his share in the discussion. This behavior is quite likely to persist, as long as the remaining panelists cover his inadequacies with their participation.

After the discussion, some panels allow the audience to question the various members. The period in which the audience is allowed to ask questions is called the *forum* period. This period provides an opportunity for audience members to interact with and bring to the attention of the panel members ideas that they have overlooked, raise questions about ideas already presented, and suggest additional interpretations of the materials.

Procedure: *Panel*

1. The chairman opens the discussion with a question or statement of the topic.
2. The panel members are introduced to the audience.
3. The chairman draws the panel members into informal conversation on the topic.
4. The panel members discuss the topic; the chairman restates, clarifies, summarizes, and provides transitions as needed during the discussion.
5. (optional forum) Questions are solicited from the audience.
6. The chairman summarizes the discussion.

The symposium-forum

Imagine the following situation:

You are seated in an auditorium with 250 other students. Seated on the stage are three representatives of your ethnic studies program. Each member gives a five-minute talk. One speaks about Black studies, the second on Chicano studies, and the third on Far Eastern studies. Following their presentations, you are permitted to question the three group members.

A public discussion in which each group member gives a talk on one area or phase of the discussion topic is called a symposium. This is a relatively formal method of presentation and comparatively easy to organize. The symposium is used for much the same purposes as is the panel. Whether we select the panel or symposium depends partly on the discussion topic. If the problem is easily divided into areas, it may be better to use the symposium. Since each speaker is assigned a specific area, a symposium presentation requires more preparation than the panel.

Unlike either the panel or the round table, group members do not interact freely with each other. The group members' presentations follow a preset order. A symposium participant does not have an opportunity to respond to ideas presented by speakers that follow. It has been argued that, because no direct interaction between speakers exists, the symposium cannot be classified as a form of group discussion; we agree. The standard symposium format does not conform to our definition of group discussion. Group members do not communicate in a reciprocal fashion and therefore are not truly interacting. Speakers can adapt their comments to what other speakers have already said, but unfortunately they cannot question or communicate with the previous speaker. For a symposium to be a true form of group discussion, it must be followed by a forum and/or panel period where the group members can interact with each other or the audience.

Because group members do not interact freely during a symposium, they are usually seated in a straight line, with the chairman near the center of the group. The symposium is similar to a public speaking situation and a speaker's stand, or podium, is generally provided.

The symposium consists of a chairman and a number of group members. As is the case with the other methods of discussion, it does not have a set number of participants. The number of group members is determined by the topic and time available for discussion. The topic is divided into preselected components and each part is assigned to a specific group member. Division of the topic may be by a chronological, spatial, or problem-solution order or by any order that provides a suitable method for presenting the material to the audience. The group member is usually chosen because he represents a particular position on the problem or has special competence, expertise, or information in one area of the discussion topic. On a college campus, participants in an information-sharing symposium conducted on the role of student government might consist of the student body president, a student senator, the dean of students, and the president of the college. Each discusses the student government from his own perspective.

The chairman of a symposium does not give a speech on one area of the discussion topic. His primary responsibility is to introduce each speaker and the area of his presentation. After each speech, the chairman makes an attempt to relate the forthcoming speech to the preceding one. If a forum period follows the speeches, the chairman directs the questions and comments submitted by the audience.

Because the problem is divided into specific areas, the presentation tends to be better organized and follows a predetermined pattern with greater facility. This also helps to remedy the narrowness of having one individual deliver a speech covering the entire topic. A number of speakers can provide a number of approaches to a single topic and their variety of approaches can help to hold audience interest.

Since a symposium is organized beforehand, it is less adaptable than previously mentioned methods. But the symposium does remain somewhat flexible in that the topic can be divided to anticipate the situation and audience demands.

Unlike the panel, one mediocre or poorly prepared discussant may cause the symposium to fail. The symposium presupposes competent speakers. Yet, not all group members may be effective communicators in both formal and informal communication situations. In the panel, ill-prepared members can be covered by the other speakers, but in the symposium this may be difficult or impossible. The remaining group members may not be familiar with the area for which the discussant is responsible and thus cannot speak on that area.

You will remember we suggested that in the panel discussion some members may dominate and not allow sufficient time for other group members to participate. In the symposium a long-winded speaker may also use up time needed by the remaining speakers to present their materials. In addition, if the division of areas overlaps, it is not unusual for one speaker to cover another speaker's information, leaving that speaker with little or nothing to say. The chairman must keep strict control over the time used by speakers. He can remind the discussants of this time limit prior to the start of the symposium, or he can stop a discussant if he has exceeded his time limit and ask him to summarize his remaining talk in one or two sentences.

Procedure: *Symposium-forum*

1. The chairman introduces the question for discussion and the areas to be covered by the speakers.
2. The chairman introduces each speaker and his specific area.
3. The speaker discusses his area of the topic.
4. The chairman provides transitions between the speakers.
5. The chairman conducts the forum period. If a panel discussion follows the symposium, the chairman and panelists follow the procedures listed in our discussion of the panel.
6. At the completion of the discussion, the chairman summarizes the materials presented.

The dialogue

Sometimes a discussion may consist of a conversation between two people in front of an audience or in private. In both cases, we have a dialogue. Imagine, if you will, two television commentators analyzing a speech delivered by the president of the United States. This is a public dialogue. If you were ever interviewed for a job, you have participated in a private dialogue. A dialogue is defined as a group discussion between two individuals. If it is held before a listening audience, it is usually followed by a forum period. Radio and television dialogues may or may not have an audience or forum. The *Tonight* show has an audience, but no forum. A dialogue between a newsman and potential candidate for public office rarely has an audience.

The interaction between the group members is direct. They discuss the topic freely between themselves. Often one of the discussants is an expert on the topic, and the other acts as a questioner or, sometimes, the devil's advocate. Many newsmen when interviewing political candidates or officeholders assume this devil's advocate role. While the format of the dialogue is preplanned, the participants do not rehearse or prepare speeches. The interviewer may, however, come prepared with a list of questions he wishes to ask. We can see that this method is somewhat less formal than the symposium and provides many of the same opportunities for conversational exchange that we find with the panel and round-table methods of discussion.

The physical arrangement of the dialogue is flexible. It may consist of two persons seated across a desk from each other as in a job interview, or two people seated on a stage, one questioning the other. In the public dialogue, the participants and audience should be able to see each other easily.

During the discussion, one of the two participants must act as the leader, guiding the conversation, questioning, providing transitions, and so on. The leader may also conduct the forum period, if any. He guides the dialogue in such a way that it will be most intelligible and in the best interests of the audience, whenever the dialogue is public. With the chairman in control, it is easy to keep the dialogue within the established time limits. When an expert does not have time to prepare a lecture or is ineffective as a lecturer, this method may be the most advantageous in imparting his ideas.

Caution must be taken to ensure that the topic of discussion is interesting to the audience as well as the dialogue participants. Since many experts have a tendency to talk above the heads of their listeners, they should exercise caution by discussing their subject at a level that can be understood by the audience. Listen to a dialogue between TV newscasters attempting to discuss U.S. economic policy and you'll see what we mean by trying to simplify very technical material. If the topic is presented in technical terms, the chairman must use questions to promote clarification and definition of the materials. Since the major interaction is between dialogue participants, they should not become so involved with each other that they forget the audience. Finally, like the panel, this method induces a tendency to wander and to become disorganized at times.

Procedure: *Dialogue*

1. The chairman introduces himself and the other participant.
2. The chairman presents the area to be covered and begins to question the other group member.
3. If an audience is present, the dialogue may be followed by a forum period conducted by the chairman.
4. The chairman completes the discussion by summarizing the materials covered.

The colloquy

The colloquy is unique among discussion methods, as well as the least known or used method. It was created for the purpose of working out problems and for devising new methods in the field of adult education. Originally, the colloquy consisted of questioning and reporting of information by a group of experts. Unfortunately, the questioning during the discussion period tended to slow down the proceedings and there was a tendency for the discussion to turn into a question-and-answer session between the experts and audience.

Since then, two different formats for the colloquy have been developed. In the first format (single panel) there is a chairman and panel of experts. The discussion process is identical to the panel discussion with one notable exception. If the chairman or member of the panel feels that a solution is being neglected, or that a disagreement exists, or that the material is unclear, then the audience is asked to comment or ask questions. The forum continues until the issue is resolved. The panel then continues its regular discussion until another need for the audience exists. The physical arrangements of this method are identical with those of the panel discussion.

The second format (two panels) retains much the same format used in the original colloquy. A lay panel is chosen in advance to prepare the discussion. An expert panel is selected consisting of individuals with special knowledge of the subject. The lay panel, with the assistance of the chairman, proceeds as in the regular panel discussion. When special information is needed, the lay panel and chairman may ask questions of the experts. The experts do not take an active part in the regular discussion phase, although they may introduce information that is being overlooked by the lay panel. Immediately following the discussion, the audience may react to the comments made by both panels.

The physical arrangements are identical with those of the panel, except that in this case we have two panels. The chairman is seated at the center of the stage flanked by both panels. This allows the two panels to see each other and be seen and heard by the audience.

The first colloquy procedure is probably the most efficient method for utilizing experts and meeting audience needs. The second procedure has the advantage of making use of both lay and expert personnel. Since the major part of the discussion is conducted by the lay panel, the communication is more likely to be understood by the audience. At the same time, expert advice is immediately available. If the experts use technical language, the lay panel can clarify the information for the audience.

In the first colloquy format, intermittent questioning can consume too much time. The experts may also talk over the heads of their audience. In the second colloquy format, the experts may not be needed or used very little. This is a waste of time, talent, and effort on the part of the experts. Sometimes this format has a tendency to turn into a question-and-answer period between the lay and expert panels. It is also possible for the expert panel to dominate the discussion and usurp the responsibilities of the lay panel. Despite these disadvantages the colloquy is an effective, though not the most efficient, method of discussion.

Procedure: *Colloquy* (Single Panel)

1. The chairman introduces the expert panel and topic.
2. Remainder of the discussion follows the panel discussion format with the exception that the audience is allowed to question or comment when an important issue arises.

Procedure: *Colloquy* (Two Panels)

1. The chairman introduces the lay panel, expert panel, and discussion topic.
2. The discussion topic is open to comments by the lay panel.
3. The lay panel and chairman ask questions of the experts when information is needed; experts add information that the lay panel has overlooked.
4. A forum period follows the regular discussion; questions can be directed to both lay and expert panels.
5. The chairman closes the discussion by summarizing the proceedings.

Lecture-forum

Throughout the semester your instructor will present a number of lectures dealing with group communication. You will be permitted to question and comment on your instructor's remarks. This method of discussion is called the lecture-forum.

The lecture-forum is the form of group discussion used when the audience listening to the speaker is given an opportunity to make comments and ask questions regarding his presentation. The lecture-forum is always public. It is the most formal method of discussion. Some people might argue that the lecture-forum is not really a form of discussion, but a type of public speaking. The basis for this argument rests in part on the fact that during the lecture we do not have group interaction—communication is one-way from speaker to audience. However, during the lecture the audience interacts continually with the speaker on a nonverbal level. At times audience members may interrupt or are permitted to question the speaker, and during the forum period audience and speaker interact. Thus the lecture-forum is in fact a two-way process and is a form of discussion.

The lecture-forum has two purposes. First, it supplies new information and motivation about a topic or problem. Second, it allows the audience a chance to participate in the discussion—to clarify obscure points, obtain additional information, and express their opinions. Often an audience will benefit more from a thorough coverage of a single subject. When this is the case, a single speaker exploring a subject, presenting information, arguing a point of view, and answering questions for his audience is the best discussion method.

The physical arrangements for this method are simple. A speaker sits either at floor level or on a stage in front of an audience. Many times a chairman will be used to introduce the speaker to the audience.

The lecture-forum is used because of the ease with which it can be arranged. With only one speaker, it is usually better organized, and the use of an expert speaker can guarantee a complete and detailed presentation. Since the audience cannot comment or question until after the lecture, information can be conveyed quickly without distractions or interruptions.

There are, however, some problems associated with this method. The speaker who is recognized as an authority rarely has his judgments questioned. How often have you seriously questioned your own instructor's lectures? An irresponsible speaker may distort facts, use emotional appeals, or selectively bias the materials. (Listen to a white supremicist discuss the validity of using IQ tests in schools consisting predominately of black or Chicano students.) It also may be difficult to keep a speaker from exceeding his time limit. If his speech is too long, he may leave little or no time for audience participation. When this occurs, group discussion does not exist. Because the speaker may be an expert, there is always the danger he may use language above the level of his audience's ability to comprehend. If the lecturer is a poor speaker, he could ruin the entire program.

exercise 2

SELECTING A DISCUSSION METHOD

What discussion method would you choose for the following situations?

1. A group of thirty students, all in the same social club, are having a meeting at which the topic for discussion is "How can group membership be increased?"
2. A group of students must plan how to present their topic "What should be done about prison reform?" to your class.
3. At a meeting open to all students the student senate must deal with alternative methods for funding the Economic Opportunities Program on campus.
4. Ralph Nader is coming to campus to speak on the latest safety devices on automobiles.
5. Your ecology club usually has thirty members in attendance at its meetings. The club will discuss "How can we prevent oil pollution of our waterways?" The club is composed of interested college students and ecology experts from the biology department.

In selecting the discussion method ask yourself the following questions:

1. Is the method private or public?
2. What is the goal of the group discussion?
3. Can the information be presented in more than one way?
    If your answer is yes, why did you select one method over another?

exercise 3

PRESENTING A GROUP DISCUSSION

1. The class should be divided into small groups (six members maximum).
2. Each group should select a topic for discussion and a method for presenting that discussion.
3. Since this will be a public discussion and perhaps your first, we recommend that the first discussion be concerned with presenting information to the class, rather than attempting to solve a problem.
4. Present a thirty-minute discussion.

The chapter has examined methods or procedures for presenting a group discussion. Group discussion has been defined as the face-to-face interaction of two or more persons engaged in the task of information sharing, problem solving, and self-maintenance. Group discussion is viewed as a type of group communication.

The six methods for presenting group discussions were viewed on a continuum with three dimensions: (1) public-private; (2) informal-formal; and (3) control over interactional patterns. It was pointed out that the more formal, public group discussion exercised greater control over the interaction of group members, their messages, communicators, and the structure of the situation.

ADDITIONAL READINGS

Potter, David, and Anderson, Martin P., *Discussion: A Guide to Effective Practice* (Belmont, Calif.: Wadsworth, 1963–64). Here is a readable book, full of exercises, which emphasizes the application of discussion principles to practice.

Beal, George M., Bohlen, Joe M., and Randabaugh, J. Neil. *Leadership and Dynamic Group Action* (Ames: Iowa State Univ. Press, 1962). The authors give a "how to" approach for using group discussion methods. Each method is examined by answering the following questions: Why?, When?, and How?.

Gulley, Halbert E. *Discussion, Conference and Group Process*, 2d ed. (New York: Holt, Rinehart & Winston, 1968), chapters 2–3. These chapters provide a description of the functions and limits of group discussion.

Bormann, Ernest G. *Discussion and Group Methods* (New York: Harper & Row, 1968). This book blends group discussion procedures within the context of the group process.

Harnack, Victor R., and Fest, Thorrell B. *Group Discussion Theory and Technique* (New York: Appleton-Century-Crofts, 1964). A good basic text in the area of group discussion with emphasis on problem-solving groups.

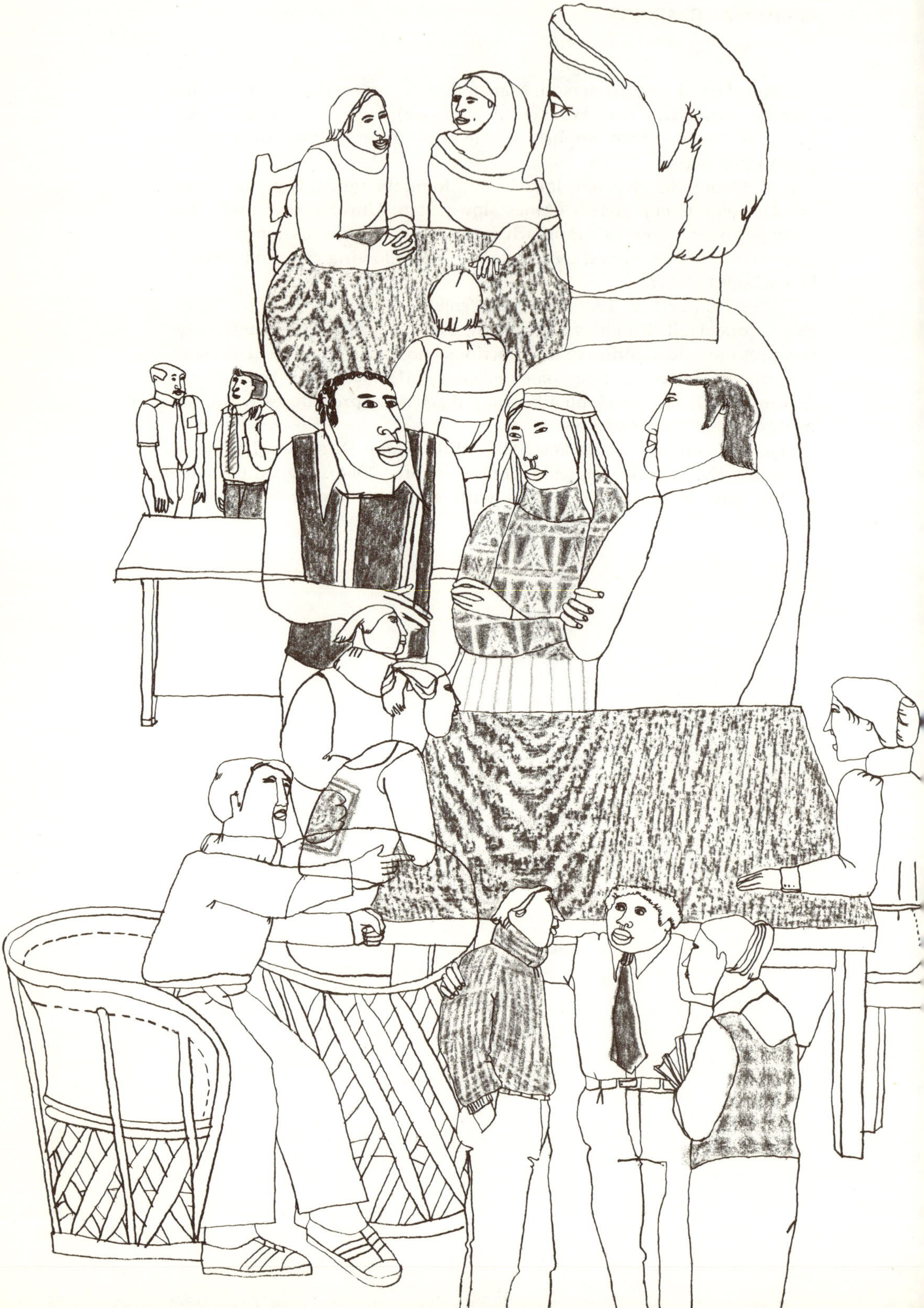

11. Small-group techniques

PREVIEW

What are discussion techniques?
   Four discussion techniques developed either to assist group interaction or to promote an understanding of roles within the group are investigated. The discussion techniques explored are
      brainstorming
      buzz sessions and Phillips 66
      posting
      role playing

What is Laboratory training?
   Laboratory training includes a wide range of approaches to human relations, group dynamics, and organizational development using verbal and nonverbal experiences to increase awareness and functioning of group members in group situations.

In chapter 1 we stressed the critical function of communication in affecting social interaction in the group. No matter what the nature of the group may be, or what its purpose is, the tool it uses to establish social interaction, to achieve its goals, is communication. In chapter 10, we examined six methods of discussion. We must now recognize that the use of these methods does not ensure a group's success. They do not guarantee group interaction. Discussion methods merely provide a format for information sharing or problem solving. They do not provide the information or solutions. Only group members, through their interaction, can provide the ideas needed by a group.

There are times, however, when individuals are reticent about expressing their solutions to a problem; for example, a group member may feel that his solutions are foolish or unacceptable. Many times in public discussions questions or comments are not made by group members because they fear being criticized. To prevent such occurrences and facilitate communication by group members, a number of discussion techniques have been developed. Group discussion techniques are used in conjunction with group methods to assist the overall group or audience interaction. In the first section of this chapter we shall examine three techniques used to promote or assist group interaction: (1) brainstorming; (2) buzz sessions and Phillips 66; and (3) posting.

In chapter 8, we discovered that a group member's role is a crucial element in the group process. We found that discrepancies between perceived roles and role expectations of group members can result in conflict, inhibiting the group efforts and, at the same time, the group members' adaptation and integration within the group process. So it becomes important that each group member understand his role and the role of others within the group. The last technique examined in the first section, role playing, has as its primary purpose the attempt to provide a group member with a clearer understanding of his own role and the roles of the other group members.

In the second section of this chapter we shall explore laboratory training, a technique for promoting self-maintenance among group members.

Discussion techniques

Brainstorming

Brainstorming is a technique of small-group discussion designed to encourage the introduction of ideas on an unrestricted basis. In many group discussions, we may lack self-confidence, may be discouraged from contributing by certain members, or may lack the opportunity to be creative. The purpose of brainstorming is to remove these inhibiting factors in order to promote group interaction.

The brainstorming process is simple. For example, if a group wants to find a number of solutions to a problem, members get together in a round-table fashion, appoint a chairman, and begin suggesting solutions. All solutions are recorded regardless of their value or merit. As Osborn (1957) has stated, "the wilder the idea, the better; it is easier to tame down than to think up." If a solution is proposed and another group member wishes to amend or add to it, he may do so. Participants are encouraged to add to, subtract from, combine, and modify the solutions of others. This process is called *piggy-backing*. Adverse judgments and weighting of ideas are withheld until the session is completed. In brainstorming, a free exchange of ideas between group members is not only desired—it is an absolute necessity.

Research upon the usefulness of brainstorming has provided some inconsistent results (Shaw, 1971). However, there is some indication that with longer work periods groups produce more under brainstorming than do individuals working alone; that is, groups continue to produce ideas, whereas individuals tend to run dry.

We can list four basic rules for conducting a brainstorming session:

1. Evaluation and criticism by group members is forbidden.
2. All contributions are to be encouraged.
3. An attempt should be made to create the greatest quantity of ideas.
4. A combination of ideas and solutions should be sought.

We must also recognize that the use of brainstorming does not guarantee successful results. Group members must possess the ideas to be drawn out in a brainstorming session. If the group does not possess the needed ideas, the productivity of the session will be minimal. It is also not unusual for group members to evaluate or criticize the group member's ideas occasionally. If a group member does not refrain from criticizing, he may be asked to remain quiet or leave the group. However, this maneuver could reduce the desired free exchange of ideas. Let us observe how the brainstorming activity is conducted.

Procedure: *Brainstorming*

1. Decide on the area or issue with which the group must cope; state the problem clearly.
2. Appoint a secretary to write down all ideas. The role of secretary may rotate, thus permitting each member to contribute his ideas to the brainstorming session.
3. Set a time limit for the session.
4. Appoint a chairman to enforce brainstorming rules.
5. Establish an informal physical arrangement.
6. Ask the group to discuss the selected area or issue freely.
7. Bring the session to a halt when the time limit is reached.

---

exercise 1

Below you will find a list of topics suitable for a brainstorming session in your classroom. Divide the class into groups of five or six. Each group is given four problems. Each group discusses the problem for seven minutes. After the brainstorming sessions, answer the following questions:

1. Did you want to evaluate the contributions of other group members?
2. Did one individual or leader dominate the session?
3. Did members piggy-back ideas or solutions?
4. Did you feel free to communicate as the session progressed? If your answer is no, why not?
5. Did some group members contribute more than other members?
6. Did all group members have an opportunity to participate?

Answer the next two questions in relation to all the groups in your classroom:

1. Did certain groups arrive at more solutions?
2. Did some groups have a higher quality of solutions?

BRAINSTORMING PROBLEMS

1. How can we create equality among races in America?
2. What should be done about water pollution?
3. How can we improve the quality of teachers in college?
4. What subjects should all students take before graduation?

Buzz sessions and Phillips 66

Brainstorming is concerned with promoting interaction in an already existent group. It is not concerned with drawing ideas from individuals outside the primary discussion group—for example, an audience. However, in chapter 10 we found that many times an audience can play an integral role in a group discussion. If we reflect upon our own experience, we may remember times when we were hesitant about participating in the forum period of a discussion. Two techniques often used to encourage audience participation are *buzz groups* and *Phillips 66*.

The label *buzz group* is used when referring to a small group drawn from a listening audience that converses on a specific question dealing with the discussion topic. By dividing the audience into small groups, all individuals have an opportunity to participate. To assure participation, each group member is given the chance to express his reaction to the question. At the end of the buzz group discussion, the chairman presents the group's opinion to the primary discussion group. Each group member takes an active role and still remains anonymous, because his opinions are forwarded through a chairman. The chairman's presentation, in turn, allows the entire audience to benefit from the group's findings. Let's examine a buzz group in operation. Imagine that you are in an audience of forty students. You have just heard a panel discussion dealing with the problem "What can be done to clean up our environment?" At the completion of the panel discussion, their chairman asks the audience to divide into eight groups of five. Each group is given a specific question to discuss.

Just pretend that your group was given the question "How can we rid our air of smog?" The group decides to elect you to serve as chairman. The group then discusses the problem in a round-table format. Following the discussion, you present your conclusions to the panel and the other audience groups.

The term *buzz groups* has also been used in reference to groups of two. The procedures and functions of this buzz group are identical with those of the larger buzz groups. Groups of this size virtually guarantee participation by every individual and have a greater potential for involvement than larger buzz groups.

The label *Phillips 66* is sometimes used when referring to a small group whose function is to develop questions about an area of the problem. Phillips refers to the creator's name. The number 66 symbolizes six persons discussing for six minutes. The method is more flexible than the title appears. Some problems are discussed longer than six minutes and groups vary in size from three to eight.

Phillips 66 functions somewhat differently than the buzz group. The time spent in discussion is used to formulate questions dealing with an area of the discussion topic. When the time period is completed, the chairman of the Phillips 66 group presents the questions to the primary discussion group. This procedure gives each group member a feeling of participation. An alternate procedure is for the chairman of the primary group to collect the questions from the smaller discussion groups and present them to the primary discussion group. This action may deprive the Phillips 66 group member of a feeling of active participation.

The success of either the buzz groups or the Phillips 66 technique rests upon five principles. First, the participants must feel qualified to discuss or question the primary discussion group. The topic under discussion must be of interest and relevance to the members of the group. Second, the groups must know what is expected of them. Requesting a decision is more specific than just asking a group to comment on a problem. In one group, members might merely add their opinions together and have the chairman report a summary of their contributions. This would not accomplish the group's goal of reaching a specific decision. Third, the group size must be small enough so that the members can interact freely with each other. The larger the group, the harder it is to achieve that interaction. When you have a large group that is subsequently divided into many small groups, only brief reporting of conclusions is feasible. Fourth, the time allotted for the discussion should be influenced by the nature of the topic and size of the groups. The question might be "What can be done to save our schools?" If the topic takes more than one hour to discuss, buzz groups or the Phillips 66 technique should not be used. Fifth, the prime goal of a smaller group is to encourage participation; thus the group must be careful to maintain a free and informal climate.

A note of caution should be exercised. These techniques are not as well planned and carefully prepared as many small-group discussions. We should not expect the results to be comparable. These techniques are most useful in situations calling for quick reactions to simple assignments. They are much better in pointing up problems than in solving them. Moreover, the time allocated is generally too short to go through the entire problem-solving process.

Procedure: *Buzz Group*

1. The audience is divided into smaller groups of four to ten.
2. A chairman is appointed for each group.
3. Each group discusses one aspect of the problem/topic presented to the entire audience.
4. The buzz group chairman presents the group's opinions to the entire audience.

Procedure: *Phillips 66*

1. The audience is divided into smaller groups of three to eight.
2. A chairman is appointed for each group.
3. A time limit of between six and ten minutes is usually established for the group discussion.
4. The group attempts to develop questions dealing with the discussion topic for the primary discussion group.
5. The chairman presents the group's questions to the primary discussion group.

exercise 2

Following the first formal discussion in your class, divide the class into groups of five or six students. Each group will formulate and select two questions dealing with the discussion topic. Assign each group to respond to the questions. After the forum period, ask yourself the following questions:

1. Did every group member have an opportunity to participate?
2. Was there a duplication of questions and, if so, how was it handled by the performing group?
3. Did you feel as if you were involved in the discussion?

Posting

There are times during a discussion when questions are asked prematurely or out of context by group or audience members. Such questions could put the group on the defensive or put the questioner in an embarrassing situation. Also, the group may not be able to answer the question because needed information has not as yet been provided by group members. To handle this problem, the chairman sets aside a time for raising orienting questions and problems. The chairman records the questions, usually on a blackboard, where they can be seen by group members and the audience. A time is then set aside for discussing the orienting questions. Posting is a technique for listing questions or ideas that the group or audience members may have regarding the discussion topic.

If questions are gathered after a presentation, a skilled group may develop a supplementary presentation built around the questions which are then subjected to open discussion. If the questions are gathered during a formal discussion presentation, the extent to which the posted problems are used will depend on the time available. If time is limited, the scope and importance of the questions may necessitate future discussions. When time is short, the group may also select the most important questions for consideration. If the questions or problems are gathered before the formal discussion, they can be used as a basis for organizing the discussion. This also assures both group members and audience that the information desired will be discussed.

Posting serves a number of functions. First, it can raise the level of interest among group members and audience. Through posting, group members may find that they have common questions or problems. Group members often believe that their questions are unique. By selecting the most important questions, the group can address itself to problems that are familiar and capable of competent, adequate analysis. This reduces the fear of having to discuss unknown problems.

Second, posting can assist in clarifying problems. Many problems have an emotional overtone. By stating various orientations (attitudes, biases) which individuals bring to a problem, posting alleviates possible future hostility over personal interpretation of materials. For example, a group could meet to consider the problem of racism in America. While some members might see racism as an issue concerning morals, others may see it as an economic problem.

Third, a discussion may falter because the group cannot agree on their specific problem. Members may be dealing with different parts of a complex problem. For example, a group discussion on the United States policy towards China may find group members discussing two different areas—social and cultural. In this case each group member would be asked to state his view of the problem, and all ideas would be posted. Once the problem is posted, the group can decide which area would be the most fruitful for discussion. If each area is handled separately, the chance for group agreement on solutions will be increased.

Like brainstorming, all contributions during posting are accepted by and listed by the leader. This can be a definite asset to group member participation. In posting the problem, the leader or recorder must try to understand the meaning that is intended to be evoked by the questions raised. He must be able to translate the contributions into an understandable form. For example, a chairman may ask other group members to assist in the interpretation of questions and thus give group members an additional opportunity to interact. If an attempt is made to clarify and resolve differences, the results of posting could be the improvement of group cohesiveness and communication.

The method does have at least two potential drawbacks. First, it is time-consuming. If the group allows posting during the discussion process, time is spent listing and selecting questions for future discussion. Second, the success of the technique depends on the leader, who must act as recorder and sometimes evaluator of questions. The discussion leader who is perceived as a critic and judge, rather than an aid to the discussion process, may cause group members and audience participants to become reticent in contributing their problems and questions.

> Procedure: *Posting*
>
> 1. The chairman states the time when posting will be conducted: prior to the discussion, during the discussion, or immediately following the discussion.
> 2. The chairman records all questions or problems.
> 3. If the list is long and time is limited, the chairman or group ranks the questions in order of importance.
> 4. The group then discusses the questions selected.

Role playing

In chapter 3, we observed that each group member learns a way of behaving that is acceptable to other group members. That behavior is the role one is expected to play in the group. Our role is, in part, a consequence of our communication with other group members. Roles are affected by the group environment and the group members' perceptions of that situation. Frequently, a group member's perceptions of a group situation are not realistic. He may not have had prior experience with the other group members or the problem under discussion and so he probably cannot evaluate his behavior in the group setting. We should realize that it is necessary that the group member be able to clarify his expected role. One technique that can provide group members with an understanding of their roles within the group is called role playing. It was first used in psychological therapy and has since been applied to a wide range of human activities from education to business.

Role playing is an individual dramatization of a problem or situation. The goal is to have group members literally put themselves into specific roles in specific situations and then evaluate their performances. It provides an opportunity for group members to act out various roles in a laboratory situation and thereby clarify and gain understanding of group roles and processes.

Role playing is a frequently used technique for entertainment as well as educational purposes. As children we played "cowboys and Indians" and "cops and robbers"; these roles were not taken to provide understanding, but rather to provide entertainment. In many American cities, one day a year is set aside for high school students to switch roles with officials in the community.

One student may play the role of mayor, another the fire chief, and so on. This role-playing experience is educational, and endeavors to provide students with an understanding of the roles of city officials. It does not, however, provide a base from which to judge one's own role in group situations.

Role playing has been used in labor and management relations to settle contractual disputes. For example, management might assume the role of labor, and labor the role of management. The two parties would be placed in a negotiating situation to enact their new roles. Each party can, by playing the role of the other, gain new insight into the other's behaviors or acquire new sensitivity to the other's position on an issue. When the parties resume their real-life roles, quite possibly more realistic bargaining may be conducted.

In group discussion, role playing is utilized for two general purposes; first as a tool for demonstration. For example, a group is concerned with increasing its productivity (defined in this case as formulating as many solutions to a problem as possible). The group creates a problem-solving situation and attempts to view how the group arrives at solutions to the problem. The role-playing situation provides a concrete example for subsequent analysis. When role playing is used for demonstration, the evaluation of the member's interaction taking place is crucial. The primary concern of the group is not how much a group member learns while he participates, but how much knowledge he gains from the evaluation of the situation.

Second, role playing is often used for practicing discussion skills. For example, a group may desire to develop their members' ability to solve problems. An imaginary problem-solving situation is developed. Students are then asked to go through the problem-solving process. The group effort is then analyzed by the group participants and observers. Unlike role playing for demonstration, the group members use the play acting as a basis for learning how they should play in that group. The role-playing situation provides a vehicle for modifying one's behavior. The evaluation process serves to refine the observations of the group and suggest methods for improving group behavior.

Role playing stimulates enactment of a situation by people who may or may not have experienced the roles they portray. You might have already noticed that three different types of roles are enacted. The first is "straight" acting, in which the individual plays himself. He attempts to learn more about how he acts rather than how others feel or act in the group. Since role playing is more informal, flexible, and permissive than a real-life situation, it releases the inhibitions that normally cloak group members' interaction with each other. The more freedom of expression that group members feel, the greater the communication of true feelings, attitudes, and beliefs. The second and third types of roles can be called role switching and role reversal. The role players take different roles than they would under normal group conditions. Our example of the labor representative taking the role of management would be a form of role reversal. Role reversal can provide a better understanding of ourselves and of the individuals whose roles we are playing. By assuming the role of another person, we often feel freer to communicate true feelings and attitudes. The comments we make can be ascribed to the person we are playing and not ourselves. Thus some anxiety concerning what is said can be removed and we are not as pressured to control our comments.

Role-playing techniques can assist the individual in the group as well as the group as a whole. On the individual level, this technique can provide insight into the effectiveness of individual roles in the group. When others take our role, we have a unique opportunity to see ourselves as others see us. While this may be occasionally embarrassing, it can illustrate areas of our behaviors that need readjustment. It can point out more effective behaviors that we can use in the future. We may find that the comments and lines of argument we've been using are not clear, logical, or supported by sufficient information. With this new knowledge, we could improve the clarity and effectiveness of our communication.

On the group level, role playing can help the group to function more effectively as a unit. It can help forestall or remove problems of communication that arise from failure to understand how the group should operate. Ideally, all members of the group are part of the role-playing situation either as role players or as observers and evaluators. This allows each member to play a part in the group's development. It not only provides a learning vehicle for the discussion skills, but provides a greater amount of group satisfaction.

However, since role playing is time-consuming, we should understand its problems and limitations. Players often lose their sense of reality when involved in role playing. Many participants tend to embellish their roles, which does not produce a realistic context in which to study either an issue or an interpersonal problem. While role playing is likened to acting on the stage, the participants are not asked to perfect their roles. The situation is fictional and unreal. It only approximates reality. Role players are to behave as they normally would with the exception of the specific role requirements that they have been given. That is, they are to do the best job of communicating in a group that they can except in those cases where the requirements of their role specifically demands ineffective communication behavior.

Role playing is not a cure-all and cannot be used to solve all problems related to understanding individual and group needs. It depends heavily on the group members' abilities to be creative. If the participants cannot use their imagination, it would be a waste of time. Role playing should start with simple situations. It is important that the objectives be clear and well defined. Many role players have difficulty assuming roles. They do not perceive the situation as even resembling real life. If the group members are receptive, creative, and cooperative, role playing can be an effective tool for improving the effectiveness of groups and the communication within the group environment.

exercise 3

Ameriville, a town of 20,000 in the West, has some industry and a heterogeneous population of various religious, racial, and nationality groups. There are four grade schools, one junior high school, and one high school.

Mr. White, the superintendent of schools, has been on the job in Ameriville for three years. It is now spring and his contract is expiring. For several weeks the board of education has been discussing whether Mr. White's contract should be renewed. A decision has to be made at this meeting of the board, since he must be given adequate notice if he is to be released.

There is a great deal of controversy over the issue of retaining Mr. White. The major questions over which the controversy seems to have been raging are three:

1. Progressive education. Some people in the community feel that Mr. White has gone much too far in bringing so-called progressive methods of education into the schools. It is asserted that not enough attention is given to the fundamentals of reading, writing, and arithmetic and that a lot of time is devoted to "social adjustment" and discussion of controversial social and political issues that children are not adequately prepared to talk about. Other people feel that the most up-to-date knowledge about the psychology of learning is being employed, and that children should be informed on questions such as the United Nations, racial prejudice, sex education, and so on.

2. Administrative abilities. Complaints have been voiced by some teachers, principally the older, more conservative ones, that Mr. White's methods of dealing with his staff leave much to be desired. They complain of the amount of extra time they are expected to devote

to various kinds of faculty committees, and they feel that teachers who try to maintain high standards and discipline are discriminated against when it comes to promotions, favorable teaching assignments, and the like. Other teachers seem to feel that Mr. White is a dynamic administrator who is simply trying to inject more democracy into the running of the schools.

3. Off-the-job activities. Many members of the community are disturbed at the off-the-job activities of Mr. White. He is an active member of the local chapters of the Americans for Democratic Action and the American Civil Liberties Union and, when asked to give speeches before the Rotary Club and other service organizations, often delves into controversial political and social issues, such as advocating the elimination of racial and religious barriers in the community and elimination of censorship. Many people feel that the superintendent of schools should remain a more impartial figure. Others feel that it is not only his right but his duty as a private citizen to engage in whatever activities off the job he see fit to.

Procedure:

1. Ask for six volunteers from the class.
2. Assign the following roles:
    a) Mr. White
    b) Chairman, board of education
    c) Four board of education members, two who support and two who oppose an extension of Mr. White's contract
3. Situation: The six role players will assume they are in the board of education conference room and their task is to decide if Mr. White's contract should be extended.

Immediately after the role-playing situation, answer the following questions:

1. Were the role players realistic?
2. What communication problems did the role players confront and/or create?

Examine the role-playing group in terms of the following questions:

1. Did group norms develop?
2. What communicator variables influenced the discussion?
3. Was conflict present? How was it resolved?
4. Was the group cohesive?
5. Was group conformity an important variable?
6. What styles and functions of leadership were manifest in the situation?
7. What types of messages were communicated? Which messages had the greatest impact in the role-playing situation?

There are many procedural variations for implementing role playing. A procedure can be selected for its ability to provide the group with the greatest understanding of its problem or develop the skill necessary for dealing with group or individual problems. In the suggested readings section of this chapter, a number of texts have been listed which explain the different types of role-playing procedures.

In this section we examined four techniques frequently used in conjunction with discussion methods. In the next section we will be concerned with group training laboratories, which are concerned primarily with individual development through group interaction. Unlike the previous discussion techniques, this group technique is never used with discussion methods. However, some of the discussion techniques have been used with this group technique.

Laboratory training

Origin and function

Lecture and discussion techniques are widely used in education and industry to improve individual performances in groups. These techniques have been somewhat effective, particularly in conveying knowledge about group processes. An additional group technique frequently used as a learning tool is laboratory training. Laboratory training adds to conventional techniques by providing situations in which group members experience through their own interaction the group conditions usually talked about in the classroom. Group members learn how to improve their performance by experimenting with their behaviors in simulated group experiences.

Interest in group training has steadily gained momentum since its inception over twenty-five years ago. The term *laboratory training* is used loosely to include a wide range of laboratory training approaches in human relations, group dynamics, and organizational development, as well as a number of verbal and nonverbal experiences that seek to increase awareness and release human potential (Birnbaum, 1969). The first training center at Bethel, Maine, fathered the National Training Laboratories (NTL) and nurtured the training group (T-group) as a basic technique in the laboratory movement. The T-group is a relatively unstructured group in which individuals participate as learners under the guidance of a trainer or group facilitator using the interactions between members as tools for self and group improvement.

A T-group may be sponsored by a church, school, college, civic group, YMCA, business, or industry. There is no doubt that business and industry have profited considerably from providing laboratory training for personnel.

The T-group or training group is not an easy technique to describe. As Schein and Bennis (1965) point out, laboratories vary as to goals, design, group composition, length of training, and setting. However, most training groups have certain commonalities: (1) face-to-face interaction; (2) planned activities involving communication (verbal and nonverbal) between individuals and groups; (3) feedback and analysis of group experiences; (4) analysis of problems necessitating new behavior patterns on the part of group members; and (5) arriving at conclusions about group and personal behaviors based on an analysis of group experience (Buchannan, 1965).

The T-group is kept small to allow each group member the opportunity to communicate with other members, allowing individuals to communicate according to their needs and capabilities. As Egan (1970) suggests, if the group is too small each member is "on call"; if the group is too large, it is too easy for an individual to hide in the group. The ideal group is one just large enough to provide diverse opinions and contributions.

Group interaction is carried on through face-to-face communication. The group members may discuss lectures or independently read materials, or participate in exercises. The lectures or exercises are used to stimulate participation, introduce missing elements into the group experience, and highlight various aspects of participant behavior. For example, a group may be presented with a problem-solving exercise that necessitates group members assuming leadership behavior to complete a task. The group members work through the exercise until either the problem is solved or the allotted time is used up. The group then discusses the group process, concentrating upon their leadership behavior. The group members learn by doing. However, a potentially greater learning experience occurs with a discussion of the group action. The group concerns itself with what has happened in the here-and-now —that is, it concerns itself with group behavior during the experiment. Past behavior of group members is important only if it has contributed to the present group interaction. Learning takes place on the basis of evaluating behavior occurring during the group experience.

Because the purpose of a training group is to have group members learn new interactional behavior, they are encouraged to experiment. In a real-life situation, the group member may not possess the freedom to assume different behavioral styles. In fact, many T-group exercises are designed to force group members out of previous behavior patterns. For example, an exercise in problem solving that demands a certain type of leadership behavior may necessitate that members assume new behavior patterns to complete the group task successfully.

Since the learning experience concerns the actual behavior of group members, the behavior itself is part of the discussion during and after the learning experience. Opportunities are provided in the T-group for giving and receiving feedback concerning individual and overall group behavior. Since one problem in group discussion is effective communication, a T-group might examine the personal and interpersonal problems that inhibit free communication within the group and hinder the group from reaching its goal. Members might observe and evaluate the communication necessary for proper functioning of their group. Exercises can be developed to focus on communication and assist in developing new communication behavior patterns between group members.

The trainer. The leader of a training group is called the trainer. Although physically present, he is not a member of the learning group. He is a resource person. He does not impose goals or control the interaction of group members. Seashore (1968) states that his "role is to facilitate the examination and understanding of group experiences. He helps group participants to concur on the way the group is working, the style of individual participation, or the issue that is facing the group." He also trains the group members to be observers as well as participants. If the participants learn how to observe what is happening in the group, the end product of the training session will be a greater understanding of the total group process. A group member does not merely assume the role of trainer. The role requires extensive schooling in laboratory techniques. Most qualified trainers have been certified under the auspices of the NTL.

Persons who have never participated in a training group generally perceive a group leader or trainer in the traditional position of authority. They judge him to be efficient if he acts as a chairman, gives the group an agenda, and conducts the meeting according to parliamentary procedure. Thus they are apt to become confused and disorganized when they attempt to assess the T-group trainer's role as that of a nonleader.

Blake (1958) says that the T-group trainer should be able to (1) identify the motivation of the behavior that occurs in the group; (2) examine the subjective feelings produced by the interaction; (3) evaluate procedural assumptions on which the group is approaching the task at hand; and (4) understand the manner in which membership functions are being exercised. He states further that the trainer "provides a working model by creating conditions under which members become participant-observers, themselves interrupting the action now and then to evaluate the meaning of the discussion."

Sensitivity training. Sensitivity training is the most controversial laboratory training method. It has been praised by some, and condemned by others. Sensitivity training developed from the work of specialists in group dynamics and therapeutic counseling. In contrast to role playing, which is a pleasant way of learning about oneself in the group, sensitivity training is usually not pleasant, at least in the initial stages. Some participants have labeled their experiences as frustrating, uncomfortable, and confusing.

Sensitivity training is a controlled group experience in which personal and interpersonal problems are the principal focus. Learning a method of solving problems or becoming an expert in analyzing group structure is not the primary emphasis. Egan (1970) prefers to use the label *self-actualization* or *interpersonal-growth experience* to differentiate sensitivity training groups from regular training groups. According to Schein and Bennis (1965), sensitivity training has two major objectives: (1) to help people learn how to behave in groups in such a way that they can solve the problems for which they are assembled; and, (2) to ensure that the individuals have a meaningful and rewarding group experience. The goal is valid communication; each member should be able to express freely his own feelings about himself and others and to accept others as individuals who have the right to express their feelings, beliefs, and values. If sensitivity training deals with personal and interpersonal problems, we might ask, "How does it differ from group psychotherapy?" In both instances the techniques attempt to develop man's fullest potentialities in his interaction with others; both attempt to show people how they can live with themselves and others more effectively.

The sensitivity group is designed for "normal" people—those who have good coping skills and who can learn readily from experience—whereas a person is selected for therapy because he is deficient in ego skills and unable to learn from real-life experiences. The extent of a trainee's ability to cope with the T-group depends upon whether he is a patient in therapeutic terms or a trainee in sensitivity training terms. (Gottschalk and Pattison, 1969)

The director of the NTL Midwest Group for Human Resources cautions, "this is learning, not therapy. It is not intended for sick people, but for the normal neurotic who wants to get more out of his relations with people." (Rakstis, 1970) We must realize, however, that the reasons why participants seek a group experience may vary from wanting a quick emotional "kick," to wanting to grow personally by being part of a session on interpersonal functioning, to wanting to scout or observe the trainer in order to learn new techniques.

Group participants whose expectations in sensitivity training are based on reports of critics may be disappointed in the methodology and techniques actually used by most trainers. Although trainers may use relaxation exercises, body movements, sensory awareness, and fantasy, the purpose and interpretation of the experience make the difference. Many trainers develop an individual personality and style as group leaders and acquire their own repertoire of skills and techniques to motivate and involve participants in learning experiences. Thus the techniques used are as varied as the personalities, training, and experience and specialization of the trainers. For example, a few trainers are authorities on workshops for police; some specialize in working with management personnel; others work primarily with youth groups.

Role playing, which we discussed in an earlier section, is one technique that has become a basic tool for most trainers. The trainee may play himself or he may assume the identity (role taking) of another in a simulated situation that is an imitation of an experience or a projected real-life episode. To deepen the experience and help participants gain insight, the trainer may use the technique of role reversal. For example, a student may reverse roles with a person playing the role of his instructor in order to experience the responsibilities of an authority figure. Brainstorming, also discussed earlier, has been used to establish a problem inventory, or problem census. The problem census makes up a relevant agenda for extensive task group work.

Most exercises are warm-ups, for the group is technically leaderless, and the agenda is generated by the interaction of the group members. Sometimes data generated during introductions engage the attention of the group for several days. When a technique is used, it may be to get the group to cope on a deeper level, or to move off dead center when stalemated. Knowing what technique to use and when to use it demands skill.

The use of sensitivity training has been successful in a number of cases. Evidence suggests that some immediate gain in positive personal behavior results from training, but that change may not carry over into normal life situations. The real problem, as the movie satire *Bob and Carol, Ted and Alice* suggests, may not reside in the training group. The real problem arises with the difficulty many participants experience trying to apply their laboratory training experience to an insensitive environment.

We have examined a number of techniques for either promoting group interaction or teaching individuals how to function more effectively in groups. The group-discussion techniques examined in this chapter are used because members of the group or audience are at times hesitant about participating in the group process. Unless the group can establish an environment in which members of the group or audience feel free to interact, the success of the group is in jeopardy. Increased participation by the group or audience members may lead to increased group involvement, increased group and audience satisfaction with group product, and increased group cohesion. Using role-playing techniques with group-discussion methods or other group laboratory techniques can provide increased awareness of group, thereby clarifying and possibly solving problems developed during group interaction. If a group member has a greater understanding of his own role and the roles of others in the group, it may facilitate social interaction, thereby enhancing the group's potential for success. The laboratory techniques concentrate on personal improvement, changes in behavior, or alteration of values of individual group members. It provides a vehicle for the individual to develop more of an understanding of his own needs and wants, adequacies, and inadequacies, and to improve members' understanding of others.

ADDITIONAL READINGS

Coon, Arthur M., "Brainstorming: A Creative Problem-Solving Technique, "*Journal of Communication* 7 (Autumn 1957), 111–18. This article provides a good overview of the brainstorming process.

Beal, George M.; Bohlen, Joe M.; and Raudabaugh, J. Neil. *Leadership and Group Action* (Ames: Iowa State Univ. Press, 1962), pp. 197–99, 246–60. This text provides an excellent outline of brainstorming, buzz groups, and role-playing techniques. It provides procedures, advantages, and disadvantages of the group techniques.

Maier, Norman R. F. *Problem-Solving Discussion and Conferences* (New York: McGraw-Hill, 1963), pp. 161–71. The text provides an excellent overview of the posting technique and its specific application to management situations.

Egan, G. *Encounter: Group Processes for Interpersonal Growth* (Belmont, Calif.: Brooks/Cole, 1970). An excellent, easy-to-read text about the interpersonal-growth-oriented T-group.

References

Adorno, T. W.; Frenkel-Brunswik, E.; Levinson, D. J.; and Sanford, R. N. *The Authoritarian Personality*. New York: Harper, 1950.

Andrews, R. E. *Leadership and Supervision*. U.S. Civil Service Commission, Personnel Management Series, no. 9. Washington, 1955.

Argyle, M.; Gardner, G.; and Cioffio, F. "Supervisory methods related to productivitiy, absenteeism, and labor turnover." *Human Relations* 11 (1958): 23–42.

Argyle, M., and Dean, J. "Eye contact, distance, and affiliation." *Sociometry* 28 (1965): 289–304.

Argyle, M., and Kendon, A. "The experimental analysis of social performance." In *Advances in Experimental Social Psychology*, edited by L. Berkowitz, vol. 3, pp. 55–98. New York: Academic Press, 1967.

Argyris, C. *Interpersonal Competence and Organizational Effectiveness*. Homewood, Ill.: Dorsey Press, 1962.

_____. *Integrating the Individual and the Organization*. New York: Wiley, 1964.

Asch, S. E. "Effects of group pressure upon the modifiation and distortion of judgments." In *Groups, Leadership and Men*, edited by H. Guetzkow. Pittsburgh: Carnegie Press, 1951.

Athos, A., and Coffey, R. *Behavior in Organizations: A Multidimensional View*, pp. 159–82. Englewood Cliffs, N. J.: Prentice-Hall, 1968.

Bales, R. *Interaction Process Analysis: A Method for the Study of Small Groups*. Cambridge, Mass.: Addison-Wesley, 1950.

_____. "A theoretical framework for interaction process analysis." In *Group Dynamics: Research and Theory*, edited by D. Cartwright and A. Zander. 1st ed. New York: Harper & Row, 1953.

Bales, R., and Slater, P., "Role differentiation in small decision-making groups." In *Family, Socialization, and Interaction Process*, edited by T. Parsons and R. Bales, pp 259–306. New York, Free Press, 1955.

Barch, A. M.; Trumbo, D.; and Nangle, J. "Social setting and conformity to a legal requirement." *Journal of Abnormal and Social Psychology* 55 (1957): 396–98.

Barnlund, D. C. "Experiments in leadership training for decision-making groups." *Speech Monographs* 22 (1955): 1–14.

_____. *Interpersonal Communication*. Boston: Houghton Mifflin. 1968.

Bass, B. M. *Leadership, Psychology and Organizational Behavior*. New York: Harper & Row, 1960.

Bass, B. M.; McGehee, C. R.; Hawkins, W. C.; Young, P. C.; and Gebel, A. S. "Personality variables related to leaderless group discussion." *Journal of Abnormal and Social Psychology* 48 (1953): 120–28.

Bass, B. M., and Wurster, C. R., "Effects of the nature of the problem of LGD performance." *Journal of Applied Psychology* 37 (1953): 96–99.

Bavelas, A. "Leadership: Man and function." *Administrative Science Quarterly* 22 (1960: 494.

Baxter, J.; Winter, E.; and Hammer, R. "Gestural behavior during a brief interview as a function of cognitive variables." *Journal of Personality and Social Psychology* 8 (1968): 303–7.

Bayless, O. L. "An alternate pattern for problem-solving discussion." *Journal of Communication* 17 (1967): 188–97.

Beal, G.; Bohlen, J.; and Raudabaugh, J. N. *Leadership and Dynamic Group Action*, pp. 31–37. Ames: Iowa State Univ. Press, 1971.

Beck, D. "Communication through confrontation: A case study in intergroup conflict reduction." Paper presented to the International Communication Association Convention, Atlanta, 1971.

Beer, M. *Leadership, Employee Needs, and Motivation*. Ohio State Univ., Bureau of Business Research Monograph no. 129, 1966.

Bell, G. B., and Hall, H. E. "The relationship between leadership and empathy," *Journal of Abnormal and Social Psychology* 49 (1954): 156–57.

Benne, K. D., and Sheats, P. "Functional roles of group members," *Journal of Social Issues* 4 (1948): 41–49.

Berelson, B., and Steiner, G. *Human Behavior: An Inventory of Scientific Findings*. New York: Harcourt, Brace & World, 1964.

Berg, I. A., and Bass, B. M. *Conformity and Deviation*. New York: Harper & Row, 1961.

Berkowitz, L., "Sharing leadership in small decision-making groups." *Journal of Abnormal and Social Psychology* 48 (1953): 231–38.

Berkowitz, L., and Cottingham, D. "The interest value and relevance of fear-arousing communications." *Journal of Abnormal and Social Psychology* 60 (1960): 37–43.

Berlo, D. *The Process of Communication*. New York: Holt, 1960.

Berlo, D. K. "An empirical test of a general construct of credibility." Paper presented to the Speech Association of America, New York, 1961.

Birdwhistell, R. *Kinesics and Context: Essays on Body Motion Communication*. Philadelphia: Univ. of Pennsylvania Press, 1970.

Birnbaum, M. "Sense about sensitivity training." *Saturday Review* 52 (1969): 82–83.

Blake, R., and Mouton, J. "Improving organizational problem solving through increasing the flowing and utilization of ideas." *Training Directors Journal* 17 (1963): 48–57.

Blake, R. R. *Group Training vs. Group Therapy*. New York: Beacon House, 1958.

Blau, P. *The Dynamics of Bureaucracy*. Chicago: Univ. of Chicago Press, 1955.

Borg, W. "The behavior of emergent and designated leaders in situational tests." *Sociometry* 20 (1957): 95–104.

Borg, W. R. "Prediction of small group role behavior from personality variables." *Journal of Abnormal and Social Psychology* 60 (1960): 112–16.

Borgatta, E.; Bales, R.; and Couch, A. "Some findings relevant to the great man theory of leadership." *American Sociological Review* 19 (1954): 755–59.

Bormann, E. G. *Discussion and Group Methods*. New York: Harper & Row, 1969.

Bormann, E. G., and Bormann, N.C. *Effective Small Group Communication*. Minneapolis: Burgess, 1972.

Bradford, L. *Group Development*. NTL, Selected Readings Series no. 1. Washington: National Education Association, 1961.

Brilhart, J. K., and Jochem, L. M. "Effects of different patterns on outcomes of problem-solving discussion." *Journal of Applied Psychology* 48 (1964): 175–79.

Browne, C. "A study of executive leadership in business: I. The R, A, and D scales." *Journal of Applied Psychology* 33 (1949): 521–26.

Browne, C., and Cohn, T., eds. *"The Study of Leadership."* Danville, Ill.: Interstate Printers & Publishers, 1958.

Buchannan, P. C. "Evaluating the effectiveness of laboratory training in industry." In *Explorations in human relations training and research*. Washington: NTL, 1965.

Bugenthal, D., and Lehner, G. "Accuracy of self-perception and group perception as related to two leadership roles." *Journal of Abnormal and Social Psychology* 56 (1958): 396–98.

Burke, P. "Authority relations and behavior in small discussion groups." *Sociometry* 29 (1966): 273–49.

———. "Task and social-emotional leadership role performance." *Sociometry* 34 (1971): 22–40.

Campbell, B. T. "An error in some demonstrations of the superior social perceptiveness of leaders." *Journal of Abnormal and Social Psychology* 51 (1955): 694–95.

Campbell, D. "A study of leadership among submarine officers," Columbus: Ohio State Univ., Personnel Research Board, 1953.

Campbell, D. T. "Systematic error on the part of human links in communication systems." *Information and Control* 1 (1958): 334–69.

Carter, L. "Leadership and small group behavior." In *Group Relations at the Crossroads*, edited by M. Sherif and M. O. Wilson. New York: Harper & Row, 1953.

Carter, L.; Haythorn, W.; and Howell, M. "A further investigation of the criteria of leadership." *Journal of Abnormal and Social Psychology* 45 (1950): 350–58.

Carter, L.; Haythorn, W.; Meirowitz, B.; and Lanzetta, J. "The relations of categorizations and ratings in the observation of group behavior." *Human Relations* 4 (1951): 239–54.

Carter, L.; Haythorn, W.; Shriver, E.; and Lanzetta, J. "The behavior of leaders and other group members." *Journal of Abnormal and Social Psychology* 46 (1951): 589–95.

Cartwright, D. R. "The nature of group cohesiveness," In *Group Dynamics*, edited by D. Cartwright, and A. Zander, 3d ed. New York: Harper & Row, 1968.

Cartwright, D. R., and Zander, A. *Group Dynamics: Research and Theory*. New York: McGraw-Hill, 1968.

Cattell, R. B. "New concepts for measuring leadership in terms of group syntality." *Human Relations* 4 (1951a): 161–84.

———. "New concepts for measuring leadership in terms of group syntality." *Human Relations* 11 (1951b): 41–53.

Cattell, R. B.; Saunders, D.; and Stice, G. F. "The dimensions of syntality in small groups." *Human Relations* 6 (1953): 331–56.

Cattell, R. B., and Stice, G. F. "The dimensions of groups and their relations to the behavior of members." Champaign, Ill.: Institute for Personality and Ability Testing, 1960.

Clifford, C., and Cohn, T. S. "The relationship between leadership and personality attributes perceived by followers." *Journal of Social Psychology* 64 (1964): 57–64.

Coch, L., and French, J. "Overcoming resistance to change." *Human Relations* 1, no. 4 (1948): 512–32.

Cohen, A. *Attitude Change and Social Influence*. New York: Basic Books, 1964.

Coleman, J. C. "Facial Expression of Emotion," *Psychological Monographs* 63 (1949): 1–36.

Collins, B., and Guetzkow, H. *A Social Psychology of Group Processes for Decision-Making*, pp. 149–51, 183–87. New York: Wiley, 1964.

Coser, L. *The Functions of Social Conflict*. New York: Free Press, 1956.

Crockett, W. "Emergent leadership in small, decision-making groups." *Journal of Abnormal and Social Psychology* 51 (1955): 378–83.

Deutsch, M. "Conflict and its resolution." Paper prepared for the Interdisciplinary Colloquium sponsored by the Speech Association of America and the U.S. Office of Education. Racine, Wis., 1967.

———. "Conflicts: productive and destructive."*Journal of Social Issues* 25 (1969): 7–41.

———. "Toward an understanding of conflict." *International Journal of Group Tension* 1 (1971): 42–54.

Deutsch, M., and Krauss, R. *Theories in Social Psychology*. New York: Basic Books, 1965.

Dewey, J. *How We Think*. Chicago: D. C. Heath, 1910.

Druckman, D. "Dogmatism, prenegotiation experience and simulated group representation as determinants of dyadic behavior in a bargaining situation." *Journal of Personality and Social Psychology* 6 (1967): 279–90.

Duncan, S., Jr. "Nonverbal communication." *Psychological Bulletin* 72 (1969): 118–37.

Durbin, R. "Stability of human organizations." In *Modern Organization Theory*, edited by M. Haire, pp. 247–48. New York: Wiley, 1959.

Dyson, J.; Fleitas, D., and Scioli, F. "The interaction of leadership, personality, and decisional environments." *Journal of Social Psychology* 86 (1972): 29–33.

Efran, J., and Broughton, A. "Effect of expectancies for social approval on visual behavior." *Journal of Personality and Social Psychology* 4 (1966): 103–7.

Egan, G. *Encounter: Group Process for Interpersonal Growth*. Belmont, Calif.: Brooks/Cole, 1970.

Ekman, P., and Friesen, W. F. "Head and body cues in the judgment of emotion." *Perceptual and Motor Skills* 24 (1967); 711–24.

Evan, W., and Zelditch, M. "A laboratory experiment on bureaucratic authority." *American Sociological Review* 26 (1961): 883–93.

Exline R., and Winters, L. "Affective relations and mutual glances in dyads." in *Affect, Cognition and Personality*, edited by S. Tomkins and C. Izard, pp. 319–30. New York: Springer, 1965.

Fearing, F. "Toward a psychological theory of human communication." *Journal of Personality* 22 (1953–54); 73–76.

Festinger, L. *A Theory of Cognitive Dissonance*. Evanston, Ill.: Row, Peterson, 1957.

Festinger, L.; Schachter, S.; and Beck, K. *Social Pressures in Informal Groups*. Stanford, Calif.: Stanford Univ. Press, 1950.

Fiedler, F. "A contingency model for the prediction of leadership effectiveness." Office of Naval Research Contract NR–177–472, Nonr-1834(36), Technical Report no. 10, 1963.

––––––. "A contingency model of leadership effectiveness." In *Advances in Experimental Social Psychology*, edited by L. Berkowitz, vol. 2, pp. 237–64. New York: Academic Press, 1966a.

––––––. "The effect of leadership and cultural heterogeneity on group performance: A test of the contingency model." *Journal of Experimental Social Psychology* 2 (1966b): 237–64.

––––––. *Leader Attitudes and Group Effectiveness*. Urbana: Univ. of Illinois Press, 1958.

––––––. "The leader's psychological and group effectiveness." In *Group Dynamics*, edited by D. Cartwright and A. Zander. 2d ed. New York: Harper & Row, 1960.

––––––. *A Theory of Leadership Effectiveness*. New York: McGraw-Hill, 1967.

Fiedler, F.; O'Brien, G.; and Ilgen, D. "The effect of leadership upon the performance and adjustment of volunteer teams operating in successful foreign environment." *Human Relations* 22 (1969): 503–14.

Fisher, B. "Decision emergence: Phases in group decision-making." *Speech Monographs* 37 (1970): 53–66.

Fitzsimmons, S., and Marcuse, F. "Adjustment in leaders and nonleaders as measured by the sentence completion projective technique." *Journal of Clinical Psychology* 17 (1961): 380–81.

Fleishman, E., and Harris, E. "Patterns of leadership behavior related to employee grievances and turnover." *Personnel Psychology* 15 (1962): 43–56.

Fleishman, E.; Harris, E.; and Burtt, H. *Leadership and supervision in industry*. Ohio State Univ., Educational Research Monograph no. 33, 1955.

Freed, A. M.; Chandler, P. J.; Mouton, J. S.; and Blake, R. R. "Stimulus background factors in sign violation." *Journal of Personality* 23 (1955): 499.

French, J. R., and Raven, B. "The bases of social power." In *Studies in Social Power*, edited by D. R. Cartwright. Ann Arbor: Univ. of Michigan Press, 1959.

French, J. R., and Snyder, R. "Leadership and interpersonal power." *Studies in Social Power*, edited by D. R. Cartwright. Ann Arbor: Univ. of Michigan Press, 1959.

Geier, J. "A trait approach to the study of leadership in small groups." *Journal of Communication* 17 (1967): 316–23.

Gibb, C. "Leadership." In *Handbook of Social Psychology*, edited by G. Lindzey. Cambridge, Mass: Addison-Wesley, 1954.

Gold, M. "Power in the classroom." *Sociometry* 21 (1958): 50–60.

Goldstein, M. "The relationship between coping and avoiding behavior and response to fear-arousing propaganda." *Journal of Abnormal and Social Psychology* 59 (1959): 252.

Gottschalk, L. A., and Pathison, E. M. "Psychiatric perspectives on T-groups and the laboratory movement: An overview." *American Journal of Psychiatry* 126 (1969): 823–39.

Gouldner, A. W. *Studies in Leadership*. New York: Harper & Row, 1950.

Gouran, D. "Conceptual and methodological approaches to the study of leadership." *Central States Speech Journal* 21 (1970): 217–23.

Greer, F. L. "Small group effectiveness." Institute Report no. 6, Contract Nonr-1229(00), Institute for Research in Human Relations, Philadelphia, 1955.

Guetzkow, H. "Communication in organizations." In *Handbook of Organizations*, edited by J. G. March, pp. 558–59. Chicago: Rand McNally, 1956.

———. "Differentiation of roles in task-oriented groups." In *Group Dynamics*, edited by D. R. Cartwright and A. Zander, pp. 512–26. New York: Harper & Row, 1968.

Hall, E. T. "Adumbration as a feature of intercultural communication." *American Anthropologist* 66 (1964): 154–63.

———. *The Hidden Dimension*. Garden City, N.Y.: Doubleday, 1966.

———. *The Silent Language*. Garden City, N.Y.: Doubleday, 1959.

Hamblin, R. "Leadership and crisis." *Sociometry* 21 (1958): 322–35.

Hare, A. *Handbook of Small Group Research*. New York: Free Press, 1962.

——— "Situational differences in leader behavior." *Journal of Abnormal and Social Psychology* 55 (1957): 132–34.

———. "Small group discussions with participatory and supervisory leadership." *Journal of Abnormal and Social Psychology* 48 (1953): 273–75.

Hare, A., and Bales, R. "Seating position and small group interaction." *Sociometry* 26 (1963): 480–86.

Harvey, O., and Consalvi, C. "Status and conformity to pressure in informal groups." *Journal of Abnormal and Social Psychology* 57 (1960): 182–87.

Haythorn, W. "The influence of individual members on the characteristics of small groups." *Journal of Abnormal and Social Psychology* 48 (1953): 276–84.

Haythorn, W.; Couch, A.; Haffner, D.; Langham, P.; and Carter, L. "The effects of varying combinations of authoritarian and equalitarian leaders and followers." *Journal of Abnormal and Social Psychology* 53 (1956): 210–19.

Heinecke, C., and Bales, R. "Developmental trends in the structure of small groups." *Sociometry* 16 (1953): 7–38.

Hemphill, J. K. "A proposed theory of leadership in small groups." Second preliminary report. Columbus: Ohio State Univ., Personnel Research Board, 1954.

Hewgill, M., and Miller, G. "Source credibility and response to fear-arousing communications." *Speech Monographs* 32 (1965): 95.

Hoffman, L., and Maier, N. "Valence in the adoption of solutions by problem-solving groups: II. Quality and acceptance as goals of leaders and members." *Journal of Personality and Social Psychology* 6 (1967): 175–82.

Hollander, E. "Competence and conformity in the acceptance of influence." *Journal of Abnormal and Social Psychology*, 61 (1960): 365–70.

———. *Leaders, Groups and Influence.* New York: Oxford Univ. Press, 1964.

Hollander, E., and Hunt, R., eds. *Current Perspectives in Social Psychology*, pp. 487–522; 607–14. New York: Oxford Univ. Press, 1971.

Homans, G. *The Human Group.* New York: Harcourt, Brace, 1950.

Hovland, C. I., and Janis, I. R. *Personality and Persuasibility.* New Haven: Yale Univ. Press, 1959.

Hovland, C. I., and Mandell, W. "An experimental comparison of conclusion drawing by the communicator and by the audience." *Journal of Abnormal and Social Psychology* 47 (1952): 581–88.

Jacobson, W. *Power and Interpersonal Relations*, pp. 129–47. Belmont, Calif.: Wadsworth, 1972.

Janis, I., and Feshback, S. "Effects of fear arousing communications." *Journal of Abnormal and Social Psychology* 47 (1953): 78–92.

Jennings, E. "The anatomy of leadership." *Management of Personnel Quarterly* 1 (1961): 2.

Jones, E.,; Davis, K.; and Gergen, K. "Role playing variations and their informational value for person perception." *Journal of Abnormal and Social Psychology* 63 (1961): 302–10.

Katz, D., and Kahn, R. *The Social Psychology of Organizations.* New York: Wiley, 1966.

Katz, K.; Macoby, N.; and Morse, E. "Productivity, supervision, and morale in an office situation." Ann Arbor: Univ. of Michigan, Institute for Social Research, 1950.

Keltner, J. *Interpersonal Speech-Communication.* Belmont, Calif.: Wadsworth, 1970.

Kepner, C., and Tregoe, B. *The Rational Manager: A Systematic Approach to Problem Solving and Decision Making.* New York: McGraw-Hill, 1965.

Kiessling, R., and Kalish, R. "Correlates of success in leaderless group discussion." *Journal of Social Psychology* 54 (1961): 359–65.

Kipnis, D., and Cosentino, J. "Use of leadership powers in industry." *Journal of Applied Psychology* 53 (1969): 460–66.

Klubeck, S., and Bass, B. "Differential effects of training on persons with different leadership status." *Human Relations* 7 (1954): 59–72.

Knapp, M. *Nonverbal Communication in Human Interaction.* New York: Holt, Rinehart Winston, 1972.

Koontz, H., and O'Donnell, C. *Principles of Management: An Analysis of Managerial Functions*, pp. 556–78. New York: McGraw-Hill, 1972.

Krech, D., and Crutchfled, R. *Theory and Problems of Social Psychology.* New York: McGraw-Hill, 1948.

Lana, R.; Vaughan, W.; and McGinnies, E. "Leadership and friendship status as factors in discussion group interaction." *Journal of Social Psychology* 52 (1960): 127–34.

Larson, C. E. "Forms of analysis and small group problem-solving." *Speech Monographs* 36 (1969): 452–55.
―――. "The verbal response of groups to the absence or presence of leadership." *Speech Monographs* 38 (1971): 177–81.
Leavitt, H. "Some effects of certain communication patterns on group performance." *Journal of Abnormal and Social Psychology* 46 (1951): 38–50.
Lefkowitz, M.; Blake, R. R.; and Mouton, J. S. "Status factors in pedestrian violation of traffic signals." *Journal of Abnormal and Social Psychology* 51 (1955): 704–6.
Leventhal, H., and Singer, R. "Affect arousal and positioning of recommendations in persuasive communication." *Journal of Personality and Social Psychology* 4 (1966): 137–46.
Levi, M. " 'Group atmosphere' and completion of survival instructor training." Reno, Nev.: Stead Air Force Base, Crew Research Laboratory, February 1956.
Lewin, K., and Lippitt, R. "An experimental approach to the study of autocracy and democracy: A preliminary note." *Sociometry* 1 (1938): 292–300.
Lewin, K.; Lippitt, R.; and White, R. "Patterns of aggressive behavior in experimentally created 'social climates.' " *Journal of Social Psychology* 10 (1939): 272–99.
Lindgren, H. *An Introduction to Social Psychology*. New York: Wiley, 1969.
Lippitt, R., and White, R. "The 'social climate' of children's groups." In *Child Behavior and Development*, edited by R. G. Barker, J. Kounin, and H. Wright, pp. 485–508. New York: McGraw-Hill, 1943.
Lott, D. F., and Sommer, R. "Seating arrangements and status." *Journal of Personality and Social Psychology* 7 (1967): 90–95.
McCandless, B. "Changing relationships between dominance and social acceptability during group democratization." *American Journal of Orthopsychiatry* 12 (1942): 529–35.
McClintock, C. "Group support and the behavior of leaders and nonleaders." *Journal of Abnormal and Social Psychology* 56 (1958): 245–55.
McCroskey, J. "Scales for the measurement of ethos." *Speech Monographs* 33 (1966): 65–72.
―――. "A summary of experimental research on the effects of evidence in persuasive communication." *Quarterly Journal of Speech* 36 (1969): 169–76.
McCroskey, J.; Larson, C.; and Knapp, M. *An Introduction to Interpersonal Communication*, chapter 8. Englewood Cliffs, N.J.: Prentice-Hall, 1971.
McDavid, J., and Harari, H. *Social Psychology: Individuals, Groups, Societies*, pp. 348–66. New York: Harper & Row, 1968.
McGrath, J. "Assembly of quasi-therapeutic rifle teams." Mimeographed. Urbana: Univ. of Illinois, Group Effectiveness Research Laboratory, 1961.
Mack, R., and Snyder, R. "The analysis of social conflict—Toward an overview and synthesis," *Journal of Conflict Resolution* 1 (1957): 212–48.
Maier, N. "An experimental test of the effects of training on discussion leadership." *Human Relations* 6 (1953): 161–73.

Mann, R. D. "Dimensions of individual performance in small groups under task and social-emotional conditions." *Journal of Abnormal and Social Psychology* 62 (1961): 674–82.

———. "A review of the relationships between personality and performance in small groups." *Psychological Bulletin* 56 (1959): 241–70.

Maslow, A. H. *Motivation and Personality.* New York: Harper & Row, 1954.

Mehrabian, A., *Silent Messages.* Belmont, Calif.: Wadsworth, 1971.

Merei, F. "Group leadership and institutionalization." *Human Relations* 2 (1949): 23–39.

Merton, R. "The social nature of leadership." *American Journal of Nursing* 69 (1969): 2614–18.

Miller, G., and Burgoon, M. *New Techniques of Persuasion.* New York: Harper & Row, 1973.

Moberg, D. O. "Church membership and personal adjustment in old age." *Journal of Gerontology* 8 (1953): 207–11.

———. "Leadership in church and personal adjustment in old age." *Sociological Society Research* 37 (1953): 312–16.

Morris, C., and Hackman, J. "Behavioral correlates of perceived leadership." *Journal of Personality and Social Psychology* 13 (1969): 350–61.

Mortensen, C. D. *Communication: The Study of Human Interaction.* New York: McGraw-Hill, 1972.

Murphy, A. "A study of the leadership process." *American Sociological Review* 6 (1941): 674–87.

Nakamura, C. Y. "Conformity and problem solving." *Journal of Abnormal and Social Psychology* 56 (1958) 315–20.

Newcomb, T. M. *Personality and Social Change: Attitude Formation in a Student Community.* New York: Holt, Rinehart & Winston, 1943.

Newport, M. "Middle management development in industrial organizations." Unpublished doctoral dissertation. Urbana: Univ. of Illinois, 1963.

Ort, R. S. "A study of role conflicts as related to happiness in marriage." *Journal of Abnormal and Social Psychology* 45 (1950): 691–99.

Osborn, A. F. *Applied Imagination.* New York: Schribner, 1957.

Partridge, E. "Leadership among adolescent boys." *Contributing Education* (Teachers College, Columbia University), no. 608, 1934.

Pelz, D. "Leadership within a hierarchical organization." *Journal of Social Issues* 7 (1951): 49–55.

———. "Some social factors related to performance in a research organization." *Administration Science Quarterly* 1 (1956): 310–25.

Phillips, G. *Communication in the Small Group.* Indianapolis: Bobbs-Merrill, 1966.

Phillips, G., and Erickson, E. *Interpersonal Dynamics in the Small Group.* New York: Random House, 1970.

Pittenger, R., and Smith, H., Jr. "A basis for some contributions of linguistics to psychiatry." *Psychiatry* 20 (1967): 61–78.

Preston, M., and Heinz, R. "Effects of participatory versus supervisory leadership on group judgment." *Journal of Abnormal and Social Psychology* 44 (1949): 345–55.

Rakstis, T. J. "Sensitivity training: Fad, fraud or new fronter?" *Today's Health* 48 (1970): 20–25, 86–87.

Redl, F. "Resistance in therapy groups." *Human Relations* 1 (1948): 307–13.

Reitan, H. T., and Shaw, M. E. "Group membership, sex-composition of the group and conformity behavior." *Journal of Social Psychology* 64 (1964): 45–51.

Reusch, J. "Nonverbal language and therapy." *Psychiatry* 18 (1955): 323–330.

Reuter, E. *Handbook of Sociology.* New York: Dryden Press, 1941.

Rokeach, M. *The Open and Closed Mind.* New York: Basic Books, 1960.

Rosenbaum, M. E., and Blake, R. R. "Volunteering as a function of field structure." *Journal of Abnormal and Social Psychology* 50 (1955); 193–96.

Russo, N. "Connotation of seating arrangements." *Cornell Journal of Social Relations* 2 (1967): 37–44.

Schachter, S. "Deviation, rejection, and communication." *Journal of Abnormal and Social Psychology* 46 (1951): 190–207.

Scheidel, T. M. *Speech Communication and Human Interaction.* Glenview, Ill.: Scott, Foresman & Company, 1972.

Schein, E., and Bennis, W. *Personal and Organizational Change through Group Methods: The Laboratory Approach.* New York: Wiley, 1965.

Scott, W. G., and Mitchell, T. *Organization Theory: A Structural and Behavioral Analysis*, chapter 8. Homewood, Ill.: Richard D. Irwin, Dorsey Press, 1972.

Seashore, C. "What is sensitivity training?" *NTL Institute News and Reports* 2 (1968): 1–2.

Sereno, K. K. "Ego involvement: A neglected variable in speech communication research." *Quarterly Journal of Speech* 55 (1969): 69–77.

Sereno, K. K., and Mortensen, C. D. "The effects of ego-involved attitudes on conflict negotiation in dyads." *Speech Monographs* 36 (1969): 8–12.

Sharp, H., Jr., and McClung, T. "Effects of organization on the speaker's ethos." *Speech Monographs* 32 (1966): 182–83.

Shartle, C. *Executive Performance and Leadership.* Englewood Cliffs, N.J.: Prentice-Hall, 1956.

Shaw, M. E. "A comparison of two types of leadership in various communication nets." *Journal of Abnormal and Social Psychology* 50 (1955): 127–34.

———. *Group Dynamics.* New York: McGraw-Hill, 1971.

Sherif, C. W.; Sherif, M.; and Nebergall, R. E. *Attitude and Attitude Change.* Philadelphia: Saunders, 1965.

Sherif, M., and Sherif, C. W. *An Outline of Social Psychology.* New York: Harper & Row, 1956.

Showel, M. "Interpersonal knowledge and rated leader potential." *Journal of Abnormal and Social Psychology* 61 (1960): 87–92.

Simmel, G. *Conflict.* Translated by K. H. Wolff. Glencoe, Ill.: Free Press, 1955.

Simons, H. W. "Introduction: Interpersonal perception, similarity, and credibility." In *Advances in Communication Research*, edited by C. D. Mortensen and K. K. Sereno. New York: Harper & Row, 1973.

Smith, C. G., and Tannenbaum, A. "Organizational control structure: A comparative analysis." *Human Relations* 16 (1963): 299–331.
Sommer, R. "Leadership and Group Geography" *Sociometry* 24 (1961): 106.
———. *Personal Space: The Behavioral Basis of Design.* Englewood Cliffs, N.J.: Prentice-Hall, 1969.
Steinzor, B. "The spatial factor in face-to-face discussion groups." *Journal of Abnormal and Social Psychology* 45 (1950): 552–55.
Stogdill, R. M. "Personal factors associated with leadership." *Journal of Psychology* 25 (1948): 35–71.
Strodtbeck, F., and Hook, L. "The social dimensions of a twelve man jury table." *Sociometry* 24 (1961): 397–415.
Tannenbaum, R., and Schmidt, W. "How to choose a leadership pattern." *Harvard Business Review* 36 (1958): 95–101.
Terman, L. M., and Miles, C. C. *Sex and Personality: Studies in Masculinity and Femininity.* New York: McGraw-Hill, 1936.
Thompson, E. "An experimental investigation of the relative effectiveness of organizational structure in oral communication." *Southern Speech Journal* 26 (1960): 59–69.
Tomkins, S. S., and McCarter, R. "What and where are the primary effects? Some evidence for a theory." *Perceptual and Motor Skills* 18 (1964): 119–58.
Trapp, P. "Leadership and popularity as a function of behavioral predictions." *Journal of Abnormal and Social Psychology* 51 (1955): 452–57.
Tubbs, S. "Explicit versus implicit conclusions and audience commitment," *Speech Monographs* 35 (1968): 14–19.
Tuddenham, R. D.; MacBride, P.; and Zahn, V. "The influence of the sex composition of the group upon yielding to a distorted norm." *Journal of Psychology* 46 (1958): 243–51.
Tyler, B. A study of factors contributing to employee morale. Unpublished master's thesis. Columbus: Ohio State Univ. 1949.
Uesugi, T. T., and Vinacke, W. E. "Strategy in a feminine game." *Sociometry* 26 (1963): 75–88.
Wagner, R. H., and Arnold, C. C. *Handbook of Group Discussion.* Boston: Houghton Mifflin, 1950.
Weisbrod, R. "Looking behavior in a discussion groups." Unpublished report cited by M. Argyle and A. Kendon in "The experimental analysis of social performance. In *Advances in Experimental Social Psychology,* edited by L. Berkowitz, vol. 3, pp. 55–98. New York: Academic Press, 1967.
White, R., and Lippitt, R. *Autocracy and Democracy.* New York: Harper & Row, 1960.
Whyte, W. *Human Relations in the Restaurant Industry,* New York: McGraw-Hill, 1948.
Williams, J. "Personal space and its relation to extroversion-introversion." Unpublished master's thesis. Univ. of Alberta, 1963.
Wilson, R. "Personality patterns, source attractiveness, and conformity." *Journal of Personality* 28 (1960): 186–99.
Zajonc, R. "Distortion at the receiving end." *Communication in Organiza-*

tions: Some New Research Findings, p. 6. Ann Arbor: Univ. of Michigan, Foundation for Research on Human Behavior.

―――. "The process of cognitive tuning in communication." *Journal of Abnormal and Social Psychology* 61 (1960): 159–67.

Zeleny, L. "Characteristics of group leaders." *Sociology and Social Research* 24 (1939): 140–49.

Zimbardo, P., and Ebbesen, E. *Influencing Attitudes and Changing Behavior*. Reading, Mass.: Addison-Wesley, 1969.

Index

Acceptance, 62–63, 66–67
  factors influencing, 66–67
  ambiguity, 66
  congruency, 67
  credibility, 67
  reality, 66
Adorno, T., 40
Argyle, M., 81, 82, 87
Asch, S., 138
Attitude, 35–37, 196–98, 200
  ego involvement, 36
  latitude, 35–37
  nature of, 35–36
Attraction, 161–67

Bach, K., 159, 206
Bales, R., 87, 97
Barch, A. M., 140
Barnlund, D. C., 151
Bass, B., 39, 41, 44, 235
Baxter, J., 79
Bayless, O., 120
Beck, D., 192
Bell, G., 41
Benne, K. D., 145–46
Bennis, W., 289, 291
Berg, I., 39
Berkowitz, L., 242
Berlo, D., 10
Birdwhistell, R., 233
Birnbaum, M., 288
Blake, R., 290
Blake, R. R., 140–41
Body movements, 77–79
Borg, W., 41
Bormann, E. G., 143, 145, 146, 152, 234
Brainstorming, 276–78
Broughton, A., 81
Buchannan, P. C., 289
Burgoon, M., 149
Burke, P. 234
Buzz session, 278–81

Campbell, D., 67
Cartwright, D., 146, 162, 163, 206
Cartwright, R., 206

Cattell, R., 41
Censure, 57–60
  individual rights, 59–60
Chandler, P. J., 141
Coch, L., 242
Coercive power, 201–2
Cohen, A., 14, 33, 196
Cohesiveness, 159–79, 206–7
  and attraction, 161–67
  and communicator, 175–76
  definition, 160–61
  and message, 177–78
  and productivity, 171–78
  and satisfaction, 167–71
  and situational context, 176–77
Collins, B., 67
Colloquy, 266–67
Communication
  communicators, 14-15
  definition, 8–9
  interaction, 16–17
  message, 15–16
  model, 8–12
  situational context, 17–21
Communicator, 14–15, 29–45, 137–38, 149–50
  characteristics, 29–45
    attitude, 35–39
    credibility, 30–34
    intelligence, 43–45
    personality, 13–14, 39–43
    sex, 37–39
  cohesiveness, 175–76
Competitive orientation, 191–95
Conflict, 183–211
  and communicator, 196–203
    attitude, 196–99
    dogmatism, 199–200
    power, 200–203
  and interaction, 205–10
    cohesiveness, 206–7
    member satisfaction, 207–9
  interpersonal, 147–48, 185–88
  intrapersonal, 148, 184–85
  and message, 204–5
  nonproductive, 189–91
  and orientation, 191–94

Conflict (cont'd)
  competitive, 192–94
  cooperative, 193–94
  productive, 189–91
  and situational context, 208–9
  types, 184–89
Conformity, 136–37
Cooperative orientation, 193–94
Coser, L., 186, 189, 196, 203, 206
Credibility, 30–34
  determinants, 31–32
  dimensions, 32
    authoritativeness, 32–34
    competence, 32–34
    trustworthiness, 32–34
  effects, 32–34
Criticism, 57–60
  individual rights, 59
Crutchfield, R., 229

Davis, K., 151
Dean, J., 87
Decoding, 10–12
Deutsch, M., 186, 190, 191, 193, 207
Dewey, J., 101–3, 112
Dialogue, 264–65
Discussion techniques, 275–88
  brainstorming, 276–78
  buzz session, 278–81
  Phillips 66, 278–81
  posting, 281–83
  role playing, 283–88
Discussion, methods of, 249–71
  colloquy, 266–67
  dialogue, 264–65
  lecture-forum, 268–69
  panel, 259–61
  round table, 257–59
  symposium-forum, 262–64
Distortion, 63–64
  points of origin, 63
Dittman, A., 78
Dogmatism, 199–200
Druckman, D., 200
Dubin, R., 66

Ebbesen, E., 14, 196
Efran, J., 81
Ego involvement, 36–7
Ekman, P., 78
Emotional stability, 42–3
Encoding, 9–12
Erickson, E., 94
Exline, R., 81
Expert power, 201–2
Eye contact, 77, 81–2

Facial expressions, 77–82
Fearing, F., 53, 67
Feedback, 11, 52
Festinger, L., 65, 159, 206

Fiedler, F., 222
Filtering, 63, 64–65
Finado, S., 78
Fisher, B. A., 122, 124, 126–28
Fitzsimmons, S., 224
Freed, A. M., 141
French, R., 190, 201, 242
Frenkel-Brunswik, E., 40
Friesen, W., 78

Gebel, A., 41, 44
Geier, J., 222
Gergen, K., 151
Gonsalvi, C., 224
Gouran, D., 221, 242
Greer, F., 41
Group atmosphere, 159–60
Group-attraction, 161–67
Group-communication process 21–22
  characteristics, 21–2
  complex, 21
  dynamic, 21
  simultaneous cause and effect, 21–22
  systemic, 21
Group discussion, 249–55
  characteristics 251–55
  definition, 250–53
Group performance, 170
Group Process Model, 160
Groups, 5–8
  definition, 7
  functions, 5–6
  nature of, 7–8
Guetzkow, H., 64, 67, 146

Hall, H., 13, 41
Hammer, R., 79
Hare, A. P., 7, 87
Harvey, O., 224
Hawkins, W., 41, 44
Haythorn, W., 42
Heintz, R., 240
Hollander, E., 152
Homans, G., 134
Hook, L., 232
Hovland, C., 42
Huenergardt, D., 78

Ideal-Solution Form, 109, 117–19
Idiosyncrasy credits, 152
Individual orientation 191–94
Instructions, 60–61
  techniques, 61
Interaction, 16–17, 93–100, 205–6
  phases, 94–96
    deliberation, 95
    orientation, 95
Interaction process analysis, 97
Interpersonal attraction, 161–67

Interpersonal conflict, 147–48, 185–88
Intrapersonal conflict, 148, 184–85

Janis, I., 42
Jennings, E., 222
Jones, E., 151

Kahn, R., 218
Kalish, R., 224
Katz, D., 218
Keltner, J., 191
Kendon, A., 81
Kiessling, R., 224
Knapp, M., 16, 18, 68, 86
Krauss, R., 207
Krech, D., 229

Laboratory training, 288–93
  origin and function, 288–90
  sensitivity training, 103–4, 291–93
  trainer, 290–91
Language, 50–52
Larson, C., 68, 119, 121
Leader
  definitions, 218–21
  as communicator, 218–26
Leadership, 215–45
  functional approach, 228–31
  interaction with members, 235–44
  message factors, 233–35
  roles, 228, 230–32
  situational approach, 226–30
  styles, 235–43
  traits, 221–26
Leadership attribution, 218–21
  by appointment, 221
  by emergence, 220
  by sociometric choice, 218–19
Leadership emergence, 321–33
  physical determinants, 232–33
Leadership roles, 228, 230–32
  consideration, 231
  social-emotional, 228, 230
  structure-initiation, 231
  task-facilitation, 228, 230
Leadership styles, 235–43
  autocratic, 236–43
  democratic, 236–43
  laissez-faire, 236–43
Leadership traits, 221–26
  adjustment, 224
  deviancy, 224
  intelligence, 224
Leavitt, H., 232
Lecture-forum, 268–69
Lefkowitz, M., 140
Legitimate power, 201–3
Levinson, D., 40
Lewin, K., 236

Lindgren, H., 224
Lippitt, R., 236

MacBride, P., 38
McCarter, R., 76, 77
McClintock, C., 225
McCroskey, J., 68
McGehee, C., 41, 44
Mack, R., 206
Mann, R., 44
Marcuse, F., 224
Meaning, 51
Mehrabian, A., 79, 233
Message factors
  content, 233–35
  method, 233–35
  nonverbal response, 233–35
  verbal response, 233–35
Message overload, 66
Message sharing, 62–67
  dysfunctions, 62–67
    acceptance, 62–63, 66
    distortion, 63–64
    filtering, 63, 64–65
    message overload, 63, 66
    pathologies, 62–67
Message strategies, 53–62
  criticism and censure, 57–60
  instructions, 60–62
  praise, 54–56
Messages, 15–16, 49–88, 138–39, 150–51, 204–5
  and cohesiveness, 177–78
  types 15–16
    nonverbal, 15–16, 73–88
    verbal, 15–16, 49–68
Miles, C., 39
Miller, G., 149
Models, nature of, 9–12
Mortensen, C. D., 37, 78, 84, 85
Motives, 6
Mouton, J. S., 141

Nakamura, C., 44
Nangle, J., 140
Nebergall, R., 35, 36
Newcomb, T. M., 141
Nonproductive conflict, 189–91
Nonverbal cues, 73–79
Nonverbal language signals, 73–88
  clarification of verbal messages, 82–84
  control and direction, 79–80
  emotions and feelings, 75–79
  interpersonal orientation, 80–82
  seating arrangements, 84–88
  social distance, 84–88
Norms, 133–41
  characteristics, 135–36
  and communicators, 137–38
  and conformity, 136–37
  definition, 134–35

Norms (*cont'd*)
  development, 135
  and interaction, 139–40
  and messages, 138–39

Ort, R., 38
Osborn, A. F., 276

Panel, 259–61
Personality, 39–43
  ascendant tendencies, 41
  authoritarianism, 40–41
  dogmatism, 40–41
  emotional stability, 42–43
  self–reliance, 42
  social sensitivity, 41
  unconventionality, 42
Phillips, G., 114
Phillips 66, 278–80
Pittinger, R., 84
Posting, 281–83
Power, 200–203
  coercive, 201–2
  expert, 201–2
  legitimate, 201–3
  referent, 201–2
  reward, 201
Praise, 54–56
Preston, M., 240
Problem questions, 110–11
  fact, 110
  policy, 110
  value, 110
Problem-solving groups, 93–128
  and the communication system, 125–28
  and decision making, 122–24
  definition, 93
  interaction, 94–96
Productive conflict, 65–66, 189–91
Productivity, 171–75
  definition, 172

Raven, B., 190, 201
Referent power, 71, 201–2
Reflective-thinking process, 101–18
  analysis, 101–3, 114
    test of materials, 114–16
  definition, 101–3, 113
  problem recognition, 102–3, 112
  solution criteria, 101–3, 116–18
  solution selection, 101–5, 116–18
Reward power, 201
Rokeach, M., 14, 40, 197, 199
Role conflict, 147–49
Role expectations, 141
Role formation, 142–45
Role performance, 141
Role playing, 283–88

Roles, 141–54
  characteristics, 141–42
  and conflict, 147–49
  definition, 141
  formation, 142–45
  and small-group behavior, 149–52
    communicator, 149–50
    interaction, 151–52
    message, 150–51
  types, 145–47
    social, 146–47
    task, 145–46
Rosenbaum, M. E., 141
Round table, 257–59
Russo, W., 85

Sainsbury, R., 78
Sanford, R., 40
Satisfaction, 167–71, 207–8
  definition, 167
Schachter, S., 159, 206
Schein, E., 289, 291
Self-esteem, 42
Sensitivity-training, 291–93
Sereno, K., 37, 197
Sex, 37–39
Shaw, M., 7, 38, 40, 43, 242, 276
Sheats, P., 145, 146
Sherif, C., 35, 36, 138
Sherif, M., 35, 36, 138
Showell, M., 224
Simmel, G., 206
Simons, H., 34
Single-question form, 109, 119
Situational context, 17–21, 176–77, 208–9
  and cohesiveness, 176–77
  physical setting, 17–18
  purpose or task, 18–19
    information sharing, 18
    problem solving, 18
    self-maintenance, 18
    social climate, 19
  structure, 19
Small-group techniques, 275–93
  discussion, 276–88
  laboratory training, 288–93
Smith, H., 84
Snyder, R., 206
Social roles, 146–47
Sommer, R., 85
Steinzor, B., 88
Stice, G., 41
Stogdill, R., 42, 221
Strodtbeck, F., 232
Symposium-forum, 262–64

Task roles, 145–46
Terman, L., 39

T-group, 288–91
Tomkins, S., 76, 77
Trumbo, D., 140
Tuddenham, R., 38

Uesugi, T., 38

Verbal message, 49–68
   difficulties, 62–63
   environment, 67–68
   function, 52–53
Vinacke, W., 38
Vocal cues, 83

Weisbrod, R., 80
White, R., 236–40
Williams, J., 85
Winter, E., 79
Winters, L., 81

Young, P., 41, 44

Zahn, V., 38
Zajonc, R., 67, 151
Zander, A., 146
Zimbardo, P., 14, 196

This book was designed and illustrated by Barbara Ravizza,
set in Palatino with Helvetica display by
Holmes Composition of San Jose,
then printed and bound by the
Kingsport Press of Kingsport,
Tennessee. Edited by George Oudyn.
Communications editor, Frank Geddes
Cover by Ravizza

4567/5432

Kirtley Library
Columbia College
8th and Rogers
Columbia, MO. 65201